藤县非遗传录

藤县文化广电体育和旅游局 编

TENGXIAN
FEIYI
CHUANLU

广西人民出版社

图书在版编目（CIP）数据

藤县非遗传录：汉文、英文 / 藤县文化广电体育和旅游局编 . — 南宁：广西人民出版社，2024.11
　　ISBN 978-7-219-11744-6

Ⅰ . ①藤… Ⅱ . ①藤… Ⅲ . ①非物质文化遗产—藤县—名录—汉、英 Ⅳ . ① G127.674-62

中国国家版本馆 CIP 数据核字（2024）第 062419 号

责任编辑　彭青梅
责任校对　陈　威
美术编辑　李彦媛
版式设计　翁襄媛
翻　　译　林叶芊芊　梁峻豪　麦　研

出版发行	广西人民出版社
社　　址	广西南宁市桂春路 6 号
邮　　编	530021
印　　刷	广西民族印刷包装集团有限公司
开　　本	787 mm × 1092 mm　1 / 16
印　　张	24
字　　数	330 千字
版　　次	2024 年 11 月　第 1 版
印　　次	2024 年 11 月　第 1 次印刷
书　　号	ISBN 978-7-219-11744-6
定　　价	158.00 元

版权所有　翻印必究

《藤县非遗传录》编委会

主　　　任　　杜　诚　蒙中平

常务副主任　　蒙土金

副　主　任　　秦　燕　唐宏飞

主　　　编　　李燕霞

副　主　编　　杨　愈　韦杰川　李华祥　江武坤　李　前
　　　　　　　李世孝　黄　弘　邓海燕　江　欣　苏炎萍

编　　　辑　（按姓氏笔画为序）

　　　　　　　韦　相　韦照林　甘丽云　江雨潞　苏　海
　　　　　　　李秋芳　何　柏　何锦奋　欧伟文　罗金霞
　　　　　　　莫　姗　黄　静　梁斯瑜　霍雨锋

Editorial Committee of Records of Tengxian County Intangible Cultural Heritage

Directors   Du Cheng   Meng Zhongping

Executive Deputy Director   Meng Tujin

Deputy Directors   Qin Yan   Tang Hongfei

Editor in Chief   Li Yanxia

Deputy Editors in Chief   Yang Yu   Wei Jiechuan   Li Huaxiang

  Jiang Wukun   Li Qian   Li Shixiao

  Huang Hong   Deng Haiyan   Jiang Xin

  Su Yanping

Editors (sort by chinese surname strokes)

  Wei Xiang   Wei Zhaolin   Gan Liyun   Jiang Yulu   Su Hai

  Li Qiufang   He Bai   He Jinfen   Ou Weiwen   Luo Jinxia

  Mo Shan   Huang Jing   Liang Siyu   Huo Yufeng

序

北京大学中文系教授 | 王娟

　　非物质文化遗产是人类文化的一个重要组成部分。所谓非物质文化遗产，按照联合国教科文组织的官方定义，即"被各社区、群体，有时是个人，视为其文化遗产组成部分的各种社会实践、观念表述、表现形式、知识、技能以及相关的工具、实物、手工艺品和文化场所"。该定义重点关注的是以普通民众为主体的，以口头表述、表演、仪式、节庆和传统手工艺等方式传承的那部分文化遗产。

　　非物质文化遗产的一个显著特点是其活态性。实际上，我们都生活在一种文化环境当中，除了阅读书籍，我们还会以口耳相传和参与、模仿的方式获取知识，文化借助于文字、习俗、物质等媒介，将我们塑造成为文化人。我们创造了文化，文化又借助我们的言谈举止而延续，没有文化就没有人类，反过来，没有人类也就没有文化。文化对于我们来说，不是一种游离于我们之外的东西，而是体现在我们每一个人身上，并通过我们之间的相互交流、相互沟通而形成的一种共同的东西。

　　人类的民俗生活是随着人类文化的产生而产生的，有着上万年的历史，但是，民俗生活成为研究对象却只有200多年。在这200多年的历史中，从发现民俗生活之美，到发现民俗生活的意义和价值，再到现在将民俗生活作为一种非物质文化遗产，作为文化的重要财富，人们经历了一个文化觉醒的过程。我们发现，其实每一个人都是文化的创造者，同时也是文化的载体和文化的传播者。将我们的生活记录在册，不仅是对人类文化历史的重要贡献，还是对我们自己——文化主体的肯定。

21世纪初，联合国教科文组织缔约国签署了《保护非物质文化遗产公约》。现在，我们国家越来越重视保护非物质文化遗产。习近平总书记曾作出重要指示，强调要扎实做好非物质文化遗产的系统性保护，更好满足人民日益增长的精神文化需求，推进文化自信自强。《关于进一步加强非物质文化遗产保护工作的意见》里，也强调要坚持创造性转化、创新性发展，坚守中华文化立场、传承中华文化基因……切实提升非物质文化遗产系统性保护水平，为全面建设社会主义现代化国家提供精神力量。

《藤县非遗传录》正是在这个背景下收集、整理、编纂而成的。该书内容非常丰富，堪称是藤县民俗生活的百科全书。该书涵盖了藤县民俗生活的各个方面，有民间文学，如古藤州传说、藤县龙母传说、藤县道家村传说、藤县袁崇焕故事、藤县神仙脚迹传说；有传统音乐，如藤县元宵歌、藤县上灯歌、藤县水上船歌、藤县八音等；有传统戏剧，如藤县牛歌戏、藤县杖头木偶戏；有传统舞蹈，如藤县狮舞；有传统技艺，如藤县太平米饼制作工艺、藤县鱼生制作工艺、藤县彩龙编织技艺、藤县木偶制作技艺、藤县疳积散制药技艺等；有传统节庆民俗，如藤县赛龙舟习俗、藤县乞巧节、藤县龙母诞、藤县做社习俗、藤县太平二帝庙装色出游等；有传统体育、游艺与杂技，如斗鸡、斗蟋蟀、藤县抢花炮等；有传统美术，如彩扎（藤县狮头）。

该书对当地民俗生活的记录详细而准确。以藤县狮舞为例，该篇不仅梳理了藤县狮舞的历史，而且对藤县狮舞中狮子的造型、角色、装饰、舞蹈动作套路等也进行了详细的描述，对狮舞的表演场合和环境也有所记录。此外，对狮子的彩扎技艺，无论是材料，还是染色、组装等都一一记录在案，具有很高的史料价值。另外，该书还收录了各种图片资料，图文并茂的形式大大提高了该书的实用性和观赏性。

该书的另一大特点是书中的许多非遗项目增加了传承人谱系部分。例如，介绍藤县牛歌戏时不仅详细介绍了牛歌戏的历史源流、行当、脸谱、服装、唱腔、剧本、表演、舞美、演出场合和过程，还列出了藤县牛歌戏的传承谱系，即对牛歌戏六代传承人的姓名、性别、民族、学历、学艺时间和传承方式等内容进行了记录。

总之，这部书是中国保护非物质文化遗产的一个缩影，所谓麻雀虽小，五脏俱全。按照联合国教科文组织的观点，每一种本土文化的表达，都应该作为人类天赋的表达而加以保留。藤县正是以实际行动努力践行了这一观点。该书对地方传统文化的记录和描述，不仅可以加深我们对藤县地方民俗生活的了解，而且也会促使我们思考如何更积极、更有效地传承和保护非物质文化遗产，将中华优秀传统文化发扬光大。

Preface

Prof. Wang Juan
Department of Chinese language and Literature,
Peking University

Intangible Cultural Heritage (ICH) constitutes a vital component of human culture. According to the United Nations Educational, Scientific, and Cultural Organization (UNESCO), ICH encompasses "the social practices, representations, expressions, knowledge, skills, and associated tools, objects, artefacts, and cultural spaces that communities, groups, and, in some cases, individuals recognize as part of their cultural heritage." This definition emphasizes the elements of cultural heritage transmitted primarily by the public through oral traditions, performances, rituals, festivals, and traditional crafts.

One of the defining features of ICH is its living nature. We inhabit a cultural environment where, alongside reading, we acquire knowledge through oral transmission, participation, and imitation. Culture shapes us into cultural beings through language, customs, and material objects. We create and perpetuate culture through our speech and actions. Without culture, there is no humanity, and conversely, culture is embodied in each of us and sustained through our interactions with others.

Folk life has existed since the emergence of the development of human culture, spanning over tens of thousands of years. However, it was not until over two hundred years ago that folk life became a subject of scholarly interest. Over the past two hundred years, cultural awareness has gradually evolved—from recognizing the beauty of folk traditions to exploring their deeper significance and value, and now, to preserving them as ICH, a vital cultural treasure. This realization affirms that each of us is not only a creator but also a custodian and disseminator of culture. Consequently, documenting our lives not only contributes to the cultural history of humanity but also serves as an affirmation of ourselves as cultural beings.

At the beginning of this century, the States Parties to UNESCO signed the *Convention for the Safeguarding of Intangible Cultural Heritage*. China has placed significant emphasis on this endeavor. President Xi Jinping has emphasized the need for systematic safeguarding of ICH to meet the growing spiritual and cultural needs of the people and to promote cultural confidence and self-improvement. The *Opinions on Further Strengthening the Protection of Intangible Cultural Heritage* calls for creative transformation and innovative development, the preservation of Chinese cultural identity, and the enhancement of ICH protection as a means of providing spiritual strength to China's modernization.

It is in this context that the *Records of Tengxian County Intangible Cultural Heritage* was compiled. This comprehensive volume serves as an encyclopedia of the folk life in Tengxian County, encompassing a wide range of content. It includes a wide range of folk literature, such as legend of ancient Tengzhou, legend of loong mother in Tengxian County, legend of Daojia Village in Tengxian County, story of Yuan Chonghuan in Tengxian County, and legend of the fairy footprints in Tengxian County. Additionally, it features traditional music, including lantern festival song, song of lighting up, the boat song, and eight-tone music, as well as traditional dramas such as ox-song opera and the cane-head puppet show. Traditional dance (the lion dance) and traditional crafts in Tengxian County are included, such as production of Taiping rice cake, preparation of *Yusheng*, weaving technique of colorful Loong, puppet-making, and pharmaceutical technique of making Ganji San. Traditional festivals, and folklore, including the loong boat racing, Qiqiao Festival, loong mother's birthday celebration, custom of worshipping the god of land, and the Taiping Two Emperor's Temple parade, are also documented. The volume further addresses traditional sports, games, and acrobatics, such as cockfighting, cricket fighting, and fire cracker ball, as well as traditional arts like the lion head tying craft.

The book provides a detailed and accurate account of local folk traditions. For example, regarding the lion dance in Tengxian County, it not only traces its historical development but also offers elaborate descriptions of the lion's appearance, roles, decorations, behaviors, and choreography. It further details the contexts and occasions in which the lion dance is performed. The book also meticulously documents the intricate techniques used to create the lion, from materials and dyeing to assembly, adding to its historical significance. The inclusion of various photographs enhances its richness and vividness.

Another notable feature of the book is the inclusion of genealogical records for many ICH items, particularly regarding their inheritors. For instance, the chapter on the ox-song opera not only introduces its historical origins, roles, facial paintings, costumes, singing style, scripts, performances, choreography, and performance contexts, but it also lists the inheritance lineage of the ox-song opera in Tengxian County. This includes the names of inheritors across six generations, along with details about their gender, ethnicity, educational background, learning timeline, and means of inheritance.

In summary, this book is a microcosm of China's intangible cultural heritage. As an old Chinese proverb states, "The sparrow may be small, but it possesses all the essential organs." According to UNESCO, every expression of indigenous culture should be preserved as a testament to human creativity—a principle that Tengxian County has actively embraced. Through the records and descriptions of local traditional culture in this volume, we not only gain a deeper understanding of the folk life of Tengxian County but are also inspired to consider how to pass on and safeguard ICH more effectively. In doing so, we contribute to the preservation and flourishing of traditional Chinese culture.

目录

CONTENTS

目录

018　藤县狮舞
Lion Dance in Tengxian County　　034

048　藤县牛歌戏
Ox-song Opera in Tengxian County　　062

074　藤县水上船歌
The Boat Song in Tengxian County　　081

088　藤县乞巧节
Qiqiao Festival in Tengxian County　　095

102　藤县杖头木偶戏
Cane-head Puppet Show in Tengxian County　　106

110　藤县八音
Eight-Tone Music in Tengxian County　　114

118　藤县龙母传说
Legend of Loong Mother in Tengxian County　　122

128　藤县太平米饼制作工艺
Taiping Rice Cake Production Craft in Tengxian County　　134

140　彩扎（藤县狮头）
Lion Head Colorful Tying Craft in Tengxian County　　145

150 采茶歌
Tea-Picking Song 153

158 同心米粉制作工艺
The Craft of Making Tongxin Rice Noodles 163

168 藤县元宵歌
Lantern Festival Song in Tengxian County 177

184 藤县袁崇焕故事
The Story of Yuan Chonghuan in Tengxian County 192

200 藤县鱼生制作工艺
The Craft of Making Yusheng in Tengxian County 203

208 龙母出巡
Loong Mother Parade 211

214 古藤州传说
The Legend of Ancient Tengzhou 218

222 藤县道家村传说
The Legend of Daojia Village in Tengxian County 228

目录

- 234 藤县神仙脚迹传说
  The Legend of the Fairy Footprints in Tengxian County　237

- 240 藤县思罗河传说
  The Legend of Siluo River in Tengxian County　244

- 248 藤县咸酸菜制作工艺
  The Technique of Making Pickled Mustard Greens in Tengxian County　253

- 258 藤县抢花炮
  Hua Pao (Fire Cracker Ball) in Tengxian County　262

- 266 藤县木偶制作技艺
  Puppet-Making Craft in Tengxian County　270

- 274 藤县赛龙舟习俗
  The Custom of Loong Boat Racing in Tengxian County　278

- 282 藤县彩龙编织技艺
  The Weaving Technique of Colorful Loong in Tengxian County　286

290 木面筛
Mumian Shai: A Wooden Mask Performance　292

294 藤县黑米饭制作工艺
Preparing Black Rice in Tengxian County　298

302 藤县龙母诞
Loong Mother's Birthday Celebration in Tengxian County　305

308 斗鸡
Cockfighting　310

312 斗蟋蟀
Cricket Fighting　314

316 藤县古龙舞豹节
Gulong Town's Leopard Dance Festival in Tengxian County　318

322 藤县太平二帝庙装色出游
Taiping Two Emperors' Temple Parade in Tengxian County　326

目录

- 330 　上灯
  Shang Deng: The Lantern Lighting Ceremony　333

- 336 　藤县发糕制作技艺
  The Craft of Making Fagao in Tengxian County　340

- 344 　藤县山歌
  Folk Songs of Tengxian County　349

- 354 　藤县上灯歌
  The Songs of Lighting Up in Tengxian County　357

- 360 　藤县做社习俗
  The Custom of Sacrificing to the God of Land in Tengxian County　365

- 368 　藤县疳积散制药技艺
  Pharmaceutical Technique of Making Ganji San in Tengxian County　370

- 372 　藤县青砖烧制技艺
  Firing Technique of Greenish-black Brick in Tengxian County　377

- 381 　后记
  Afterword　383

藤县狮舞

○ 廖金胜　周雄

狮舞，藤县民间又称"舞狮""舞狮子"。藤县素有"舞狮之乡"的美称。据史料记载以及流传下来的实物佐证，藤县狮舞形成于唐朝年间（约718年）至清乾隆十四年（1749年），成熟兴盛于清乾隆至新中国成立初期，发展创新于当代，至今已有1300多年的历史。古时候狮舞又称"太平乐"。藤县狮舞是藤县劳动人民在长期的社会生活中创造的文化瑰宝，具有浓郁的地域特色和民族特色。

舞狮运动，是中华民族优秀的传统文化和民族体育活动。中国舞狮分南北两派。藤县狮舞属"南狮"，具有浓郁的乡土气息，有自成体系的两种表演，一种是侧重于地面表演的传

藤县狮舞

藤县2019年举办世界狮王争霸赛现场 / 欧伟文 摄

2023年春节，奶茶街舞狮活动中群众对狮舞的喜爱 / 欧伟文　摄

统套路狮舞即地狮，如拆蟹、拆蜈蚣等；另一种是侧重于高桩上技艺表演的高桩狮。无论是地狮还是高桩狮，在表现形式上都有着自己独特的风格而备受世人所关注喜爱。

　　藤县狮舞的行头一般由狮子、大头佛、马骝（"猴子"的粤语表述）等组成，配以锣、鼓、镲等打击乐器。这些乐器演奏起来节奏明快、雄壮热烈、气势磅礴。狮子由一人舞狮头，另一人弯腰舞狮尾。狮子造型威武雄壮，形神俱似。藤县狮舞的狮子分文狮、武狮、少狮三大类。文狮以刘备、关公作脸谱，以黄色和红色为主色调，表现温驯和善；武狮以张飞作脸谱，以黑色为主色调，表现勇猛刚烈；少狮即幼狮，多为彩色调，憨态可爱，一般随文武狮同场表演。大头佛由一人扮演，扮演者戴上一个满脸慈祥笑容的佛面具，穿上袈裟，手执葵扇引领、戏弄狮子，动作笨拙，诙谐幽默，令人捧腹大笑。马骝是由一人戴马骝面具，扮演孙悟空的角色，头戴紧箍咒，手拿金箍棒，跳跃舞棒，挤眉弄眼，咧嘴叫，举手望远，在前方护卫引行表演队伍。

大头佛、马骝的伴舞一般出现在传统的地狮中，高桩狮不采用大头佛、马骝作伴舞。

富有特色的传统地狮

藤县狮舞是清乾隆十四年（1749年）至清宣统二年（1910年）期间由藤县濛江富炉社子孙堂（现濛江子孙堂醒狮团）的前辈们，在传承历史流传的狮舞技艺基础上，吸纳各时期各地狮舞队的特点，模仿表现狮子喜、怒、醉、乐、醒、惊、疑、猛、动、静十大神态，创造出具有当地地域特色和民族特色的狮舞技艺。

民国初年，广东佛山的吴细牛、陈添二人来到濛江，担任富炉社子孙堂狮舞打击乐和狮舞技艺的师傅，富炉社子孙堂老前辈何兆元、黄渭清等不断把传统套路技艺传承发扬，逐步形成并完善了一整套舞狮传统的节目套路、表演技法和打击乐技法，从而规范了狮舞技艺，增加了表演的艺术性。

南狮传统套路的主要特征是侧重于地面技艺表演，传统节目有雄狮拆蟹、狮子吃柚、狮子拆蜈蚣、大头佛梳妆照镜、高台采青、狮子摘银圆等。采青是藤县传统狮舞的精髓。所谓"青"有狭义和广义之分。狭义的"青"指的是一份采物，代表狮子需要采摘、捕获的食物。这个"食物"在当地民间通常用几棵带根的生菜和一封红利市（红包）扎成一扎代替，寓意生财有道、大吉大利。广义的"青"是指狮子所要表演或者需要去破解的阵法，比如千百年来在当地民间流传至今的蟹青、蛇青、银牌等，就是主家为了考究狮子的功架、技艺、智慧、技能而设置的一种青阵。藤县舞狮青阵和套路的形式是藤县民间老艺人根据人们生产生活和历史人物、传奇故事的内容设计的，乐器的使用套路和技法是按照狮子的形态、神态、动态设计完成的。目前，仍保留下来的传统表演套路（技法）主要有参拜、起狮、三星、抛狮、洗脚、食青等六种。参拜（行礼）是分三次，先由左边开始，依次为左、右、中，要求前进约五步，退后约五步，再以四平马步法开狮口，举狮向左、向右；起狮是用右手握起，左手按狮口，左右摆动狮头走一个圈；三星是阴阳手按狮口，四平马、弓步马（如寻找食物动态，四五次左右不等）；抛狮是准备去试探食物，步法有四平马、合脚跳前一步和开四平三个动作；洗脚是先左脚摆前用狮头洗脚的动作，洗完左脚、洗右脚、再洗左脚，后举起狮头摇动；食青是狮子开口吃东西慢

大头佛戏醒狮表演 / 霍雨锋　摄

藤县狮舞

地狮表演——狮子拆蜈蚣 / 欧伟文　摄

慢咬嚼，左边吐，右边吐，中间再吐生菜，吃完后洗脚。

乐器使用的传统套路（技法）主要有擂鼓、起狮鼓、行狮鼓、抛狮鼓、七星鼓、洗牙鼓、拆蟹鼓、大头佛鼓、桩狮鼓等九种。擂鼓是开始拜神或行礼时，左、右、中擂鼓三次作为仪式的开始。起狮鼓是拜完神或行完礼后开始起舞时使用的鼓点。具体打法是先打鼓边后打鼓心。行狮鼓（三星鼓）是狮子左望右望，寻找食物的动作，循环二至三次。抛狮鼓是狮子试探食物或食青的动作，循环三次。七星鼓是狮子咬七星试探动作，看其动作判断可否进食，循环三次……

地狮在舞动时，由戴着顽皮马骝面具和满脸笑容的大头佛面具的队员（引狮人）带路引逗、护卫，在燃放的爆竹声中和锣鼓打击乐的配合下按不同套路进行表演。地狮表演以活泼可爱、滑稽顽皮、威武雄壮、动作细腻为特点，多用于节日庆典、集会、拜年、祝贺、婚庆等喜庆活动以及娱乐。

精彩绝伦的时代高桩狮

1995年,藤县南安镇禤洲村的武术和狮舞教练祝启春、邓明华,组建了一支年龄在8～16岁的青少年禤洲武术队,并在次年的县春节文艺表演中以精彩的武术节目赢得了群众的赞赏和关注。而后,团县委和县体育局敏锐地意识到可以把这支武术队打造成

藤县狮舞

一支狮舞队，于是指导成立了以祝启春、邓明华为队长的藤县体校禤洲武术醒狮队，在禤洲初中球场露天场地开展训练。

为掌握狮舞技艺，禤洲武术醒狮队组织队员到远近闻名的濛江子孙堂醒狮团学习传统狮舞基本技艺，随后在传统套路的基础上，通过录像资料、上门请教等方式学习上高桩狮舞的基本技术，运用传统技艺和现代技艺相结合的方法，根据狮子的神态并借用武术、舞蹈、杂技的表现手法，创新设计形成了竞技性很强的藤县民间高桩狮舞新形式。高桩狮是在极其简陋的条件下，大部分利用自制的器材，历尽千辛万苦，经受无数挫折，在多年磨炼中不断探索逐渐成熟的。

高桩狮，是从中国武术的梅花桩阵中得到启发，在传统套路采青的基础上形成的，强调动作惊险、刺激和高难度。由于要在高桩上表演，其采青的表意性受到高桩的限制而难度更大、更惊险。

国际龙狮运动联合会对高桩狮的桩阵规格设有统一的规定，但藤县高桩狮的要求更高，其桩阵共18根桩，桩与桩之间距离为0.7

2024年6月2日，在中国—东盟国际龙舟公开赛开幕式上的高桩狮表演 / 霍雨锋 摄

米，最大跨度达 2.8 米，飞距达 3.5 米。最高的桩为 2.8 米，最低的桩为 1.6 米（开始时按 1.4 米），每个桩柱顶面直径只有 0.35 米。这样的高桩，一般人上桩行走都非常困难，而禤洲武术醒狮队要在高桩上跳跃翻飞，用快、稳、准、灵活、协调、惊险的动作来表现造型的力量美、艺术美和完整套路，难度可想而知，特色也是十分鲜明的。

高桩狮的主要特征是侧重于空中技艺表演。桩阵结构为长方形，一般情况下，桩摆放在观众视觉效果最好的位置。藤县高桩狮的套路设计，是根据狮子的神态（喜、怒、醉、乐、醒、惊、疑、猛、动、静、寻、望、探、烦等）和狮子的面对物（山、岭、溪、涧、索、桥、水等）来完成的，目前已形成了包含"飞攀上桩""侧空翻下桩""桩上钢线前滚翻""钢线一字腿""飞桩 3.5 米""独桩挟腰转体 450 度""金狮倒挂"

2023年春节，藤县泗洲岛水上高桩狮表演 / 霍雨锋 摄

等13个精湛的国家专项狮舞绝技的套路。这些绝技，传统与现代相结合，武术与舞艺相结合，需要教练员和运动员有扎实的武术功底、良好的体能、敏捷的身手、高度的团队合作意识、过硬的心理素质、不俗的创新能力。运动员需要从七八岁就开始训练，经过时间的磨炼，风雨的锤打，精气神的凝聚契合，在漫长的岁月里成就高超的本领。

不负青春世界封王

1999年12月，藤县狮队参加广西狮王大赛荣获金奖。

2004年7月，藤县狮队走出国门，赴马来西亚参加第六届云顶世界狮王争霸赛。

云顶世界狮王争霸赛，逢双年举行，是世界级大赛，从

1994年至2002年共举办了5届，前来参赛的各个狮队都是各有特色的世界顶尖狮队。印度尼西亚、泰国、文莱、越南和中国台北等国家和地区狮队，富有多次参加国际大赛并获奖的经验。新加坡和中国香港、中国澳门的狮队在国际大赛中也屡有建树。中国广东佛山是南狮的发源地，狮队表演有细腻的表情、过硬的技术和丰富的大赛临场经验，他们对夺冠充满信心。马来西亚号称舞狮王国，蝉联了前五届云顶世界狮王争霸赛的冠军，又是举办赛事的东道主，占尽天时、地利、人和。为了继续称王，2004年，他们派出3支强队参赛，志在构筑夺冠保杯三重保险。

第六届云顶世界狮王争霸赛于2004年7月9日至11日举行，分预赛和决赛两个阶段。这个赛事共有来自亚洲、欧洲、大洋洲、美洲等的14个国家和地区的23支狮队参加，预赛阶段的前十名方能进入决赛。藤县狮队以9.19分的最高分夺得预赛第一名，顺利杀入决赛。

决赛阶段，藤县狮队的队员以敏捷的侧空翻进场，朝气蓬勃，雄姿英发。行礼完毕，狮子在赛场四周绕场作出野外玩耍、寻青、见青、惊青、戏青等传统动作。比赛动作正式开始，狮子面对

藤县狮舞

2023 年，中国龙狮公开赛（广西藤县站）南狮高桩自选套路决赛 / 霍雨锋　摄

东方狮王出少年 / 何锦奋 摄

1.3 米的高桩（其他狮队只有 0.5 米）飞身上桩，接着在最高 2.7 米、最大桩距 1.95 米的 18 根桩阵上，施展金鸡独立、2.2 米距离往返 180 度转身飞桩、追星赶月、探峰攀岩、天狗追月、雄狮抖威、饿狮擒猪、雄狮过天桥、雄狮坐头走钢绳、雄狮行空飞天桥、狮子侧空翻下桩等绝技。藤县狮队凭借独创的绝活和超高难度的技术，行云流水，一气呵成，最终以 9.23 分与马来西亚麻坡关圣宫龙狮团并列第一名。藤县狮队从此世界封王，获得"东方狮王""世界狮王"美誉，开启了高光时刻。

弦歌不断薪火相传

藤县狮队荣获"东方狮王""世界狮王"称号后，继续南征北战，参赛表演，在各种赛事斩金夺银的同时，在精神提炼、文化升华方面不断走向成熟，形成了艰苦奋斗、刻苦训练、团结协作、勇于创新、顽强拼搏、敢闯高峰的"东方狮王"理念。

藤县狮舞从襦洲出发，走向全国，走向了世界，影响力不断扩大。2004 年，广西电视台拍摄并播出狮队的故事《小岛狮队出国》。2006 年，北京东方明星数字影视中心拍摄的数字电影《东方狮王》，于 2007 年上映并获得第六届美国圣地亚哥国际儿童电影节优秀影片奖。藤县狮队不断受邀在中央电视台和全国各地省级电视台参加系列节目演出，藤县狮队的故事也多次获中央电视台、新华社、人民网等主流媒体宣传。藤县狮队 2019 年受邀上中央广播电视总台春节联欢晚会演出，2022 年、2023 年连续两年受邀参加中央广播电视总台元宵晚会，并多次随中国文化交流团到法国、瑞典、蒙古国、新加坡等地参加文化交流活动。据不完全统计，截至 2024 年 8 月，藤县狮队在国内外舞狮大赛中累计获金、银、铜奖 300 多项。藤县现有国际级舞狮裁判（教练）8 人，国家一级舞狮裁判（教练）15 人，国家二级舞狮裁判（教练）36 人。2000 年，藤县狮队成为国家 A 级狮队。

国外不少舞狮权威人士、专家表示，中国广西藤县狮队对世界舞狮难度技术发展起到了非常重要的推动作用。最主要的难度技术有：2 米高空腾空飞跃 3.5 米（雄狮飞天桥）、2.8 米高空单桩间飞跃 1.95 米（雄狮闯天涯）、接狮子挂桩（倒挂金狮）、钢绳前滚翻（雄狮前滚翻下天桥）、侧空翻下桩（雄狮空翻）、飞身上桩 1.6 米（猿猴攀树）。这些动作改变了舞狮上高桩一直是以 0.5 米或 0.8 米为桩起点的高度。另外，于 2006 年 9 月在梧州市举办的国际狮王争霸赛中，藤县狮队的狮尾采青，经现场专家审核鉴定并签字通过为独创的新难度动作。

独创的飞身上桩、侧空翻下桩、狮尾采青等高难度技艺成为藤县狮队的秘密武器，影响了世界舞狮界，引得其他狮队争相效仿。

多年来，藤县狮队一直在守正创新，接续奋斗。一些队员到自治区各市县和广东等地传道授业，把"东方狮王"的技艺发扬光大。坚守藤县本土的队员，继续顽强拼搏，不断取得新成绩。藤县县委、县政府还出台文件、政策，推动狮舞进校园，在幼儿园、小学、中学、中专校园开设特色课堂，不断传承和发扬藤县狮舞。

2007 年，藤县狮舞技艺列入第一批市级非物质文化遗产代表性项目名录，同年列入第一批自治区级非物质文化遗产代表性项目名录。2011 年，藤县狮舞列入第三批国家级非物质文化遗产代表性项目名录。2016 年，藤县被评为广西十大民族传统体育保护传承示范基地，藤县世界狮王争霸赛被命名为广西少数民族传统体育品牌赛事项目。2021 年，藤县狮舞入选中华体育文化优秀民族项目。2023 年，藤县世界狮王争霸赛入选 2023 中国体育旅游精品项目。

藤县狮舞代表性传承人

级别	姓名	性别	出生时间（年）	认定时间（年）
国家级	邓明华	男	1941	2018
自治区级	苏德威	男	1982	2015
自治区级	祝盛清	男	1982	2021
自治区级	邓植伦	男	1991	2021
市级	邓彬光	男	1990	2015
市级	江龙潘	男	1993	2015
市级	邓剑文	男	1986	2015
市级	苏伟海	男	1984	2015
市级	徐贵标	男	1989	2015
县级	唐载鹏	男	1998	2018
县级	邓文海	男	1991	2018
县级	祝家志	男	1990	2018
县级	邓华金	男	1986	2018
县级	祝家俊	男	1988	2018
县级	邓静安	男	1986	2018
县级	邓慧婵	女	1981	2018

Lion Dance in Tengxian County

· Liao Jinsheng and Zhou Xiong ·

Lion dance, also referred to as the "dance of the lion" in Tengxian County, is a significant element of local folk tradition. Tengxian County is widely known as the "town of lion dance". Historical records and physical evidence suggest that lion dance in this region originated during the Tang Dynasty (circa 718 AD) and continued to develop through the 14th year of Emperor Qianlong's reign during the Qing Dynasty (1749 AD). The practice matured and flourished from the reign of Emperor Qianlong through to the early days of the founding of the People's Republic of China, and it continues to evolve in the present day. With a history spanning more than 1,300 years, lion dance has deep cultural roots. In ancient times, it was also known as "*Taipingyue*", meaning "dance of peace". Rich in both regional and national characteristics, the lion dance stands as a cultural treasure created by the working people of Tengxian County throughout their long social history.

The lion dance is not only a prominent feature of Chinese culture but also a recognized national sporting activity. In China, lion dance is divided into two schools: The Northern Lion and the Southern Lion. The lion dance of Tengxian County belongs to the Southern Lion tradition and possesses a strong local flavor, manifesting in two distinct styles. The first is the traditional routines named "ground lion", which emphasizes performance on the ground, also known as the "Caiqing lion". This style includes a variety of techniques, such as "splitting crabs" and "splitting centipedes". The second style is the "high-pile lion", which focuses on acrobatics performed on elevated platforms. Both the ground lion and high-pile lion exhibit unique performance characteristics, earning widespread admiration both locally and globally.

Costumes for the lion dance in Tengxian County typically consist of the lion, the big-headed Buddha, and the monkey, with these roles supported by percussion instruments such as gongs, drums, and cymbals. Accompanied by lively and energetic rhythms, the performance is marked by enthusiasm, majesty, and vitality. The lion is performed by two individuals: one manipulates the lion's head, while the other supports the front performer by holding onto a

2024年2月17日，藤县龙狮巡游活动中的狮舞表演 / 许景才　摄

belt and bending forward to form the lion's tail. The lion's movements are vigorous and lifelike, creating a powerful visual effect. Tengxian County's lion dance has inherited the three major categories of the Southern Lion tradition: "Wen Shi", "Wu Shi", and "Shao Shi". The "Wen Shi" lion, representing the figure of Liu Bei, is characterized by a yellow face and displays gentleness and kindness. The "Wu Shi" lion, modeled after Zhang Fei, features red, black, and white colors, embodying bravery and strength. "Shao Shi" represents a young lion and is characterized by its colorful, innocent, and playful nature. The big-headed Buddha is portrayed by an actor wearing a large smiling mask and a robe, who wields a fan and interacts humorously with the lion, often evoking laughter from the audience through exaggerated, clumsy movements. The monkey, portrayed as Sun Wukong, wears a mask with the "incantation headbands" and carries a golden staff, performing acrobatic movements that include jumping, dancing, and leading the team.

While both the big-headed Buddha and the monkey appear in the ground lion performances, they are not part of the high-pile lion dance.

The Special Group Lion

The lion dance in Tengxian County was created by the predecessors of the "Mengjiang Fulushe Zisuntang" (now known as the Mengjiang Zisuntang Lion Dance Troupe) between the 14th year of the Qianlong period (1749 AD) and the 2nd year of the Xuantong period of the Qing Dynasty (1910 AD). Based on traditional lion dance skills passed down through generations, and incorporating the unique characteristics of lion dance troupes from across Tengxian County, they imitated ten expressions of the lion: joy, anger, drunkenness, happiness, wakefulness, surprise, suspicion, fierceness, movement, and stillness. This led to the development of lion dance techniques imbued with both local and national characteristics.

藤县狮舞

狮子踩砂煲 / 廖金胜　供图

　　In the early Republic of China, Wu Xiniu and Chen Tian from Foshan, Guangdong Province, came to Mengjiang, Tengxian County. Wu served as the percussion master and Chen as the lion dance technique master of Fulushe Zisuntang. Old-timers such as He Zhaoyuan and Huang Weiqing continued to refine these traditional techniques, gradually developing standardized routines, performance skills, and percussion methods. This standardization enhanced the artistic expression of the lion dance.

　　The defining feature of the Southern Lion dance is its emphasis on ground techniques. Traditional performances include routines such as "Male Lion Splitting Crab", "Lion Eating Grapefruit", "Lion Splitting Centipede", "Big-Headed Buddha Dressing Up and Looking in the Mirror", "High Platform Caiqing", and "Lion Picking Silver Dollar". Caiqing is not only the essence of lion dance in Tengxian

藤县非遗过大年舞狮表演活动 / 霍雨锋 摄

County but also the core of lion dance activities. The term "Qing" has both narrow and broad meanings. In the narrow sense, "Qing" refers to the objects the lion must "pick", often representing food. This "food" typically consists of a few pieces of knotted lettuce with roots, accompanied by a red packet (*hongbao*), symbolizing wishes for wealth and good fortune. In the broad sense, "Qing" refers to the formations the lion must navigate or break, such as the Crab Formation, High Formation, or Bagua Formation. These formations, passed down in local folklore for centuries, are designed by the host family to test the lion's strength, skill, wisdom, and ability. The formations and performance routines (skills) of the lion dance in Tengxian County were crafted by senior folk artists from Tengxian County. These routines are based on the people's daily life, production, historic figures and legends. The use of musical instruments and the choreography are aligned lion's appearance, expressions and movements. Currently, traditional routines still performed include: (1) Worshiping (Worshiping the Immortal): This involves three stages. The lion moves forward five steps, then back five steps, making four Shaolin Temple-style "flat horse steps".

The lion's mouth is opened, and the lion is lifted from left to right. (2) Raising the Lion: The performer holds the lion's head with the right hand and uses the left hand to press its mouth, moving the lion's head in a circular motion. (3) Three-Stars: The performer uses "Yin and Yang" hands to press the lion's mouth, combined with four flat horse steps and lunge horse steps, while the lion searches for food. (4) Throwing the Lion: The lion "tastes" the food, performed with four flat horse steps and one forward step, repeated three times. (5) Washing Feet: The lion washes its feet by swinging its head left, right, and back again, followed by shaking its head. (6) Eating "Qing": The lion mimics slow eating, chewing, and spitting lettuce to the left, right, and center, followed by washing its feet after eating.

The musical accompaniment follows traditional drumming patterns, which include: (1) Drumming for Worship: The drum is struck three times, left, right, and center, to begin worship or rituals. (2) Drumming for Starting: After worship, the drum plays, striking the side and then the center of the drum skin. (3) Drumming for Acting (Three-Star Drum): The lion looks left and right, searching for food, repeated two to three times. (4) Drumming for Throwing: Preparatory drumming for approaching the food, repeated three times. (5) Seven-Star Drum: Drumming to test the lion's actions, repeated three times. (6) Drumming for Washing Teeth: Accompanied by specific movements for cleaning the lion's mouth. (7) Drumming for Demolishing the Crab: For the lion's act of breaking a crab. (8) Drumming for the Big-Headed Buddha: Accompanying the playful performance of the Big-Headed Buddha. (9) Drumming for the Pile Lion: A routine where the lion climbs on a stack.

During the ground lion dance, team members guide and guard the lion, wearing masks such as the mischievous monkey or the smiling Big-Headed Buddha. The lion performs alongside firecrackers and percussion music, following distinct routines. The ground lion dance is characterized by its lively, adorable, playful, powerful, and intricate movements. It is performed during festive occasions such as festival celebrations, New Year greetings, weddings, and other joyous gatherings.

The Outstanding Modern High-Pile Lion

In 1995, Zhu Qichun and Deng Minghua, both martial arts and lion dance instructors from Xuanzhou Village, Nan'an Town, Tengxian County, formed a youth martial arts team composed of members aged 8 to 16. This team gained public recognition and appreciation following a remarkable lion dance performance during the county's Spring Festival cultural celebration the following year. Recognizing the potential of the team, the County Youth League Committee and the County Sports Bureau decided to transform the martial arts group into a lion dance team. Thus, the Xuanzhou Martial Arts Lion Dance Team of the Tengxian County Sports School was established, with Zhu Qichun and Deng Minghua serving as captains. Training was conducted in the open field at Xuanzhou Junior High School.

To master lion dance techniques, the Xuanzhou team began by learning the basic skills of traditional lion dance from the renowned Mengjiang Zisuntang Lion Dance Troupe. Building upon the traditional routines, they furthered their skills by studying the high-pile lion dance through video materials, in-person guidance, and other methods. Merging traditional and modern techniques, they developed a new, highly competitive form of folk lion dance in Tengxian County, known as the "High-Pile Lion". This innovative form draws upon martial arts, dance, acrobatics, and lion's traditional expressions to create a distinctive performance. Training for the high-pile lion dance was conducted under extremely modest conditions, with much of the equipment being homemade. The team faced many challenges, setbacks, and failures, but over years of exploration and refinement, they matured into a skilled and disciplined troupe.

The high-pile lion dance emphasizes thrilling, exciting, and difficult movements. It is inspired by the quincuncial piles array of Chinese martial arts and is rooted in the traditional Caiqing lion dance. However, due to the physical restrictions imposed by the high piles elevated nature of the performance, the expressiveness of "Caiqing" is more challenging and breathtaking.

The International Dragon and Lion Federation has established standard specifications for the stakes used in High-Pile Lion Dance. However, the standards in Tengxian County are more demanding. The pile formation consists of 18 piles, with spans between them ranging from 0.7 to 2.8 meters, and in some cases up to 3.5 meters. The highest pile stands at 2.8 meters, and the lowest at 1.6 meters (initially 1.4 meters). Each pile top is only 0.35 meters wide, making it difficult for the average person to walk on, let alone perform complex routines. The Xuanzhou Martial Arts Lion Dance Team not only dances and jumps on these high piles but does so while showcasing the power, grace, and artistry of the lion dance with movements that are fast, steady, precise, flexible, harmonious, and thrilling. Despite the difficulty, these characteristics define the high-pile lion dance.

The main feature of the High-Pile Lion Dance is its focus on aerial acrobatics. The pile formation is typically arranged in a rectangular pattern to maximize visual impact for the audience. The dance routines are designed around the lion's traditional expressions (such as happiness, anger, drunkenness, joy, wakefulness, fear, suspicion, and fierceness) and the obstacles it encounters (mountains, ridges, streams, rivers, ropes, bridges, water, etc.). Today, the High-Pile Lion Dance includes a set of stunts that combine tradition with modernity, featuring movements like "fly to the pile", "side flip down pile", "steel line forward roll on pile", "steel line split on pile", "3.5-meter flying pile", "single-pile waist turn 450 degrees", and "golden lion hanging upside down" among others. These special stunts require coaches and performers with solid martial arts training, exceptional physical fitness, dexterity, mental focus, bravery, and a spirit of innovation. Athletes typically begin training at the age of seven or eight, enduring long hours and countless challenges. Over the years, they have not only mastered these skills but have also created a modern-day legend in the world of lion dance.

The Lion Dance of Tengxian County: A World-Renowned Legacy

In December 1999, the Tengxian County Lion Dance Troupe won the gold medal at the Guangxi Lion King Competition, marking the beginning of their unstoppable rise to prominence. By July 2004, the troupe had gained international recognition, participating in the 6th Genting World Lion Dance Championship in Malaysia.

The Genting World Lion Dance Championship, held biennially since 1994, is a prestigious global competition that had seen five editions prior to 2004. Competing teams represent the elite of the lion dance world, with distinctive styles and extensive experience. Teams from Indonesia, Thailand, Brunei, Vietnam, and Chinese Taipei are seasoned competitors in international tournaments. Meanwhile, Singapore, Hong Kong, and Macau have also achieved notable success on the global stage. As the birthplace of the Southern Lion, Foshan in Guangdong Province boasts a team known for its refined expressions and exceptional skill. Malaysia, often referred to as the Kingdom of Lion Dance, had won the previous five Genting Cup Championships and, as the host nation, enjoyed the advantage of home-ground support. To safeguard their championship title, Malaysia entered three strong teams, hoping to secure a triple assurance of victory.

The 6th Genting World Lion Dance Championship, held from July 9 to July 11, 2004, was divided into two stages: the preliminary

藤县狮舞

迎新春 / 欧伟文 摄

round and the final. A total of 23 lion dance teams from 14 countries and regions across Asia, Europe, Oceania, and the Americas competed in the preliminary round, with the top ten advancing to the final stage. Tengxian County's lion dance team secured first place in the preliminaries with an outstanding score of 9.19 points, earning their spot in the final.

During the final, the Tengxian County lion dance team entered the arena with an agile side somersault, radiating energy and confidence. After saluting, the lion gracefully circled the field, performing traditional movements such as playing in the wild,

舞狮进校园——在藤县一中训练 / 廖金胜　摄

searching for "Qing", discovering "Qing", expressing surprise at "Qing", and playing with "Qing". Unlike other teams, which only had to navigate 0.5-meter piles, the Tengxian team faced the daunting challenge of 1.30-meter piles. The performance began with the lion flying onto the piles, then standing on 18 stakes, the tallest of which was 2.70 meters high, with a maximum gap of 1.95 meters between them. The team's routine featured breathtaking feats such as the "Golden Rooster Standing on One Leg", "leaping across a 2.20-meter gap and spinning 180 degrees", "Chasing Stars and the Moon", "Climbing the Peak", and "The Dog Chasing the Moon". Other stunts included "The Lion Shows Its Power", "The Hungry Lion Capturing

Pigs", "The Lion Crossing the Overpass", "The Lion Walking the Steel Rope by Sitting on Its Head", and "The Lion Flipping from the Side of the Pile". Their extraordinary and difficult stunts captivated the audience, and the troupe's innovative choreography earned them a tie for first place with Malaysia's Kun Seng Keng Lion and Dragon Dance Association, with both teams scoring 9.23 points. This victory crowned the Tengxian County lion dance team as the "Lion King of the East" and the "Lion King of the World", securing their place as one of the most iconic lion dance troupes on the global stage.

The Legacy of Tengxian County Lion Dance: Passing Tradition to the Next Generation

Following its triumph as the "Lion King of the East" and the "Lion King of the World", the Tengxian County Lion Dance Troupe continued its journey across China, actively participating in performances and competitions. As the troupe accumulated numerous gold and silver medals, it matured both in skill and in the refinement of its cultural and spiritual essence. The spirit of the "Lion King of the East" evolved, embodying values such as hard work, rigorous training, unity, cooperation, innovation, resilience, and the determination to reach new heights.

Originally born in Xuanzhou, Tengxian County's lion dance has expanded its influence globally. In 2004, Guangxi Radio and Television documented this journey in a broadcast titled "The Lion Team of the Island Went Abroad". Two years later, Beijing Star Digital Film and Television Company produced "Oriental King Lion", a digital film released in 2007 and won an award at the San Diego International Kids' Film Festival. Tengxian County's Lion Dance Troupe has been invited to perform on provincial television stations across China, and their story has been featured by major media outlets, including CCTV, Xinhua News Agency, and People's Daily. Notably, they performed at the CCTV Spring Festival Gala in 2019 and were invited to the CCTV Lantern Festival Gala in both 2022 and 2023. The troupe has also engaged in cultural exchange activities, representing China in France, Sweden, Mongolia, and Singapore. As of August 2024, they had earned over 300 gold, silver, and bronze awards in both domestic and international lion dance competitions. Currently, Tengxian County is home to 8 international lion dance judges (and coaches), 15 national-level (Class 1) judges (and coaches), and 36 national-level (Class 2) judges (and coaches). In 2000, the Tengxian County Lion Dance Troupe was designated a national A-level lion dance troupe.

International lion dance authorities and experts recognize the significant contributions of the Tengxian County Lion Troupe in advancing the technical complexity of the lion dance. Some of their most challenging and iconic movements include the 3.50-meter "Lion Flying Bridge", the 2.8-meter "Single-Pile Leap" (with a 1.95-meter gap), and the "Ape Climbing Trees" stunt, where the lion leaps directly onto a 1.6-meter pile. These techniques pushed the boundaries of high-pile lion dancing, which traditionally started from a pile height of just 0.5 to 0.8 meters. Furthermore, during the International Lion Championships in Wuzhou in September, 2006, the team introduced the innovative movement, which was adopted by experts as a new, highly difficult maneuver.

The original routines of "flying pile", "side flip down pile" and "Lion Tail Caiqing" once unique to the Teng County lion dance troupe, have become their signature moves. These difficult skills have not only influenced the global lion dance community but also inspired other teams to adopt them.

Despite these accomplishments, the Tengxian County Lion Dance Troupe remains committed to its ongoing mission. Some members have traveled to other regions, such as Guangdong, to teach and promote the "Lion King of the East" spirit and skills. In recognition of the troupe's impact, the Tengxian County Party Committee and government implemented policies to integrate lion dance into educational institutions. Special lion dance classes were introduced in kindergartens, primary schools, middle schools, and specialized secondary schools, ensuring that the Tengxian County lion dance tradition is preserved and passed on to future generations.

In 2007, the Tengxian County Lion Dance was included in the first batch of both municipal and provincial intangible cultural heritage lists. By 2011, it was added to the third batch of the national intangible cultural heritage list. In 2016, Tengxian County was designated as one of Guangxi's top ten demonstration bases for the protection and inheritance of ethnic traditional sports, and the World (Tengxian County) Lion King Competition was named a Guangxi Ethnic Traditional Sports Brand Event. In 2021, the State General Administration of Sports designated the Tengxian County Lion Dance as an Outstanding Ethnic Program of Chinese Sports and Culture. In 2023, the World (Tengxian County) Lion King Competition was selected as a China Sports Tourism Quality Project.

The Representative Inheritors of the Lion Dance in Tengxian County

Level	Name	Gender	Year of Birth	Time of Certification
National	Deng Minghua	Male	1941	2018
Provincial	Su Dewei	Male	1982	2015
Provincial	Zhu Shengqing	Male	1982	2021
Provincial	Deng Zhilun	Male	1991	2021
Municipal	Deng Binguang	Male	1990	2015
Municipal	Jiang Longpan	Male	1993	2015
Municipal	Deng Jianwen	Male	1986	2015
Municipal	Su Weihai	Male	1984	2015
Municipal	Xu Guibiao	Male	1989	2015
County	Tang Zaipeng	Male	1998	2018
County	Deng Wenhai	Male	1991	2018
County	Zhu Jiazhi	Male	1990	2018
County	Deng Huajin	Male	1986	2018
County	Zhu Jiajun	Male	1988	2018
County	Deng Jing'an	Male	1986	2018
County	Deng Huichan	Female	1981	2018

藤县牛歌戏

○ 林源

　　自古以来，很多地方的人们在耕作生产和社会生活中，都会以歌舞戏曲抒怀。随着历史不断演进，各地便逐渐形成了地方特色浓郁、民族风格鲜明的独特民间艺术形式，藤县牛歌戏便是其中一种。

　　《诗经》有诗句"窈窕淑女，君子好逑""求之不得，寤寐思服"。藤县牛歌戏有唱词"亚妹生得白漂漂，好似石灰初出窑。若是嫁比我做老婆，冇使你担水劈柴烧"。牛歌戏唱词用的是藤县白话（属粤语），意思是"姑娘生得白白净净好

藤县牛歌戏

装扮好准备演出的牛歌戏演员 / 许旭芒　霍雨锋　何柏　摄

| 藤县非遗传录 |

2022年藤县牛歌戏展演活动剧照 / 何柏　摄　　　　藤县首届"牛歌戏之乡"杯戏剧大赛 / 欧伟文　摄

漂亮，好像刚出窑的石灰一样洁白无瑕，如果嫁给我做老婆，我会爱你疼你，不用你做挑水劈柴这种粗重的农活"。穿越2000多年的时空，藤县牛歌戏与《诗经》竟然有着如此相近的人间意韵。

古时候中国划分九州，藤县在荆州辖区。《汉书·地理志》记载，藤县属百越之地。无论是九州之分，还是百越之地，在以水路交通为主的年代，地处西江干流浔江边上的藤县，在中原民众源源不断迁徙岭南的进程中，南北文化交会，各种语言融合，经过一方水土的孕育和后来不断发展，最终形成继承了中古汉语较多成分的藤县白话。藤县人用白话交流，用白话唱山歌和表演。

地处丘陵山区的藤县，人们在艰苦的劳作当中，以唱白话山歌来纾解苦闷、表达喜悦。人们稻作靠水牛，水牛是人们心目中带有特殊感情的家畜。在年节期间，或重大祭祀仪式上，当地民众会跳一种叫"舞春牛"的舞蹈。作为道具的牛，是由竹篾编织、绵纸裱糊并用颜色勾画的"牛头"和布料缝制的

"牛身"组成的。"舞春牛"一般由两组人组成，一组人负责敲击锣鼓，一组人负责跳舞。跳舞者有四人，二人分别舞牛头、牛身，模仿牛的动作跳舞，类似于舞狮；一人戴人头面具、手执刀棍，按锣鼓节点吆喝或舞弄刀棍作驱牛状；一人戴猴头面具，模仿猴子动作跳来跳去戏牛。而旁边观者，深受感染，欢呼惊叹，擅山歌者便即兴赋歌。反过来，敲击锣鼓者和舞者，被歌声吸引，为听歌而暂停打击锣鼓和跳舞。双方逐渐形成默契，你敲锣打鼓和跳舞时我不唱歌，我唱歌时你不敲锣鼓、不跳舞，交替表演，甚为有趣。久而久之，唱山歌者不断提炼歌词，充分运用方言俚语，讲究平仄押韵对偶，便形成了"舞时不歌、歌时不舞"的"牛歌"。经过漫长的历史发展，"舞春牛"演变成舞台戏曲牛歌戏。

牛歌戏的流传

一方水土，一方风物。牛歌戏发源于藤县，使用的是藤县白话，民间自发流传在藤县及其周边语言相近的地区，在藤县南部地区相对较为集中，如金鸡、岭景、象棋等地，并在苍梧、梧州市区、容县、北流、平南、桂平和广东的封开、郁南、信宜等白话地区开枝散叶，覆盖人口超过1000万人。行内普遍认为，清光绪元年（1875年），藤县金鸡镇安村村坡"兆丰年"龙会演出的《亚赖卖猪》，是牛歌舞台戏的肇始。龙会把山间田头劳作唱和、"舞春牛"的山歌正儿八经搬上了戏台，"牛歌戏"之名正式流传。此后陆续产生一批名气较大的牛歌戏班，如清光绪二十三年（1897年）岭景篁村的"同庆堂"，民国十二年（1923年）金鸡乡的"群英乐"，民国三十五年（1946年）象棋乡的"群英社"。到了20世纪70—80年代，藤县牛歌戏进入成熟鼎盛时期，全县有270多个牛歌戏班。1986年，藤县牛歌戏作为我国地方剧种，编入《中国戏曲志·广西卷》。

牛歌戏的行当

藤县牛歌戏发展成为地方戏曲，与其他戏曲一样，有完整的行当表演体系，也分生、旦、净、丑等行当，人手不够时通常都需要男女串角表演。

生行是扮演男性角色的一种行当，有老生、小生、武生、红生、娃娃生之分。

旦行是扮演各种不同年龄、不同性格、不同身份的女性角色。旦行分青衣、花旦、武旦、老旦、彩旦、花衫。其中彩旦扮演滑稽诙谐的喜剧性人物，花衫是全才演员。

净行俗称花面，一般扮演男性角色，分正净、副净、武净。

牛歌戏的脸谱

藤县白话把"演牛歌戏"叫"搬戏""做戏"。牛歌戏的"做"，主要体现在脸谱上。从民国时期到新中国成立初期，由于条件的限制，藤县牛歌戏脸谱化妆大多采用面粉胭脂化妆，色彩不够鲜艳，个性特征不够突出，仅在眼、眉、口、鼻稍加变化，以区别生、旦、净、丑。生角直眉、眼角弯向上、鼻直口方。旦角弯眉、鼻细直、嘴小似樱桃。净角剑眉、眼大、脸有皱纹、嘴方阔，如果是画大花脸，一般参考民间木偶脸谱。丑角三角眼、眉梢下垂、鼻梁画一块白色。牛歌戏演员脸谱通过简单地勾线描画，就把角色分清楚了。

牛歌戏演员正在化妆 / 周雄　摄

　　随着经济社会发展，戏曲化妆材料也丰富起来。藤县牛歌戏脸谱化妆逐渐使用油彩，有黄、白、红、黑、紫等多种颜色，并根据剧中人物的身份、年龄、相貌、性格等需要，在脑门、眉、眼、鼻、嘴、脸颊等部位加以夸张渲染，描绘图案，并不断借鉴粤剧、京剧等剧种的化妆技法，使人物形象更加生动。

牛歌戏的服饰

　　藤县牛歌戏的服饰，有其基本的特点。生角扎花布头围，身穿花布长衫；文生扎头包布，左耳边插一绒球，身穿大襟长衫，腰间扎一条红布带。旦角戴盔头，上身穿花布大襟衫，下身围一条红裙；花旦身着花布大襟衫，披云肩着白裙或花裙，头包布外套花头。其他角色一般着宽松唐装，高领、袖小。

牛歌戏的伴乐

大音希声。藤县牛歌戏的伴乐，倔强地保留着简单纯粹的打击乐，没有管弦乐，是至今存世极少的不用管弦伴奏的戏曲之一。正是这种倔强，恰恰保存了牛歌戏的本真。

藤县牛歌戏的打击乐器，似乎太简陋了，只有锣、鼓、镲、竹梆四样。锣、鼓、镲奏的是热闹，一如粤剧的"喳笃撑"，响亮的金属摩擦声音和激荡的牛皮鼓点声音，驱牛赶牛的声音分贝足够了。竹梆要来干什么呢？驼有驼铃，牛有牛铃，山区放牛，自由放牧，早上赶上山，傍晚找牛回，但山高林密，牛如何去找？人们聪明得很，取一短节大竹留着两头竹节，开一条槽，吊几块厚铁片或硬木段，制成竹梆，挂在牛脖子下。牛头、脖子一动，铁片或硬木摆动敲在竹梆上，竹梆便发出"咯当咯当"悠扬动听的声音，这竹梆便是水牛的定位器。藤县白话称"咯嘞"。年复一年，竹梆与水牛总有着说不清道不明的情愫，似乎二者成为一体。于是，牛歌戏的伴奏乐器，一定得有竹梆。

就是这么简陋的乐器，"咯咯咯咚咚嚓"一响，男女老幼的精气神就上来了，大家交头接耳，猜想着今晚演什么戏、谁演什么角色，人们简单而又平淡的幸福时刻从此上演。四种打击乐器，节奏分明，在每两句唱词之间击响，唱词—击乐—圆场，反复轮回，牛歌戏带着特有的"舞时不歌、歌时不舞"的风采神韵，穿越时空向我们走来。

牛歌戏的表演

大道至简。藤县牛歌戏的表演以唱为主，唱不足时用念白补充，而表演动作也只有做手、台步、圆场等。生角甩扇子，

藤县牛歌戏

牛歌戏中的生角扮相 / 何柏 摄

旦角甩手帕，武生舞棍、棒、刀、枪，请茶、端酒、看书、写字、撑船等通通空手做动作。在发展的过程中又吸收了粤剧表演的水袖功、水波浪等程式。文生演唱缓慢而流畅，语气起伏不大，行腔平稳；武生唱得威武；旦角唱得含蓄，花腔较多注重心理变化的描述。唱法既断续，又不断不续，抑扬顿挫，回味无穷。看似简单的表演，却样样体现着"台上一分钟、台下十年功"的水平。

牛歌戏的剧本

牛歌戏原本没有文字剧本，而是先民们在观看"舞春牛"时即兴赋歌而成，随着发展进步，才逐步由一些有文化的牛歌戏爱好者编写剧本台词。在没有剧本的年代，演的都是"爆肚戏"。"爆肚"是粤剧的术语，指实时即兴创作，由有文化的点场人，在演出前讲述要演的故事梗概、扮演人物的角色要求，演员根据演出的需要，即兴作出角色表演。近代，随着演出剧本的出现，古时点场人变成了现在的导演，即兴点场变成了导演编排，演出场面感、仪式感更强。

牛歌戏的剧本唱词，运用比喻、拟人、借代、夸张、排比、双关等手法，特别是上下句对偶，唱词均衡，韵律动听。字数、音节之间有一定限制，以七言句式结构为主，四句为一组，有时候也有六句和八句的组句。偶尔也有三字、六字、八字、九字的句式。在实际演唱时，有的句子用垫字或减字的方法来求得均衡。牛歌戏的衬字由虚字构成，根据内容、行腔的需求适当使用，以完善语句的自然腔调和节奏，增强唱腔的音乐性。在词韵运用上，按照藤县白话的发音，大多唱词是用较宽的韵，如龙、连、言、张等（汉语拼音开口音），每段第一句、第二句、第四句及其他的偶数句末，需要押韵（像唐诗），且必须使用宽韵的字（如对联下联的尾字，通俗地说，是用藤县白话音拉长发音，而这个字的音始终不变）。除第一句外，其余奇数的句子，可以不押韵，但是必须使用窄韵的字如安、遮、本等（用藤县白话音拉长该字音，使语音发生变化）。每四句中的第三句尾字一定用仄声。到了现

藤县牛歌戏

在，第一句句末可以不与其他偶数句句末字押韵。有些奇数句末偶尔会用宽韵字，但是其他规则仍然不变。由于牛歌戏的字、音、韵、律都是按照藤县白话特点进行规整，就形成了藤县牛歌戏的民间传统戏曲唱词、腔调上的独特艺术风格。如"这位小姐鬼咁娇，蛤蟆腿来黄蜂腰"。意思是说姑娘长得标致，大长腿，黄蜂腰，身材苗条。"人家还礼用大担，茶人还礼使嘴倾。恕我茶人失礼仪，唯有好话讲几声。"意思是没有什么东西还礼，只能是多讲几句好话代替。

牛歌戏的舞美

藤县白话俗语说"功夫高冇使场地阔"，意思是武功高强的人，不需要有宽阔的场地也能展示功夫。牛歌戏的舞美，一场地、一屏风、一八仙桌、两椅子即可。戏曲舞台美术历来有关于"四统一"的说法：似与不似的统一，神似与形似的统一，生活真实与艺术真实的统一，有限空间与无限空间的统一。在空间处理上，用"虚拟艺术手法"，充分调动观众的想象力，从而丰富舞台环境。这样的舞台美术，既讲生活真实，又重艺术加工、提炼，讲艺术夸张。

牛歌戏里的丑角扮相 / 霍雨锋 摄

牛歌戏精彩演出的情景 / 霍雨锋 摄

牛歌戏的舞美，很好地体现了"四统一"，在简约而不简单的舞台美术面前，生、旦、净、丑粉墨登场，给观众留足了想象的空间。牛歌戏的演出从来不落幕，也不换景，不管演什么剧目，自始至终都是这种舞美摆设。剧情表现所需要的情境，任凭观众虚构想象，境随剧换，生、旦、净、丑的唱念举动，给了人们足够的情境交代。换句话说，牛歌戏在看、在听、在想、在感同身受，但不在乎舞台场景的摆设，把"功夫高"体现得淋漓尽致。随着发展变化，在藤县县城的专业场地演出的牛歌戏，舞美会有所改变，融入一些现代的舞美手段，但是，欣赏牛歌戏，始终还是要入戏才能领略她的意韵。

牛歌戏的演出习俗

藤县牛歌戏的演出活动，非常尊崇"仁义礼智信、温良恭俭让"的传统美德，有自己的演出习俗。在演出正本前，牛歌戏演员往往要唱一轮喜庆祝福的唱词。戏班保留着尊师敬贤、向观众鞠躬、正剧演完后贺封包（当地叫"猜物儿"）、演出结束全体演员登台列队唱谢幕词欢送观众等传统。

演出时间安排上，有几个方面。在春节期间，从正月初一到十五，农村白天舞狮舞龙，晚上演牛歌戏，一般一个演出点演两晚以上；在神诞或庙会期间，按诞期、会期演出若干个晚上。有店铺开张或红白事时，主家会依据自己的喜好和财力邀请戏班演出。新中国成立后，特别是改革开放后，由当地政府文化部门组织文艺演出、文艺下乡，丰富人们文化生活。

据老一辈人说，以前的牛歌戏班入村演出，有非常严苛的程序，"入村"与"出村"都没那么容易。"入村"之难，难度在于"过关"，戏队一般与狮队同行，入村先舞狮，村里的"族老"组织人员在村口摆上八仙桌，摆上芋头或其他特产，牛歌戏队即兴演唱，唱得"族老"和村民满意，才可以放行入村。有一段经典唱词是这样的："八仙桌上摆芋头，总是东家好主谋。改革开放春风好，发家致富起洋楼。"大家听得心情舒畅、春风荡漾。而"出村"之难，难度在于剧目的多少和演员水平的高低，有经济实力的村，请了牛歌戏班，会让其一直唱不停，连续几天几夜甚至十几天，唱到大家心满意足，才放戏班出村。

老一辈人对有实力有名气的戏班非常尊敬，在演员入村后，都会将演员安排在村里品德好、经济条件较好的农户家里住宿。这些经过挑选的农户觉得无上光荣，都会把主人房腾出来让演员住宿。

雨中看戏 / 霍雨锋　摄

时代在变迁，条件在变化，现在的娱乐方式已经多元化、现代化，但牛歌戏仍然受人欢迎，一些习俗也已经与时俱进，形成了与现代社会相适应的新时代风俗。

牛歌戏的保护传承

藤县牛歌戏是民间艺术，是人民的艺术，需要更多的人去参与和传承。除了有一批非遗传承人和广大的牛歌戏从业者、爱好者、支持者的不断传承发扬，藤县还通过牛歌戏进校园、不断扶持和成立牛歌戏剧队等方式来保护与传承牛歌戏。

2007年，藤县牛歌戏列入第一批市级非物质文化遗产代表性项目名录；2008年，列入第二批自治区级非物质文化遗产代表性项目名录。

藤县牛歌戏传承谱系

代别	姓名	性别	民族	学历	学艺时间（年）	传承方式
第一代	杨柱新	男	汉	私塾[①]	1921	师徒传承
	李凤堂	男	汉	私塾	1921	师徒传承
第二代	杨象明	男	汉	私塾	1940	家族传承
	陈作才	男	汉	私塾	1940	师徒传承
第三代	杨德贵	男	汉	小学	1951	家族传承
	蒙如风	男	汉	小学	1951	师徒传承
第四代	杨岳良	男	汉	小学	1965	家族传承
	陈事业	男	汉	小学	1965	家族传承
	杨寿昌	男	汉	小学	1965	家族传承
第五代	陈寿坚	男	汉	小学	1976	家族传承
	马伟文	男	汉	初中	1986	师徒传承
	黄世裕	男	汉	高中	1986	师徒传承
	陈翠芝	女	汉	初中	1986	师徒传承
	姚玉现	男	汉	高中	1986	师徒传承
第六代	陈治金	男	汉	初中	1993	家族传承
	谭秀业	男	汉	初中	1995	师徒传承
	覃伟英	女	汉	初中	1995	师徒传承

---

① 当时的传承人没能受到正规的学校教育，只能在私人办理的学校读书识字，未取得正式的学历。

Ox-song Opera in Tengxian County

· Lin Yuan ·

Since ancient times, people have expressed their emotions through songs, dances, and operas in their agricultural and social lives. As history evolved, unique folk art forms emerged, characterized by strong local traits and distinctive national styles. One such form is the ox-song opera of Tengxian County.

In *The Book of Songs,* there are verses that reflect similar themes to those found in ox-song opera, such as the following: "A good young man is wooing a fair maiden he loves." "His yearning grows so strong that he cannot fall asleep." In ox-song opera, lyrics sung in the Tengxian vernacular express sentiments like, "Girl, you are so fair, like freshly baked lime. If you marry me, I will love you and never let you do heavy farm work, such as carrying water or chopping wood." Remarkably, over 2,000 years later, the ox-song opera in Tengxian County and the earthly meanings of *The Book of Songs* resonate with each other.

Historically, China was divided into nine regions, with Tengxian County located in the Jingzhou region, roughly equivalent to modern-day Hubei and Hunan provinces. According to the *Geography Section of the History of the Former Han Dynasty*, Tengxian County belonged to the Baiyue region, where the

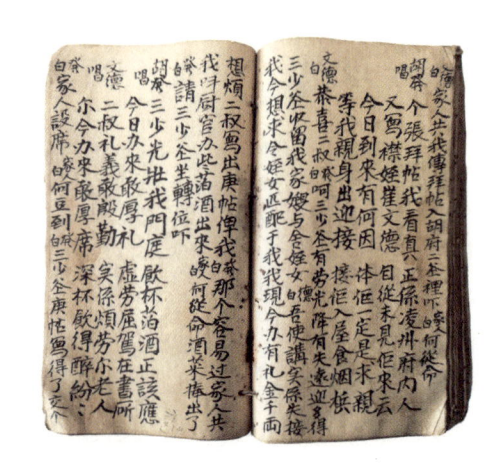

牛歌戏剧本 / 何锦奋　摄

Baiyue tribe resided in ancient China, now known as southeastern China. During the era of waterway transportation, Tengxian County was situated along the Xunjiang River, a primary tributary of the Xijiang River. As Han Chinese migrated from the Central Plains to Lingnan, cultural exchanges between the north and south led to the integration of various languages, nurturing a unique local vernacular. This vernacular, inheriting many elements of ancient Chinese, evolved into the Cantonese dialect spoken in Tengxian County. Consequently, the residents of Tengxian County communicate and perform folk songs and operas in this vernacular.

Located in a hilly, mountainous area, the people of Tengxian County sing vernacular folk songs to express their frustrations and joys amidst hard labor. Asian buffaloes are vital for rice production, and they hold a special place in the hearts of the locals. During festivals and significant rituals, a performance known as the "Dance of Spring Ox" takes place. The props used include a "ox's head", woven from bamboo and laminated with cotton paper, and a "ox's body", sewn from fabric. The "Dance of Spring Ox" is generally performed by two groups: one plays the gongs and drums while the other dances. Four dancers represent the ox's head and body, imitating the movements of ox, akin to a lion dance. Additionally, one dancer dons a human head mask, wielding a knife or stick to drive the ox, while another wears a monkey mask, mimicking monkey actions and playfully interacting with the ox. Spectators are often captivated, cheering in amazement. Talented folk singers may improvise songs, creating a dynamic interaction where performers pause to listen and react to the singing. This alternating performance style fosters a tacit understanding: dancers move in response to the music, while singers seize the opportunity to perform when the dancing halts. Over time, the folk songs evolved, with refined lyrics that employed local slang and emphasized rhyme. This led to the formation of a performance style known as the "Song of the Ox". After a long developmental history, the "Dance of Spring Ox" ultimately transformed into a stage opera called "ox-song opera".

Circulation of Ox-song Opera

Different environments shape distinct cultural landscapes. Ox-song opera, originating in Tengxian County and utilizing the local vernacular, spread organically among the folk of Tengxian and surrounding areas with similar dialects. Its circulation is concentrated primarily in the southern regions of Tengxian County, such as Jinji, Lingjing, and Xiangqi. It also reached Cangwu, Wuzhou, Rongxian, Beiliu, Pingnan, Guiping, Fengkai, Yunan, and Xinyi in Guangdong, covering a population of over ten million people. A significant milestone in its history occurred in 1875 during the "*Zhaofengnian*" Loong Celebration in Ancun Village, Jinji Town, which marked the beginning of ox-song opera. This celebration showcased local folk songs and the "Dance of Spring Ox" on stage, officially introducing the name ox-song opera to the public. Subsequently, several notable ox-song opera groups emerged, including "Tongqingtang" in 1897, "Qunyingle" in 1923, and "Qunyingshe" in Xiangqi Town in 1946. During the 1970s and 1980s, ox-song opera reached its peak, with over 270 ox-song opera classes in the county. In 1986, ox-song opera was recognized as a local opera genre in the *Annals of Chinese Opera: Guangxi Section*.

Roles in Ox-song Opera

The ox-song opera in Tengxian County has developed into a local opera with a complete system of performing roles. Similar to other operas, it comprises various roles, including Sheng (male roles), Dan (female roles), Jing (painted face), and Chou (clown). When there is a shortage of performers, men and women often switch roles to accommodate the needs of the production.

The Sheng includes male roles, encompassing elderly figures, young men, military characters, red-faced roles, and young boys.

The Dan features various female roles, differentiated by age, personality, and identity. It is further categorized into Qing Yi (main female role), Hua Dan (vivacious unmarried women), Wu Dan (martial women), Lao Dan (elderly women), Cai Dan (comic elderly women), and Hua Shan (a combination of Hua Dan and Qing Yi), with Cai Dan typically assuming a comic role.

The Jing, commonly referred to as the painted face, predominantly plays male roles, including Zheng Jing (main

藤县牛歌戏

正在梳妆的牛歌戏演员 / 霍雨锋 摄

painted face), Fu Jing (minor painted face), and Wu Jing (martial painted face).

Face Painting in Ox-song Opera

In the Tengxian County vernacular, performing ox-song opera is referred to as "moving the opera" or "doing the opera". The essence of ox-song opera is particularly reflected in its face paintings. During the Republic period and the early years of the People's Republic of China, due to limited resources, ox-song opera face paintings were primarily done using flour and rouge. Consequently, the colors often lacked vibrancy, and the characters were less distinguishable. Audiences could identify roles primarily through the facial features painted on the eyes, eyebrows, mouth, and nose. The Sheng character's face is depicted with straight eyebrows, upward-curving eyes, a straight nose, and a square mouth. The Dan character's face features curved eyebrows, a thin straight nose, and a small, cherry-like mouth. The Jing character's face is characterized by sharp eyebrows, large eyes, a wrinkled face, and a square mouth. The main painted face often resembles traditional folk puppet faces. The Chou character is distinguished by triangle eyes, downward-facing eyebrows, and a nose with a white patch. The roles are clearly delineated by the simple outlines tracing the faces of ox-song opera actors.

As economic and social conditions improved, and with greater access to diverse materials, the makeup for ox-song opera faces gradually transitioned to oil-based paints, including yellow, white, red, black, and purple. This shift allowed for more elaborate designs, with patterns exaggerated to suit the identities, ages, appearances, and characteristics of the roles. The makeup techniques continued to evolve through influences from Cantonese opera, Beijing opera, and other theatrical traditions, resulting in more vivid and dynamic portrayals of the characters.

Costumes of Ox-song Opera

The costumes of ox-song opera in Tengxian County exhibit distinctive characteristics. The role of Sheng features a colorful cloth tied around the head, complemented by a long, vibrant shirt. The Dan role includes a helmet adorned with colorful cloth and a red skirt. Other roles typically don loose "Tang" clothes with high collars and small sleeves. The Wen Sheng, a gentler and quieter variant of the Sheng, wears a head cloth and a long shirt with a large lapel, accented by a pompom on the left ear and a red cloth belt around the waist. Meanwhile, the Hua Dan sports a colorful lapel shirt paired with a white or floral skirt, also topped with a colorful headpiece.

Accompanying Music of Ox-song Opera

The greatest sound is hardly heard. The accompanying music of ox-song opera in Tengxian County is characterized by its simplicity and purity, relying solely on percussion instruments without orchestral accompaniment. This unique feature has allowed the authentic essence of ox-song opera to endure over time.

The percussion ensemble consists of four types of instruments: gongs, drums, cymbals, and bamboo clappers. The lively sounds of the gongs, drums, and cymbals resemble the "Chattering" heard in Cantonese opera. The resonant clanging of the metal instruments and the vibrant thrum of oxhide drums are intense enough to drive ox. The bamboo clapper serves a practical purpose, reminiscent of a camel bell, functioning as an "ox bell". In the mountainous terrain, where cattle graze freely, herders ascend the hills each morning and return for their animals in the evening. The dense forests and rugged mountains make locating the cattle challenging. To address this, resourceful herders fashioned bamboo clappers by cutting short segments of large bamboo, leaving two knots, and creating slots for thick iron or hardwood pieces. These bamboo clappers are attached around the ox's neck; as the animals move, the iron or hardwood strikes the bamboo, producing a characteristic "clucking" sound. Thus, the bamboo clapper becomes a vital tool for locating cattle, locally referred to as "cluck". Over time, the bamboo clapper and the cattle have developed an inseparable bond, leading to the indispensable role of bamboo clappers in ox-song opera.

Despite their simplicity, the bamboo clappers, once played, generate an infectious energy that invigorates men, women, and children alike, fostering conversation about the evening's performance and the roles to be played. This simple yet ordinary joy serves as the backdrop for the ensuing entertainment. The rhythmic interplay of the four percussion instruments punctuates the singing, creating a cycle of "singing-percussion-movement" that resonates through time and space.

The Performance of Ox-song Opera

Fundamental truths are often elegantly simple. The performance of ox-song opera in Tengxian County is primarily vocal; if singers are insufficient, Nianbai (the spoken parts of opera) serves as a supplement. The physical actions in the performance are straightforward, involving gestures, walking, and movement. The Sheng brandishes a fan, the Dan flourishes a handkerchief, and the Wu Sheng wields sticks, swords, and guns. The Wu Sheng is also capable of serving tea and wine, reading, writing, or even bracing a boat, all without prior preparation. Throughout its development, ox-song opera has absorbed elements of Cantonese opera, including water-sleeve kung fu and water wave movements. Wen Sheng delivers a slow and smooth vocal performance, marked by subtle inflections and flowing lines; Wu Sheng sings with majesty, while the Dan employs coloratura, focusing on the portrayal of psychological nuances. The singing style alternates between intermittent and continuous, employing varied intonation and staccato effects, which leave a lasting impression on the audience. While the performance may appear simple, it embodies the adage that "one minute on stage requires ten years of practice off stage".

The Script of Ox-song Opera

Historically, ox-song opera lacked a written script; performances were improvised in tandem with the "Dance of Spring Ox". As the art form evolved, script lines began to be documented by educated enthusiasts of ox-song opera. In an era devoid of written scripts, performances were characterized by "*Baodu* play", a term from Cantonese opera denoting real-time improvisation. Before each performance, educated patrons would outline the story and character requirements, and actors would improvise according to these guidelines. In contemporary times, with the introduction of performance scripts, the role of the ancient patrons has transitioned to that of modern directors, transforming improvised performances into choreographed spectacles imbued with a greater sense of ritual and grandeur.

The scripts of ox-song opera employ various literary techniques, including metaphors, similes, metonymy, exaggeration, parallelism, and puns, with a strong emphasis on antithesis. The lyrics maintain a balanced structure with a pleasing rhythm, adhering to specific limits on word and syllable counts. Primarily composed of seven-word stanzas grouped into sets of four lines, the script may occasionally feature groups of six or eight lines. In actual performances, some lines may be adjusted by adding or omitting words for balance. The lining words in ox-song opera consist of function words, used strategically to enhance the natural cadence and rhythm of the singing, thereby augmenting its musicality. The use of rhyme follows the phonetic patterns of Tengxian vernacular, predominantly featuring wide rhymes, such as "*Long*", "*Lian*", "*Yan*", and "*Zhang*".

The first, second, and fourth lines of each stanza are expected to rhyme, while the odd-numbered lines may not. However, narrower rhymes, such as "*An*", "*Zhe*", and "*Ben*", must be employed. The ending of the third line in each stanza should follow an oblique rhyme pattern. Thus, the first line's ending may not rhyme with those of the subsequent even-numbered lines. Occasionally, odd-numbered lines may use wide rhymes, but the overall structure remains intact. As the words, sounds, rhymes, and rhythms of ox-song opera are meticulously regulated according to the features of Tengxian County vernacular, they form a unique artistic style within the realm of traditional folk opera. For instance, performers use a distinctive accent to convey lyrics such as, "The girl looks beautiful, with long legs, a wasp waist, and a slim body, " and "I regret that I have nothing to offer in return, save for a few more good words."

The Setting of Ox-song Opera

A proverb in Tengxian County vernacular suggests that individuals with exceptional martial arts skills require no expansive venue to showcase their abilities. The setting for ox-song opera consists of a simple stage featuring the ground, a screen, a traditional large

藤县牛歌戏

牛歌戏的街头演出 / 黄明钊 摄

square table, and two chairs. The stage art is guided by the principle of the "four unities", which encompass the unity of likeness and unlikeness, the unity of spirit and appearance, the unity of real life and art, and the unity of limited and infinite spaces. By employing "virtual art techniques", the performance fully engages the audience's imagination, enriching the overall stage environment. Such stage art not only reflects real life but also embodies artistic refinement and exaggeration.

The setting of ox-song opera exemplifies these "four unities". The concise yet meaningful stage art invites actors to perform while leaving ample room for audience imagination. The performance does not alter its scenery; regardless of the play being presented, the same setting is maintained throughout. The scenes depicted in the narrative are left to the audience's imagination, allowing for variation as the script changes. Actors adeptly convey the scenarios outlined in the script. Consequently, ox-song opera emphasizes the importance of watching, listening, and empathizing, rendering stage settings secondary to the performance itself. As the art form has evolved, performances in professional venues in Tengxian County have gradually integrated modern elements into their settings. Nonetheless, an understanding of the play is essential for appreciating the profound meanings inherent in ox-song opera.

Performance Customs of Ox-song Opera

The performance customs of ox-song opera in Tengxian County deeply respect traditional virtues, such as benevolence, righteousness, propriety, wisdom, respect, and frugality. Prior to performances, actors often begin with a round of festive blessings. The troupe maintains customs that honor teachers and sages, including bowing to the audience and congratulating award winners post-performance (locally referred to as "guessing things"). The curtain call concludes the performance with all actors lining up on stage to bid farewell to the audience through song.

Several performance routines characterize the schedule. During the Spring Festival, from the first to the fifteenth day of the first lunar month, villagers engage in lion and loong dances during the day and perform ox-song opera in the evenings, often presenting multiple shows in the same location. During deities' birthdays or temple fairs, the opera is staged over several nights based on the event's significance. In occasions such as store openings, weddings, or funerals, hosts invite actors to perform according to their preferences and financial means. Since the founding of the People's Republic of China, particularly after the Reform and Opening-up, local government cultural departments have organized performances in rural areas to enrich community cultural life.

According to the older generation, the process for ox-song opera troupes to enter and exit a village was once highly ritualized and strictly regulated. Both entering and leaving the village were not easy tasks. The difficulty of "entering the village" was primarily in "crossing the border". Typically, the opera troupe would travel alongside a lion dance team. Upon arrival at the village, the lion dance would commence. Meanwhile, the village elders, often

藤县牛歌戏

《淑女养弃儿》剧照 / 霍雨锋　摄

referred to as "clan elders", would gather villagers at the village entrance, where they would set up a traditional large square table adorned with taro or other local specialties. At this point, the ox-song opera troupe would perform impromptu songs to gain the approval of the clan elders and the villagers. Only once they had achieved this would they be granted permission to enter the village. One famous song from this tradition goes: "The taro on the big table reflects the host's good fortune. The spring breeze of Reform and Opening-up brings prosperity, allowing the family to build a new house." As the villagers listened to the song, they would relax, their hearts lightened by the joyful, spring-like atmosphere. The difficulty of "leaving the village", however, lay in the number of performances and the skill of the actors. Wealthier villages would often hire an ox-song opera troupe and request that the actors perform for several days and nights, sometimes even up to ten days, until the villagers were completely satisfied. Only then would the troupe be allowed to depart.

In the past, villagers held immense respect for powerful and renowned opera troupes. Upon the actors' arrival in the village, they would be treated with great hospitality, provided with ample food, drink, and comfortable accommodations. It was considered an honor for a respected farmer to offer the best room in their house for the actors to stay in.

Although times have changed and entertainment options have diversified and modernized, ox-song opera continues to be popular in Tengxian County. Many of its customs have adapted to contemporary life, merging with modern practices in a way that reflects the values of today's well-off society.

Preservation and Transmission of Ox-Song Opera

Ox-song opera in Tengxian County is a form of folk art deeply rooted in the people's cultural life. Its survival and continued vitality depend on the participation and commitment of many individuals. Thanks to a dedicated group of inheritors, alongside countless practitioners, enthusiasts, and supporters, ox-song opera has been continuously passed down through the generations and further developed. Efforts to preserve and promote the art form have also been institutionalized. Tengxian County has introduced ox-song opera into schools, ensuring that younger generations become familiar with it, and the county regularly supports and organizes ox-song opera troupes to sustain its presence in the community.

Ox-song opera was included in the first batch of Wuzhou intangible cultural heritage items in 2007. A year later, in 2008, it was included in the second batch of Guangxi intangible cultural heritage items.

The Inheritance Pedigree of Ox-song Opera in Tengxian County

Generation	Name	Gender	Nationality	Education Background	Year of Craft Leanring	Means of Inheritance
First	Yang Zhuxin	Male	Han	Old-style private school	1921	Apprenticeship
	Li Fengtang	Male	Han	Old-style private school	1921	Apprenticeship
Second	Yang Xiangming	Male	Han	Old-style private school	1940	Family inheritance
	Chen Zuocai	Male	Han	Old-style private school	1940	Apprenticeship
Third	Yang Degui	Male	Han	Primary school	1951	Family inheritance
	Meng Rufeng	Male	Han	Primary school	1951	Apprenticeship
Fourth	Yang Yueliang	Male	Han	Primary school	1965	Family inheritance
	Chen Shiye	Male	Han	Primary school	1965	Family inheritance
	Yang Shouchang	Male	Han	Primary school	1965	Family inheritance
	Chen Shoujian	Male	Han	Primary school	1976	Family inheritance
Fifth	Ma Weiwen	Male	Han	Junior high school	1986	Apprenticeship
	Huang Shiyu	Male	Han	Senior high school	1986	Apprenticeship
	Chen Cuizhi	Female	Han	Junior high school	1986	Apprenticeship
	Yao Yuxian	Male	Han	Senior high school	1986	Apprenticeship
Sixth	Chen Zhijin	Male	Han	Junior high school	1993	Family inheritance
	Tan Xiuye	Male	Han	Junior high school	1995	Apprenticeship
	Qin Weiying	Female	Han	Junior high school	1995	Apprenticeship

藤县水上船歌

○ 何锦奋

地处西江水系中段的藤县，水上居民（俗称疍家）与当地民众一样操白话勾漏地区方言（称为藤县白话），但其所吟唱的船歌又与当地民众传唱的"白话歌"稍有差别，而且经久不变，因而可以说藤县水上船歌就是江河文化的"活化石"。清代戏曲理论家李调元在其《粤风》中记载了广西水上船歌："歌与民相类。第其人浮家泛宅，所赋不离江上耳。广东广西，皆有之。"乾隆三十年（1765年）藤县举人陈倜也在其《秋夜集友泛舟石壁闻渔歌》中道："邀朋探胜泛舟河，石壁凉宵寄兴多。数点渔灯人倚

疍家婚礼上，女方家拦礼船对唱｜欧伟文 摄

藤县水上船歌

棹，一川明月客闻歌。"这些就是对藤县水上船歌的很好记述。

水上居民长期泛舟江河，文化生活相对贫乏、单调，但他们能结合自己特有的船运、捕捞等水上生产生活习性，相互吟唱，自娱自乐，从而逐步产生和形成了水上船歌（民众习惯称之为"疍家歌"）。藤县的疍家历史悠久，其演唱的水上船歌自然也源远流长，但藤县水上船歌一直没有相关的文字记载，就像民族地区的盘歌那样，全凭水上人家世代口口相授而流传下来。疍家人特别是疍家女孩们自小就

疍家婚礼之迎新娘 / 欧伟文 摄

耳濡目染，自觉地跟着母亲、姑嫂学唱，在日常的船运、打鱼、摇橹、织网等生产生活中互相传唱。藤县水上船歌经过漫长的历史传承和不断完善，形成这种特有的文艺形式，而"婚时以蛮歌相迎"的习俗，更使疍家人的婚礼船歌独具一格，并成为西江流域中一种独特的文化现象。藤县水上船歌俨然一部长篇的水上人家叙事诗，且历经千百年仍然生生不息，得到不断完善和传承，并与藤县的江河流水和沃野风光一起和谐相存。

藤县水上船歌的分类

藤县水上船歌多反映行船与生产生活、婚喜寿诞、地方历史典故、社会情况、特殊事务等。行船与生产生活类如《广州至南宁水路歌》《撑船拉缆歌》《打鱼歌》《学驶船》《叹姑母》《叹船家特色饮食》《赞叹父母歌》《金玉满堂》等；婚喜寿诞类如《水上婚礼歌》《媒娘与新娘对唱》等；而特殊事务类如在丧葬仪式上唱的《百年归寿南歌》等；地方历史典故类如《唱南山风景》《赞藤州八景》等；社会情况类如《劝兄莫去赌》《禁毒歌》等。其内容信手拈来，语言浅白幽默、通俗流畅，多以朴实、简单、率直、随意为特点，便于人们随口唱答。

藤县水上船歌的演唱方式

藤县水上船歌有独唱、合唱、领唱、对唱、问答唱等演唱方式。传统的水上船歌都是清唱，全程不配音乐和其他伴奏，因而更显得婉转朴实、自然清丽。近 30 年来，藤县文化部门对水上船歌进行了整理和改编，在传统水上船歌的基础上创作出歌舞剧、舞台剧、小品等新的表演形式，使水上船歌的演唱和表演都提高到一个新的台阶。

表演时以女性为主，男性为辅。多在疍家人特有的休闲时段和观音诞、龙母诞、七姐诞（七仙女下凡）等重大节日活动中集中演唱，也有在疍家人结婚、添丁、贺寿、宝舟喜鉴（新船下水）等喜庆活动中传唱，以烘托喜庆氛围。

"绕台围"是极具地域特色的婚礼船歌。疍家女子出嫁时，女方会找一条较大的船作为举办喜庆活动的礼船，还会将礼船布置得焕然一新，在船舱内陈列男方和各方亲友送给新娘的礼物，并在礼船上唱隆重的"绕台围"，这是女子出嫁前女方最隆重、最吸引人的活动，此时的女方的船上比任何时候都热闹非凡。"绕台围"的人员以头工（指在船头持大桨的开路人）、姨仔（指水手）、新娘、办房（指行船中在船旁两侧的辅助人员）及尾舵（指舵手）等人为主，其他亲友为辅。在"绕台围"中，先由新娘出来唱盘歌，内容多是请神，唱天地公公、仙人、三界庙保平安，还要唱台上供品、礼品等，还会唱打鱼、船运等疍家工作和水路航行知识，其他"绕台围"人员轮流陪唱。盘歌内容非常丰富，疍家人的生产生活、亲人互相思念之情、家庭伦理知识、社会新闻等无所不包。演唱时间由女方定，至少唱一晚，经济条件好的家庭会连续唱三天。"绕台围"结束时，新娘走出船门，在船头与男方接亲的人对唱，接着，新娘再叹唱娘家亲戚朋友后，在媒人的搀扶下走上男方礼船，回男方的船拜堂成亲。这时，女方家庭的婚礼仪式才算结束。

藤县水上船歌的艺术特征

在歌词结构上，藤县水上船歌演唱中的歌与叹，都不脱离疍家人的日常语言和腔调。在船歌结构中，两句式或多句式都有灵活运用，以2～4小节为一句，多以两句和三四句为主，偶然也会用到五六句式结构。字数多少视内容而定，歌词相对稳定、简洁明了，既有直抒胸臆的陈述表达，又有以字（音）隐喻事物之意，多以比、赋、兴等手法来形象化地表现生活，还更多地利用衬词的重复性强化其艺术效果。歌词中包含行船知识、捕捞作业、习俗、日常用品、滩涂名称、地方特产、名胜古迹、历史传说、风俗禁忌等，甚至连常用的中草药材也拿来作比喻，生动地融入唱词中。如："借问你礼船湾边资，唔该你六亲大细报我知呀,(好)等我礼船埋好头啰。"(三句式),"篷头有条红腰带,竹丝灯笼两边排呀。船肚贴盒媒婆派,状元出入有金钗。"(四句式),"栀子我地知心同拆散啊妹,连翘踏板姑嫂又相会。"(以药材特有的性能、味道和药用来隐喻姑嫂之间的关系),"船头种棵九里香,久久返来睇爷娘。唔睇爷娘睇大细,莫比男乡水路长。"(以花草九里香意喻姑娘虽然出嫁了,也要经常回来探望爹娘等亲人)。

在曲调结构上,水上船歌的曲调结构旋律悠长,有咏和叹两种。在咏中以"歌"为主,更接近以唱的形式抒发感情;在"叹"中近似朗诵,以倾诉为先。在"歌"时,会以一句三顿、多种复句式来抒发歌者的喜怒哀乐。而在"叹"时,则会以畅所欲言的音调,将激动而复杂的心情、朴实而真挚的情感淋漓尽致地表达出来。而更多的"叹"是在节奏平稳、委婉细腻和迂回缠绕中,以长短句相结合的形式来表达的,充分运用生产生活中的大量事件、物件,用抒情与叙事相结合的方式,以反复、递进、双关、反问等手法来表现。如:"(问)四位来亲嫂呀,乜船出海插竹枝?乜船出海插红旗?""(答)亲嫂呀,礼船出海插竹枝,官船出海插红旗。"

在调式应用上,水上船歌的调式与调性相对单一,主要集中为五声宫调式,常用音域不宽(多为五度到四度之间,极具平缓特色),音域变化不大,因而曲调委婉、音色自然,音调顺畅、节奏平稳,富于抒情,并根据唱词的需要情感起伏有度,富有鲜明的地域风格。

在声腔运用上,藤县水上船歌演唱多用真声,偶尔也会用到真假声音转换来表现音调,不大强调以技巧来展示唱腔,多将情感体现在唱腔中。更多的时候,藤县水上船歌灵活地将船家人口语中特有的和谐音律与吐字艺术巧妙结合起来,因而唱腔婉转、真挚感人、声情并茂,使水上船歌蕴含浓郁的地方音色和独有的水上民歌韵味。

　　藤县水上船歌,印证了不少地方的历史知识、风物特产,保留了大量古老的语言和民间词语,在婚嫁等重要活动中,作为交流和娱乐的主要形式,并在弘扬传统孝道、礼义廉耻中起到了积极的作用,使传统文化的传承和影响达到了一个新的高度。如在《水路歌》中,将藤县在明代疏浚、裁直北流河道的情况以"天启二年通窖口"这一唱词吟唱出来,让人们从中了解古代河道疏浚的历史。

　　藤县水上船歌,记录了西江流域悠久的水上历史与文化。2008年,藤县水上船歌列入第二批自治区级非物质文化遗产代表性项目名录。

藤县水上船歌代表性传承人

级别	姓名	性别	出生时间(年)	认定时间(年)
自治区级	彭桂英	女	1939	2011
自治区级	岑月凤	女	1967	2015
市级	李贤芳	女	1948	2015
市级	麦月兰	女	1968	2015
市级	李芝兰	女	1957	2015

The Boat Song in Tengxian County

· He Jinfen ·

Tengxian County, situated in the central region of the Xijiang River System, is home to a population of floating residents, commonly known as Danjia, who speak Cantonese in the local dialect referred to as "Tengxian County Cantonese". However, the boat songs they sing differ slightly from the vernacular songs of the local populace and have remained largely unchanged over time. Thus, it can be asserted that the boat songs of Tengxian County are "living fossils" of river culture. Li Tiaoyuan, a drama theorist from the Qing Dynasty, remarked in his book *Yue Feng* on the boat songs of Guangxi, stating, "Songs are akin to people. Individuals residing in spacious houses and enjoying music by the riverside are common in Guangdong and Guangxi." During the thirty years of the Qianlong period (1765 AD), a juren (a successful candidate in the imperial examination at the provincial level in ancient China) from Tengxian County named Chen Xian also documented boat songs in his work, *Friends Gathered Around to Take a Boat in Shibi*, describing the experience of hearing boat songs on an autumn night. He wrote, "I invited friends to explore by taking a boat on the river. Shibi was cold at night, and we had much to express. Lighting some fishing lamps, we leaned on the paddles, enjoying the mountains and the moon, while guests listened to the boat songs." These descriptions vividly encapsulate the essence of boat songs in Tengxian County.

The floating residents of Tengxian County have long navigated the rivers, leading to a relatively impoverished and monotonous cultural life. However, they have managed to combine their unique production and living habits near the water—such as shipping and fishing—by singing together and entertaining themselves, gradually forming and producing boat songs, commonly referred to as "Danjia songs". The Danjia community in Tengxian County boasts a rich history, and consequently, the boat songs they sing are steeped in profound historical significance. However, there is a lack of written records related to these songs, which bear similarities to the Pan songs of ethnic group areas, being passed down orally through generations of Danjia families. Danjia members, especially Danjia daughters, learn to sing from their mothers, mothers-in-law, and sisters-in-law, often doing so in the context of daily work, such as shipping, fishing, rolling, and weaving nets. After a long history of transmission and continuous improvement, this unique form of literature and art has emerged. The custom of "welcoming people with beautiful songs during marriage" has made the wedding songs of Danjia families distinctive, creating a special cultural phenomenon in the Pearl River Basin. Tengxian County's boat songs resemble a lengthy narrative poem of the Danjia family, continuing to thrive after centuries of evolution. As a result, these songs have become more refined and resilient, coexisting harmoniously with the rivers and fertile landscapes of Tengxian County.

Categories of Boat Songs in Tengxian County

Boat songs in Tengxian County primarily reflect matters related to shipping and waterways, production activities, wedding customs, birthday celebration for elderly people, local historical allusions, social conditions, special events, and various other activities. Sailing-related songs include those pertaining to waterways, such as *Waterway Songs from Guangzhou to Nanning*, as well as songs about *Launching Boats*, *Fishing*, *Learning to Sail*, *Lamenting with an Aunt*, *Praising Local Dietary Characteristics*, and *Celebrating Wealth and Knowledge*. Additionally, there are wedding and birthday songs, including *Wedding Songs on the Water* and *Matchmaker* and *Bride Duets*. In special circumstances, such as funerals, songs related to death and the journey to heaven are performed. Local historical allusions are expressed through songs *Celebrating the Southern Mountain Scenery* and the *Eight landscapes of*

Tengxian County. Social issues are addressed in songs that *Advise against Gambling* and *Prohibit Drug Use*. The content of these songs is casual, employing simple, accessible, and smooth language. Furthermore, they are imbued with charm and humor, primarily characterized by straightforwardness and sincerity, allowing for easy communal singing.

The Singing Style of Boat Songs in Tengxian County

The singing styles of boat songs in Tengxian County encompass solo performances, choruses, lead singing, duets, and call-and-response formats. Traditional boat songs performed on the water are sung in clear voices, without instrumental accompaniment, resulting in a style that is euphemistic, simple, natural, and beautiful. Over the past thirty years, the Cultural Department of Tengxian County has arranged and adapted boat songs, creating new performance forms such as dramas that include singing and dancing, stage plays, and skits, thereby elevating the singing and performance of these songs to a new level.

The performers are predominantly female. Women primarily sing during leisure time and festivals, including Guanyin's birthday, the Loong Mother's birthday, the Double Seventh Festival (celebrating the arrival of the seven fairies on Earth), and other significant events within the Danjia community. They also perform at weddings, births, birthday celebrations, and treasure boat celebrations (marking the launch of new boats) to create a festive atmosphere.

"Running Around the Platform" is a highly regional boat song performed during weddings. When a woman from a Danjia family marries, her family seeks a larger boat as a ceremonial gift boat for the festivities, beautifully decorating it and displaying gifts from the groom's family and relatives. During the ceremony on the boat, a grand Pan song titled "Running Around the Platform" is sung, marking the most ceremonial and captivating activity before the bride's marriage. At this time, the bride's boat is livelier than any other festive boat. The participants in "Running Around the Platform" mainly include *Tougong* (those steering the front rudders), sailors, bride, Banfang (those responsible for assisting in navigation on both sides of the boat) and steering the rear rudders, while other relatives and friends serve as supplementary performers. During the ceremony, the bride initiates the Pan

疍家婚礼之新娘开面礼 / 欧伟文　摄

song, primarily focused on inviting the deities and ensuring the safety of all involved. Additionally, they sing about offerings and gifts presented on the platform, as well as the labor of the boat crew, encompassing fishing, shipping, and navigation knowledge, with others taking turns to sing along. The Pan songs cover diverse topics, including the production and life of the Danjia family, the longing among relatives, familial ethics, and social news. The singing session is determined by the bride's family, typically lasting at least one night; families with better economic conditions may sing for three days. At the conclusion of "Running Around the Platform", the bride exits the boat and performs a duet with the groom's family at the bow. After expressing her feelings for her relatives and friends, the bride, assisted by the matchmaker, walks onto the groom's boat and proceeds to the groom's hall for the marriage ceremony, marking the end of the wedding customs from the bride's family.

Musical Characteristics of Boat Songs in Tengxian County

The singing and sighing found in the boat songs of Tengxian County are deeply intertwined with the daily language and tonal patterns of the Danjia community. In these songs, two or more sentence patterns are employed flexibly,

藤县水上船歌

疍家婚礼之唱托茶歌 / 欧伟文　摄

疍家婚礼之拜堂 / 欧伟文　摄

typically using two to four bars as a single sentence. Most lyrics consist of two, three, or four sentences, with occasional use of five or six sentence structures. The word count varies according to the content, resulting in lyrics that are relatively stable, concise, and clear. These lyrics convey emotions and realities directly while employing metaphorical language to express deeper meanings. The songs frequently utilize poetic devices such as Bi, Fu, and Xing—three methods of expression commonly found in *The Book of Songs*—to visualize life experiences. Additionally, the repetition of certain phrases enhances the artistic impact of the songs. The lyrics draw upon various themes, including sailing knowledge, fishing practices, customs, daily necessities, local geographical features, historical legends, and taboos. They often incorporate metaphors derived from traditional Chinese herbs, vividly integrating these elements into the lyrics. For example: "I was wondering where your ship will be berthed; please tell me the details, so I can adjust my ship's position to welcome you." (three-sentence pattern) "There is a red belt at the bow. The bamboo lanterns are lined up on either side of the shed. The matchmaker will hand out paste boxes used to decorate the boat. The Number One Scholar (known as *Zhuangyuan*) could receive a golden hairpin when he comes in and out." (four-sentence pattern)

"We know each other's minds, yet we gradually drift apart (Gardenia). Heart-to-heart is a bridge, and the sister-in-law relationship is reconciled as before (Forsythia)." (this uniquely links medicinal properties and relationships among sisters-in-law.) "Plant a Murraya exotica at the bow, and come back to see your parents occasionally. Not only should I visit my parents, but I must also see my brothers. The journey back will not be farther than the distance to my husband's house." (where Murraya exotica signifies that although the girl is married, she should continue to visit her parents and relatives.)

The melody of the boat songs is extensive and can be categorized into two main styles: chanting and sighing. Chanting predominantly employs a "song" format, which closely resembles traditional singing to express emotions. In contrast, sighing mimics recitation, primarily reflecting spoken expression. Chanting typically includes three pauses within a single sentence and features various complex sentence structures to convey the singer's intricate emotions. Conversely, the sighing style exhibits a free tone that articulates excitement and complexity through simple and sincere expressions. Sighing is characterized by a combination of long and short sentences with a steady rhythm, creating a delicate and winding atmosphere. This style makes extensive use of events and objects from daily life and production, effectively blending lyrical and narrative elements while employing techniques such as repetition, progression, puns, and rhetorical questions. For example: (Ask) "Do your four friends come to visit your sister-in-law? Do you have a boat for the sea with bamboo poles? Do you have a boat for the sea with red flags?" (Answer) "Dear sister-in-law, the ceremonial boat will set sail to plant bamboos, and the official boat will head to sea to raise red flags..."

The modes and tonalities employed in boat songs are relatively simple, primarily focusing on the pentatonic scale. The common range is narrow, usually varying between five and four degrees, which contributes to its regional character. The limited range results in a euphemistic tone, characterized by natural sounds, smooth pitches, and steady rhythms that embody lyrical qualities. According to the lyrical context, emotional expression fluctuates appropriately, showcasing a distinct regional style.

Boat songs in Tengxian County are primarily sung in a natural voice, though there are instances of real and falsetto voice transitions to convey different tonal qualities. The emphasis is not on vocal technique but rather on reflecting emotion through melody. Often, the singing integrates the harmonious rhythm of the Danjia community's spoken language with artistic pronunciation, resulting in a graceful, sincere, and emotionally resonant performance.

These boat songs encapsulate rich local timbre and the unique charm of floating folk songs. Boat songs in Tengxian County encapsulate local historical knowledge and cultural specialties, preserving a wealth of ancient dialects and colloquialisms. In significant events such as marriages, boat songs serve as a primary mode of communication and entertainment, playing a vital role in promoting traditional values of filial piety, etiquette, and propriety. This contributes to the climax of cultural inheritance and influence. For instance, in the *Waterway Song*, the history of Tengxian County's efforts to dredge and straighten the Beiliu River during the Ming Dynasty is encapsulated in the line: "The cellar mouth was dredged in the second year of Tianqi period (1622 AD) ", providing insight into the historical practice of river dredging.

The boat songs reflect the long-standing history of life along the water in Tengxian County, as well as the cultural legacy of the region. In 2008, the boat songs of Tengxian County were included in the second batch of intangible cultural heritage items for protection by the Guangxi Zhuang Autonomous Region.

The Representative Inheritor of the Boat Song in Tengxian County

Level	Name	Gender	Year of Birth	Time of Certification
Provincial	Peng Guiying	Female	1939	2011
Provincial	Cen Yuefeng	Female	1967	2015
Municipal	Li Xianfang	Female	1948	2015
Municipal	Mai Yuelan	Female	1968	2015
Municipal	Li Zhilan	Female	1957	2015

藤县乞巧节

○ 周雄

藤县乞巧节是藤县各乡镇的民间习俗节日，而以太平镇最有代表性。这里一代又一代的妇女们，从小就听阿婆或母亲讲"牛郎织女七夕天河鹊桥相会"的神话传说。每年农历七月初六晚上，妇女们会在自家庭院里，向天上遥远的织女星和牛郎星乞求给予智慧和巧手，希望自己能有智慧的头脑、灵巧的双手与美好的姻缘。

人们各自在家进行的乞巧活动，到20世纪80年代变成以各街道名义参加的民间比巧赛。其时社会贤达热心支持，男女老幼齐参与，使得该节日成为盛大隆重的女性节日，闻名遐迩。

每年一进入农历七月，太平镇老城区的妇女们就为过乞巧节忙碌起来了。各街道乞巧活动的牵头人，都是街坊中有名望的妇女。首先，牵头人要和大家商量定下参与乞巧活动的份子钱，指定收款人。其次，定下集中制作乞巧节工艺品、食品的地点。再次，派人提前采购乞巧活动所需的材料。比如扎制"南天门""鹊桥""牛郎织女"等工艺品的纸张

色彩斑斓的精美食品 / 欧伟文 摄

用南瓜和洋葱制成的乞巧节花篮 / 欧伟文 摄

笔墨、颜料、糨糊或胶水，还有制作糍粑、米饼等食品所需的糯米粉、大米粉、花生米、黄糖、粽叶等。最后，她指定人扎制"南天门""牛郎织女""鹊桥"等工艺品，要求提前扎好，扎得精美、惟妙惟肖。她还要定下制作糍粑、面塑和负责伙房的人选。

七月初六日上午8时，锣鸣鼓响、舞起狮子，旗袍队秀起旗袍，在老城区街道巡游一番，让街坊邻舍们知道，太平街一年一度热闹的乞巧节比巧活动正式开始啰！

这时，洗漱梳妆好的七婶八姨、大小姐妹们，兴高采烈地集中到约定好的工艺品、食品制作点，如二帝庙、侯王庙等地点，听从各自牵头人分派任务。

妇女们得令后，喜气洋洋地忙碌起来。她们暂时忘记了平时谋生的劳累，操持家务、照顾儿女的辛苦及家长里短，快乐有序地忙碌着。

妇女们生火烧水、淘米煲粥、拣菜洗菜、切肉炒菜、搓粉调馅，有条不紊。她们自然围坐在一起，有说有笑，其乐融融地做糍粑、制面塑、包寿桃、打米饼，再用揉搓得大小合适的各种彩色小米粉条，在糍粑上排成不同的图案，拼成吉祥词语。妇女们费了不少功夫，制作好的糍粑、面塑、寿桃、米饼色香味俱全。红色的掺了火龙果泥，黄色的掺了南瓜泥，绿色的掺了芦荟泥，妇女们把它们弄得色彩缤纷、赏心悦目，以期博得观众认可、评委青睐。

乞巧节是女性的节日，平日里好抛头露面、八面威风、顶天立地的大老爷们，自然要退居幕后了。但是他们不是对此漠不关心、袖手旁观，也积极参与。有经济能力的，赞助或捐赠物资。有力气的，或帮厨房打下手，或在街边架梯子爬上爬下，帮挂增添节日气氛的红灯笼，拉五色彩旗、鲜红的迎乞巧节横幅。有文艺细胞的，提早准备出一台精彩的文艺节目，或练习好为演出演奏或伴奏的乐曲。有的去布置将要摆放工艺品和食品的展台，搭建展台背景墙、文艺演出的舞台。有的拉电线，准备灯光、音响设施。有的搭建食品展示一条街。总之，这一天在太平街老城区，到处呈现出男女老少齐上阵，其乐融融过乞巧节的热闹氛围。

下午3时许，妇女们将花式多样的工艺品和食品精心地摆放到展台上。许多急不可耐、好凑热闹的人早已围到德胜街、上元街、正东街、二帝庙彩旗招

乞巧节上形态各异的面塑、糍粑 / 霍雨锋 摄

藤县乞巧节

乞巧节糍粑的制作/霍雨锋 摄

展的各个展台前,开始仔细品评。

主打的工艺品有"南天门""牛郎织女鹊桥相会""七仙女下凡""八仙过海"等。"牛郎"深情款款地拉着"织女"的纤纤细手,在"鹊桥"上缓慢转动,两人痴情地相望。其他有祈求福寿的"寿星公""仙桃""金元宝""五谷丰登"等展品,还有用南瓜雕刻成的花篮,用米粉塑成的坐在牛背上吹笛的男女牧童和展翅欲飞的凤凰。色彩斑斓的糍粑上面有花草、花雀、寿龟、笑脸等图案,也有"牛郎织女""七仙下凡""吉星高照""富贵双全""花开富贵""风调雨顺""国泰民安""文武双全""代代状元""福如东海""寿比南山""少似芝兰""老

给乞巧节工艺品上色的老艺人 / 欧伟文 摄

如松柏""龙凤呈祥""老少平安""纪念乞巧"等吉祥词语。当然，乞巧节少不了"乞巧果"——桂圆、花生、红枣、瓜子。这些展品充分表达了女性期盼美好生活的思想情感，展现了她们的心灵手巧。

晚上7时，德胜码头舞台、二帝庙等地文艺表演开始。牛歌戏、民俗歌舞、民间乐器、太极拳、健身操、旗袍秀、粤剧、国学经典演绎等多个节目在舞台相继上演。这时，闻讯凑热闹的民众接踵而来，参加乞巧节活动的妇女，已从家里换上盛装来到现场。男女老幼熙熙攘攘、摩肩接踵，把旧圩心和德胜码头舞台围得水泄不通。小孩个子矮，只得骑到家长肩膀上，在人群中居高临下观看。遇到亲友在舞台上表演，他们更看得仔细入神，并大声喝彩。

食品一条街上，新鲜出炉的太平米饼香气扑鼻，引得观看者抢着品尝、购买。烧烤、果汁摊档的伙计，也忙得不亦乐乎。

藤县乞巧节

晚上 8 时 30 分是重头戏——乞巧节的比巧赛环节，评委评定出了"最佳造型""最佳人气""最佳规模""最佳组织"四大项奖项。以二帝庙、德胜街、上元街、正东街为参赛名号的各队，各有所得，皆大欢喜。

"饮了七夕水，无病又无灾。"藤县乞巧节民俗，自农历七月初七 0 时起，家中年轻的妇女就挑起水桶，到大楼江边将清澈干净的"七夕水"挑回来泡茶煮饭，并用瓶子装上几瓶收藏，相传这一天的水隔年也不变质。男女老少都会在这一天到江中泡水游泳，洗除污垢，去旧换新，祈佑身体安康。

藤县乞巧活动由民间发起、民间组织，年年岁岁、经久

流光溢彩的乞巧节街景 / 霍雨锋　摄

不衰。

2014 年，藤县乞巧节列入第五批自治区级非物质文化遗产代表性项目名录。

藤县乞巧节传承谱系

代别	姓名	性别	民族	学历	学艺时间（年）	传承方式
第一代	何振波	男	汉	私塾	1930	师徒传承
第二代	何国英	男	汉	私塾	1944	家族传承
	覃凤贞	女	汉	小学	1955	师徒传承
	覃月汉	女	汉	小学	1944	师徒传承
	韩素莲	女	汉	小学	1943	师徒传承
	欧益姬	女	汉	小学	1953	师徒传承
第三代	何月桂	女	汉	小学	1966	家族传承
	韦志群	女	汉	小学	1968	师徒传承
	何积芳	女	汉	高中	1980	师徒传承
	梁锦华	男	汉	初中	1976	师徒传承
第四代	林桂兰	女	汉	高中	1978	师徒传承
	龚凤珍	女	汉	高中	1980	师徒传承
	胡飞霞	女	汉	高中	1985	师徒传承
	黄智文	女	汉	高中	1988	师徒传承

Qiqiao Festival in Tengxian County

· Zhou Xiong ·

The Qiqiao Festival in Tengxian County is a prominent folk festival, with the most representative celebrations occurring in Taiping Town. Women in this region have passed down the myth of the "Cowherd and Weaver Girl meeting on the Magpie Bridge over the Milky Way" from generation to generation, listening to their mothers and grandmothers recount the tale since childhood. Every year, on the seventh day of the seventh lunar month, women pray to the stars Vega and Altair, hoping to gain wisdom, skillful hands, and good marital prospects.

Traditionally, each family would host "Qiqiao" activities at home, which entailed asking the weaver girl for the gift of skilled hands. By the 1980s, however, these celebrations evolved into community events organized by streets, supported enthusiastically by local scholars. Regardless of age or gender, residents would gather, transforming the festival into a grand celebration predominantly characterized as a women's festival, renowned throughout the region.

As the seventh lunar month approaches, women in the old town of Taiping become busily engaged in preparations for the Qiqiao Festival. The festival's organizers are typically respected women from the neighborhood, who first discuss the budget for activities and designate payees. They then decide on the locations for crafting activities and assign individuals to purchase necessary materials, including paper, ink, paint, paste, and glue for creating handicrafts such as "South Gate", "Cowherd and Weaver Girl" and "Magpie Bridge". Additionally, ingredients like glutinous rice flour, rice flour, peanuts, brown sugar, and bamboo leaves must be gathered to make glutinous rice cakes (known as *Ciba in* Chinese pinyin), rice cakes, and other delicacies. The organizer also appoints individuals to assemble handicrafts representing "South Gate" and the "Cowherd and Weaver Girl meeting on the Magpie Bridge", ensuring these are completed ahead of time in a visually appealing manner. Finally, women are designated to prepare glutinous rice cakes and dough, managing the kitchen operations.

Those who prepare in advance will sound gongs, drums, and lion dances at 8 a. m. on the sixth day of the seventh lunar month, while a team in cheongsams parades through the streets of the old town to announce the official commencement of the annual Qiqiao activities.

At this time, family members, including aunts, sisters, and sisters-in-law, rise early to wash and groom themselves, gathering joyfully at predetermined locations, such as the Temple of the Second Emperor or the Hou Emperor Temple, to await task assignments from their leaders.

As tasks are assigned, the women immerse themselves in the festival spirit, temporarily forgetting the burdens of daily life, such as the challenges of work and family responsibilities.

The women gather materials, boiling water for rice porridge, washing and preparing vegetables, cutting meat, and stirring fried dishes, all while sharing laughter and conversation. Together, they prepare glutinous rice cakes, dough, *Shou Tao* (a type of dessert representing longevity),

藤县乞巧节

热闹非凡的乞巧节 / 欧伟文 摄

and rice cakes adorned with vibrant colors and auspicious symbols. After considerable effort, the women create delicious treats, with the red cakes infused with loong fruit puree, yellow ones with pumpkin puree, and green ones with aloe puree. Each dessert is designed to be visually striking, aiming to impress both the audience and judges.

The Qiqiao Festival is fundamentally a celebration led by women, while men—typically more outgoing—take a supportive role. However, their participation is vital. Wealthy men contribute

乞巧节民间艺人及其制作的孔雀 / 何锦奋　摄

financially and donate supplies, while physically strong men assist in the kitchen, prepare handmade foods, or help set up decorations, such as hanging red lanterns and colorful flags to enhance the festive atmosphere. Others help establish booths for arts and crafts, construct backgrounds, and set up stages for performances. Many are responsible for wiring and preparing lighting and sound equipment. This collective mobilization of both men and women creates a vibrant and lively atmosphere throughout Taiping Street.

　　Around 3 p.m., women carefully display their exquisite crafts and foods at booths. Many eager participants gather at Desheng Street, Shangyuan Street, Zhengdong Street, and Erdi Temple, where numerous flags and impressive displays have been erected for exhibition and evaluation.

　　The main handicrafts include representations of "South Gate", "Cowherd and Weaver Girl meeting at the Magpie Bridge", "Seven Fairies Descend to the Earth", and "Eight Immortals Cross the Sea". The Cowherd tenderly holds the Weaver Girl's delicate hand as they stroll across the Magpie Bridge, gazing at each other with affection. Additional exhibits include symbols of longevity, such as the

"Longevity God", "*Shou Tao*", "Gold Coin", and "Five Grains Harvest". Also featured are intricately carved flower baskets, depicting shepherds and shepherdesses riding cows and playing musical instruments made from rice noodles, as well as phoenixes poised for flight. The display features beautiful motifs of flowers, birds, turtles, and smiling faces, alongside auspicious phrases such as "Cowherd and Weaver Girl", "Seven Immortals Descend to the Earth", "Lucky Star", "Wishing You Wealth and Prosperity", "Flourished Flowers and Prosperity", "Good Weather", "Wishing for a Prosperous Country", "Wishing You Intelligence and Quick Wit", "Top Scorer from Generation to Generation", "Wishing You Endless Happiness", "Wishing You a Long Life", "Wishing You Knowledge and Grace", "Wishing You Longevity Like Pine and Cypress", "Loong and Phoenix Represent Happiness", "Peace Across the Ages", and "Commemoration of Qiqiao", among others. The "Qiqiao fruits", including laurel, peanuts, red dates, and melon seeds, are also displayed. These exhibits vividly express the hopes and aspirations of women seeking a better life, showcasing their creativity.

At 7 p.m., artistic performances begin at Desheng Wharf Stage and Erdi Temple, featuring ox-song opera, folk songs and dances, folk musical instruments, Tai Chi, fitness exercises, cheongsam shows, Cantonese opera, and more. As news of the performances spreads, crowds gather. Women participating in the festival dress up at home, excited to attend. The bustling scene of men, women, and children enhances the vibrancy of the Qiqiao Festival activities, particularly at venues like the old Wei Xin and Desheng Wharf stage. Children often ride on their parents' shoulders to see over the crowd, and when friends and relatives perform on stage, they cheer enthusiastically.

On the food street, the freshly steamed Taiping rice cakes are a hit, enticing viewers to taste and purchase them. Stalls for barbecues and juice also attract busy patrons.

At 8: 30 p.m., the highlight of the festival, the "Qiao" competition, takes place. Judges evaluate the entries, awarding prizes in four categories: "Best Shape", "Best Popularity", "Best Scale", and "Best Organization". Teams from Erdi Temple, Desheng Street, Shangyuan Street, and Zhengdong Street achieve notable success.

A saying goes, "If you drink the Qixi water, you will be free from diseases and disasters." To honor this belief, young women collect the clear, clean Qixi water from the Dalou River on the seventh day of the seventh lunar month to make tea and cook rice. This water, collected in bottles, is said to remain fresh for a year. Adults and children alike swim in the river on this day to wash away dirt and welcome new beginnings, praying for health.

The Qiqiao Festival in Tengxian County, initiated by the community and organized by its members, has endured over time, gradually forming a rich cultural legacy.

In 2014, the Qiqiao Festival in Tengxian County was included in the fifth batch of representative items of Guangxi intangible cultural heritage.

The Inheritance Pedigree of Qiqiao Festival in Tengxian County

Generation	Name	Gender	Nationality	Education Background	Year of Craft Leanring	Means of Inheritance
First	He Zhenbo	Male	Han	Old-style private school	1930	Apprenticeship
Second	He Guoying	Male	Han	Old-style private school	1944	Family inheritance
Second	Qin Fengzhen	Female	Han	Primary school	1955	Apprenticeship
Second	Qin Yuehan	Female	Han	Primary school	1944	Apprenticeship
Second	Han Sulian	Female	Han	Primary school	1943	Apprenticeship
Second	Ou Yiji	Female	Han	Primary school	1953	Apprenticeship
Third	He Yuegui	Female	Han	Primary school	1966	Family inheritance
Third	Wei Zhiqun	Female	Han	Primary school	1968	Apprenticeship
Third	He Jifang	Female	Han	Senior high school	1980	Apprenticeship
Third	Liang Jinhua	Male	Han	Junior high school	1976	Apprenticeship
Fourth	Lin guilan	Female	Han	Senior high school	1978	Apprenticeship
Fourth	Gong Fengzhen	Female	Han	Senior high school	1980	Apprenticeship
Fourth	Hu Feixia	Female	Han	Senior high school	1985	Apprenticeship
Fourth	Huang Zhiwen	Female	Han	Senior high school	1988	Apprenticeship

藤县杖头木偶戏

○ 黄 静

木偶戏艺人在表演 / 何锦奋　摄

关于戏剧的起源，学术界可谓众说纷纭，而中国的木偶戏，目前比较认同的是"源于汉，盛于唐"。《搜神记》《通典》《封氏闻见记》《拾遗记》等古籍的记载充分说明唐朝时南方木偶艺术已经相当流行。而藤县杖头木偶戏的老艺人说起木偶戏的起源时，则颇有故事色彩：汉高祖刘邦的大军被匈奴围困，其谋臣陈平制作木偶立于城头，巧妙退敌，助其大军摆脱围困。

藤县杖头木偶戏

中国木偶戏一般分为杖头木偶戏、提线木偶戏、布袋木偶戏等。藤县木偶戏属于杖头木偶戏，流传区域遍及全县，藤南以金鸡镇大坟村为代表，藤北以和平镇、大黎镇为代表。

藤县杖头木偶戏用藤县方言演出，曲调简单，唱腔、对白相当自由。

演出内容多以中国古典小说、民间流行甚广的故事为主，并主要集中在唐、宋两朝。如薛仁贵系列、狄青系列、杨家将系列、包公系列和《龙凤再生缘》《白玉霜》等。其他范围的内容较少演出。如果是东家喜庆之事相请演出，则要先唱上一段应景祝贺之词，恭贺东家之喜。

从藤县老艺人的嘴里知道，木偶戏起源于战争，而藤县杖头木偶戏的演出内容也多是与战争有关，这究竟是巧合，还是其中有什么联系，不得而知。

藤县杖头木偶戏的演出场景非常简单，只需要一个木偶架：以3～4厘米大小的木条搭成宽约140厘米、高约240厘米的方形架子，距离地面140厘米左右。上面80～100厘米处挂一横幅为台口。木偶架除台口和后面下半部分以及架顶外，其余地方都用布围起。正对台口后面的布画成布景。演出时，艺人高举木偶，观众看到的就是台口处的木偶在唱、在打斗。

演出人员也很简单：每个杖头木偶剧队一般有2～3人。一人掌板、打锣鼓，另外的人舞动木偶，唱、做、念、打，生、旦、净、丑表演全包干。

往往越是简单的东西越不简单。试想，这么简单的一个木偶架，这么简单的2～3个演员，怎么能吸引观众？当然就靠演员的不简单了。

藤县杖头木偶戏的老艺人可以一人操纵2～3个木偶，一人扮演2～3个角色，一人模拟2～3种不同的声音。他们的

乡村木偶戏 / 杨定登　摄

双手灵活地扯动机关，让木偶做出举刀、踢腿、翻跟斗等打斗的动作；他们的嘴里唱着高亢的唱词，或者发出刀枪剑戟相撞、进攻者的吆喝和受伤者的惨叫等声音。他们在唱、做、念、打之间自由转换，游刃有余地演绎着生、旦、净、丑的角色，把观众带进金戈铁马、壮怀激烈的战场，或者花园赏花、月下诉衷肠的温馨场景，让观众不由自主地跟着剧中人物或悲或喜，整个人沉浸在剧情之中。尤其值得一提的是，木偶戏是没有剧本的，演员熟悉剧情之后，在演出时即兴编唱词，居然也能七字一句，工整押韵，有时候还诙谐幽默，让人不得不佩服演员的急才。演到紧张处，锣"锵"的一声，演出戛然而止，在观众欲罢不能之时，传来演员一句"欲知后事如何，请听下回分解"的预告，实在是吊足了观众的胃口。所以请戏往往不会只请一场，总要连续请两三个晚上，把一个故事演完，才心满意足地放木偶剧队出村。所幸木偶剧队人员和道具精少，请戏所花资费不多，管吃管住也不费什么人力。

就这样,藤县杖头木偶戏以边舞边唱、一场接一场的演出方式,吸引着那些白天在田地辛苦劳作、晚上就算点火把翻山越岭也要去看戏的群众,在物质匮乏的年代,丰富了人们的精神生活。

藤县杖头木偶戏成为深受当地群众喜爱的民间戏剧,并应邀到玉林、北流等地演出。1977年,藤县文化馆木偶艺术剧队到苍梧、蒙山、昭平、平南、贵县(今贵港市)、横县(今横州市)、邕宁、宁明、扶绥、凭祥等县(市、区)进行商业演出,所到之处,受到十分隆重的接待,演出所受欢迎程度和当时的盛况,至今仍传为佳话。

2016年,藤县杖头木偶戏列入第六批自治区级非物质文化遗产代表性项目名录。

藤县杖头木偶戏传承谱系

代别	姓名	性别	民族	学历	学艺时间(年)	传承方式
第一代	王十二公	男	汉	私塾	无从考究	师徒传承
	周业彩	男	汉	私塾	无从考究	师徒传承
第二代	黄昌和	男	汉	私塾	无从考究	师徒传承
	周业旺	男	汉	小学	无从考究	师徒传承
	林柱成	男	汉	初中	1954	师徒传承
	周发昌	男	汉	小学	1958	师徒传承
第三代	黄世宁	男	汉	小学	1970	家族传承
	黄沛英	男	汉	小学	1970	师徒传承
	黄桂荣	男	汉	小学	1987	师徒传承
第四代	黄其勇	男	汉	高中	2002	师徒传承

Cane-head Puppet Show in Tengxian County

· Huang Jing ·

The origins of drama have been the subject of considerable debate within the academic community; however, a prevailing consensus holds that Chinese puppetry first emerged during the Han Dynasty (202 BC - 220 AD) and flourished during the Tang Dynasty (618 - 907 AD). Historical texts such as *Sou-Shen Ji* (*In Search of the Supernatural*), *Tong Dian*, *Feng Shi Wen Jian Ji*, and *Shi Yi Ji* provide evidence that puppet art was prevalent in southern China during the Tang Dynasty. Elder artists associated with the cane-head puppet show in Tengxian County recount a compelling narrative regarding the origins of puppetry: during the siege of the Han Dynasty's founder, Emperor Gaozu (Liu Bang), puppets were crafted and placed on the city walls, cleverly deceiving the besiegers and allowing the defenders to break the siege.

The Chinese puppet show can generally be classified into three types: cane-head puppet shows, marionette puppet shows, and glove puppet shows. The puppet shows of Tengxian County belong to the cane-head variety and are widespread throughout the region. Dafen Village in Jinji Town represents the southern style of this tradition, while Heping Town and Dali Town represent the northern style within Tengxian County.

The cane-head puppet show in Tengxian County is performed in the local dialect, featuring simple melodies with a free-form singing and dialogue style.

The performances primarily draw on classical Chinese novels and popular folk literature from the Tang and Song dynasties. Well-known series like *Xue Rengui*, *Di Qing*, *Yang Jiajiang*, and *Bao Gong* are frequently staged, along with plays such as *Loong and Phoenix* and *White Jade Frost*. However, more modern themes are rarely performed. When a performance is held to celebrate a joyful occasion, such as a wedding or birthday, the performers sing a congratulatory song dedicated to the host.

According to elderly artists in Tengxian County, puppetry may have originated in warfare. Interestingly, the content of the cane-head puppet shows often revolves around themes of war, though it is unclear whether this is purely coincidental or whether there is a deeper historical connection.

The stage setup for these shows is simple, consisting of a single puppet stand: a square frame about 140 cm wide and 240 cm tall, built from wooden strips measuring 3 – 4 cm in width. The platform itself is elevated 140 cm from the ground. A banner is hung 80 – 100 cm above the platform, while the back of the stage and lower parts are covered in fabric. Behind the platform, the backdrop is painted to depict various scenes. During the performance, the artist manipulates the puppets so that the audience sees them singing and engaging in mock battles at the front of the stage.

The performance troupe is equally minimal, typically consisting of just two or three members. One person plays the gongs and drums, while another operates the puppets, performing all roles such as Sheng (male roles), Dan (female roles), Jing (painted-face roles), and Chou (clown roles). These roles are adapted from traditional Chinese opera.

Despite the simplicity of the setup, the artistry involved is complex. Imagine: with only a basic wooden frame and two performers, how can they captivate an audience? The answer lies in the skill of the performers.

The veteran cane-head puppet masters of Tengxian County can each control 2 – 3 puppets simultaneously, performing multiple roles with distinct voices. Their dexterity allows them to make the puppets raise swords, kick, and even somersault. Meanwhile, their voices shift seamlessly between high-pitched singing, the clash of swords, the cries of attackers, and the screams of the wounded. They effortlessly transition between the performing forms of singing, acting, reading, and fighting, embodying the different Sheng, Dan, Jing, and Chou roles. These talented artists transport the audience to the heat of battle, a serene garden, or a romantic scene under the moon. The spectators become emotionally engaged, feeling the joy and sorrow of the characters as they immerse themselves in the unfolding drama. Remarkably, there is no formal script for these performances. After becoming familiar with the basic plots, actors can improvise seven-character verses on the spot, often creating clever and humorous lines that demonstrate their talent. At a climactic moment, the sound of the gong may signal a sudden halt in the performance, leaving the audience eager to know what happens next. The actor will tease, "If you want to know what happens, come to tomorrow's performance, " thereby keeping the audience hooked. As a result, the plays are often performed over two or three consecutive nights until the story reaches its conclusion, after which the troupe moves on to another village. Fortunately, since the puppet troupe requires few members and minimal props, the cost of hiring them and providing accommodations is relatively low.

Thus, during a time when material resources were scarce, the cane-head puppet shows became a popular form of entertainment. After working hard in the fields by day, people would climb the hills at night to enjoy the performances, which enriched their spiritual lives.

Through the skill of Tengxian County artists, the cane-head puppet show evolved into a beloved folk drama, leading to performances in other places such as Yulin and Beiliu. In 1977, the Tengxian County Cultural Center's puppet troupe performed in counties like Cangwu, Mengshan, Zhaoping, Pingnan, Guixian, Hengxian, Yongning, Ningming, Fusui, and Pingxiang, where they were warmly welcomed. The popularity of these performances and the excitement they generated remain fondly remembered today.

The cane-head puppet show of Tengxian County was included in the sixth batch of the Guangxi's representative intangible cultural heritage items in 2016.

The Inheritance Pedigree of Cane Head Puppet Show in Tengxian County

Generation	Name	Gender	Nationality	Education Background	Year of Craft Leanring	Means of Inheritance
First	Wang Shiergong	Male	Han	Old-style private school	Unknown	Apprenticeship
	Zhou Yecai	Male	Han	Old-style private school	Unknown	Apprenticeship
Second	Huang Changhe	Male	Han	Old-style private school	Unknown	Apprenticeship
	Zhou Yewang	Male	Han	Primary school	Unknown	Apprenticeship
	Lin Zhucheng	Male	Han	Junior high school	1954	Apprenticeship
	Zhou Fachang	Male	Han	Primary school	1958	Apprenticeship
Third	Huang Shining	Male	Han	Primary school	1970	Family inheritance
	Huang Peiying	Male	Han	Primary school	1970	Apprenticeship
	Huang Guirong	Male	Han	Primary school	1987	Apprenticeship
Fourth	Huang Qiyong	Male	Han	Senior high school	2002	Apprenticeship

藤县八音

○ 周羽兵

八音是藤县地区主要的民间吹打乐，全县各个乡镇都有流布。据民间艺人说，藤县八音兴起于清末民初，是两广白话地区文化互相渗透、互相交融的产物。藤县八音鼎盛时期在 20 世纪三四十年代，20 世纪六七十年代一度衰落，80 年代开始复兴。藤县八音与其他地区的八音有类似之处，但历经岁月沉淀和时间洗礼，又有了自己的特色。

八音的"八"是指所用乐器很多，并非实指八种乐器。藤县八音是一种伴奏乐，通过唢呐、锣、鼓、镲、梆子、箫等吹打伴奏作乐，广泛用于城乡的庆典和红白事情。曲目有《八仙贺寿》《天姬送子》《接客》《闹酒》《十番》《小拜》《大开门》《小开门》等。

八音的活动分为坐场与走场。坐场是在特定环境中环绕八仙桌坐着演奏，以箫、梆子、小锣、小镲演奏，声音较轻柔、细腻、流畅。走场是在特定环境中走动着演奏，如迎亲、庙会游行、舞狮舞龙、拜年等，以唢呐、大镲、高边锣、苏锣等演奏，声音浑厚，音量洪大响亮，活动途中边走边吹打，乐曲活泼欢快。

婚娶之日有亲友前来祝贺，八音艺人即时演奏，

藤县八音

正在演奏藤县八音的民间艺人 / 周炎祥　摄

在屋里忙前忙后的主人闻讯立马赶到大门口笑脸相迎，其时乐声高亢，笑声朗朗，欢声笑语飘散在广袤的天空下，于是一江两岸、千树群山全都沉浸在热闹喜庆之中。

而白事请八音队演奏即为"喜丧"了。"人家之有丧，哀事也，方追悼之不暇，何有于喜。而俗有所谓喜丧者，则以死者之福寿兼备为可喜也。"（《清稗类钞》）意思就是说，死者是德高望重、福寿双全者，年纪在八九十岁，甚至寿龄更长，这样的死者葬礼可谓"喜丧"。丧事主家会停灵3～5日，亲朋好友会前来凭吊，主家会聘请八音队来演奏，以示"福、禄、寿、喜、财"五大人生愿望得到实现。

藤县八音源远流长，是一种带有习俗性的民间音乐文化。在漫长的历史岁月中，藤县八音影响着民间大众的生活，见证着藤县民间音乐文化的流传和变革，传承着中国的传统文化，对当地群众的文化生活产生很大影响，具有一定的文化价值、艺术价值和经济价值。

2016年，藤县八音列入第六批自治区级非物质文化遗产代表性项目名录。

藤县八音传承谱系

代别	姓名	性别	出生时间（年）	学历	学艺时间（年）	传承方式
第一代	周庆隆	男	不详	不详	无从考究	师徒传承
	李呈祥	男	不详	不详	无从考究	师徒传承
第二代	陈勇昌	男	1947	初中	1968	师徒传承
	李法德	男	不详	小学	无从考究	师徒传承
第三代	陈志森	男	1952	初中	1977	师徒传承
	陈惠成	男	1939	小学	1972	师徒传承
	陆丕东	男	1952	初中	1980	师徒传承
	麦柱光	男	1968	中专	1975	师徒传承

藤县八音

吹奏唢呐的老艺人 / 欧伟文 摄

Eight-Tone Music in Tengxian County

· *Zhou Yubing* ·

Eight-tone music is the predominant form of folk wind and percussion music in Tengxian County, prevalent in all towns and villages within the region. According to local folk artists, the emergence of eight-tone music can be traced back to the late Qing Dynasty and early Republic of China. It is a product of the mutual infiltration and blending of Cantonese cultural elements from Guangdong and Guangxi. The peak of eight-tone music occurred during the 1930s and 1940s; however, it experienced a decline in the 1960s and 1970s, followed by a revival in the 1980s. While Tengxian County's eight-tone music shares similarities with other regional forms, it has developed its own unique characteristics over the years.

藤县八音演奏艺人 / 欧伟文　摄

藤县八音

老艺人在演奏 / 欧伟文　摄

The term "eight" in eight-tone music refers to the variety of musical instruments employed rather than an exact count of eight instruments. This genre of music typically serves as accompaniment, featuring instruments such as the Suona horn, gong, drum, cymbal, Bangzi (a Chinese percussion instrument), and flute. It is widely utilized in urban and rural celebrations, including weddings and funerals. Notable compositions include *Eight Immortals' Birthday Celebration*, *Tianji's Sending off Children*, *Receiving Guests*, *Whingding*, *Shifan*, *Xiaobai*, *Big Door Opening*, and *Small Door Opening*, among others.

Eight-tone performances are categorized into two types: sitting performances and walking performances. Sitting performances involve performers gathering around a square table in a designated space, engaging in vocal performances accompanied by Bangzi, small gongs, and small cymbals. This style produces a soft, delicate, and smooth sound. In contrast, walking performances involve musicians moving and playing in specific contexts, such as fetching the bride, participating in temple fair parades, and celebrating the New Year. This performance style employs two Suona horns, large cymbals, high-edged gongs, and Su gongs, resulting in a deep, loud sound characterized by lively and cheerful music.

On wedding days, when relatives and friends arrive to congratulate the couple, the eight-tone artists promptly begin to play. Even if the hosts are busy inside, they will rush to the entrance with smiles to greet their guests. During these moments, the lively music mingles with joyful laughter, creating an atmosphere filled with celebration that resonates throughout the surrounding landscape.

In the context of funerals, hiring an eight-tone ensemble is considered auspicious. It is said that "having a funeral in another family is sad, as people are occupied with mourning." However, if the deceased lived a long and respected life, their funeral can be termed an "auspicious funeral". This type of funeral is characterized by the passing of an elder who enjoyed family prosperity and reached an advanced age, often 80 or 90 years or older. In such cases, the family is less inclined to mourn deeply. The mourner's family typically keeps the coffin in a temporary shelter for three to five days before burial and hosts a large banquet to entertain relatives and friends,

镲与锣 / 欧伟文　摄

hiring an Eight-tone team to perform. This celebration signifies the fulfillment of the five life wishes: "fortune, wealth, longevity, happiness, and a good death."

Eight-tone music in Tengxian County is a local folk tradition with a rich history and is deeply embedded in the cultural activities of the community. Over the years, it has influenced the lives of the people, serving as a testament to the cultural origins and transformations of Tengxian County's folk music. It plays a significant role in preserving traditional Chinese culture and has a considerable impact on the cultural life of the local populace, embodying notable cultural, artistic, and economic values.

Eight-tone music was included in the sixth batch of the Guangxi intangible cultural heritage list in 2016.

The Inheritance Pedigree of Eight-tone Music in Tengxian County

Generation	Name	Gender	Birth Time	Education Background	Year of Craft Leanring	Means of inheritance
First	Zhou Qinglong	Male	Unknown	Unknown	Unknown	Apprenticeship
First	Li Chengxiang	Male	Unknown	Unknown	Unknown	Apprenticeship
Second	Chen Yongchang	Male	1947	Junior high school	1968	Apprenticeship
Second	Li Fade	Male	Unknown	Primary school	Unknown	Apprenticeship
Third	Chen Zhisen	Male	1952	Junior high school	1977	Apprenticeship
Third	Chen Huicheng	Male	1939	Primary school	1972	Apprenticeship
Third	Lu Pidong	Male	1952	Junior high school	1980	Apprenticeship
Third	Mai Zhuguang	Male	1968	Specialized secondary school	1975	Apprenticeship

藤县龙母传说

○ 蒙土金

龙母娘娘像 / 何锦奋 摄

龙是中国等东亚国家古代神话传说中的神异动物，是中华民族具有代表性的文化之一，象征祥瑞。《说文解字》载："龙，鳞虫之长，能幽能明，能细能巨，能短能长，春分而登天，秋分而潜渊。"而《史记·五帝本纪》则说，黄帝在打败蚩尤与炎帝之后，巡阅四方，"合符釜山"，不但统一了各部军令的符号，而且确立了政治上的结盟，还从原来各部落的图腾上各取一部分元素，创造了新的图腾形象——龙。

自此，龙的形象深深地植根在中华民族的精神血脉里。

藤县，这个古时叫藤州的地方，有着大量与龙有千丝万缕联系的具象和遗迹遗存。

历史上，一个出生在藤县的姓温的女子被尊奉为龙母。《藤县志》里对龙母的出生地、生活地、墓地都有准确的考证。志曰："按龙母嬴秦祖龙时之神也。温姓或曰蒲姓……今考粤东肇庆府旧志及悦城孝通祖庙旧志，咸以为藤县人，则无论毓于何都，

藤县龙母传说

其为藤之神固可考核而无疑者，然其墓独在悦城，何也？父天瑞娶悦城梁氏，生三女，龙母其仲也……随其母到悦城，心喜其地，欲以为安厝所。因熟识之，及归于溪边，得石卵，剖之出五物，如守宫状，喜水，母豢渐长，放之江遂去，越数年，鳞甲辉煌，复来见母，母知龙子之远迎也。别其父母曰：儿当乘龙至悦城，遂跨龙，薄暮抵江口……"龙母仙逝后，"立庙祀，极显应，故至今，火独盛云"。

《藤县志》的这段文字，清楚地记录了龙母作为古藤州人氏豢养五龙的经过。龙母，作为生长在古藤州大地上的江河文明的河神形象，永远地耸立在藤县人民的心目中。

藤县与龙母生活的痕迹有关联的地方很多，比如列入了古藤州八景之一的龙巷露台，比如藤县人民耳熟能详的龙颈，比如龙母与赖法师斗法的金凤村，比如龙母曾经学道修行的龙母山，以及龙母山脚下一个叫龙腾的山环水抱、钟灵毓秀的村子……

藤州，始建于隋开皇十二年（592年），因藤江、白藤岭而得名。古藤州山川毓秀，形成了著名的藤州古八景，这八景分别是剑江春涨、石壁秋风、鸭滩霜籁、龙巷露台、东山夜月、赤峡晴岚、谷山翠叠、文岭云环。龙巷露台在县城西江河段靠西的地方，在此处宽阔的江中隐藏着一块龙巷石，据说这就是当年龙母豢养五龙戏水的地方。在长洲水利枢纽建成以前，每到秋冬时节河水干涸之时，江中的龙巷石就会显露出来。龙巷露台还有着一个凄美的传说，说的是龙母和赖法师斗法拯救黎民百姓的故事。传说当年龙母正在狮山旁边的大界脚下替凤姐的丈夫治病，她叫人连夜上山采草药。当采药人来到大界顶时，借着松木火光发现有许多石头正在往石花峡的方向移动，石花峡两旁很快就筑起了三层高的石围，只差一炷香的工夫就要把峡口封闭起来了。采药人觉得十分奇怪，便急忙赶回去告诉了龙母。龙母知道这是赖法师在赶狮山上的石头堵塞峡口，欲淹死峡口里面的人而达到独占日产黄金百两的金矿（现金凤村）的目的。为了不让赖法师的图谋得逞，龙母便叫凤姐等人到大界顶上学鸡叫，自己则连忙从狮山脚施法穿山，又赶回家（县城胜西村）取金洗盘装雨避洪。赖法师突然听到鸡叫声，以为天快要亮了，急忙停止施法匆忙逃跑，原本被他控制的石头就变成了现在石花峡上五条龙骨状的石岩，静静地伏在石花峡上。峡口里的人们终于得救了，而凤姐的丈夫由于延误了救治的时间去世了。为纪念凤姐舍夫救民的义举，人们便把她居住的村子叫作凤村，村民们开矿的地方叫作金坡村，两个村子合起来叫作金凤村，龙母穿山入口的地方叫作龙窟村，出口的江面叫作龙巷露台……

相传，龙母还曾经到过狮山拜狮山圣母为师，修仙学道、采药炼丹，治好了不少父老乡亲的病。于是，狮山山脉中的一座山便被叫作龙母山。龙母山里，"龙母赐子""龙母圣砚""龙母炼丹炉""龙母修仙岩"等遗迹遗存遍布山中，每一处都伴随着龙母的懿德昭示人间。

龙母豢养五龙，母子情深，五龙长大后，顺江而下，归于大海。秦始皇一向崇拜龙的图腾，一心求长生不老之药。当听说南方出现了五条真龙及龙母的消息时，便专门派出使者携带大批的金银珠宝来到南方，要礼迎龙母到京都长住宫中。龙母不忍离开南方的黎民百姓，被迫上了使者的官船后，一直闷闷不乐。五龙知道后便暗中保护龙母，五龙呼风唤雨，使使者的官船四次抵达桂林

龙母庙文物 / 欧伟文　摄

后，一夜之间又退回到梧州。使者知道这是五龙护母回乡的缘故，只得作罢，秦始皇也无可奈何，只好准予龙母返回家乡。龙母心系氏族，带领人们开辟山川、治理江河、利泽天下，终因积劳成疾于公元前 211 年农历八月十五日仙逝。龙母仙逝后，五龙万分悲痛，化作五位秀才披麻戴孝，像亲生儿子一样为龙母办理丧事并日夜守于墓侧，过了七七四十九天还不愿离去。

龙母就在藤县的山水里，就在藤县人们的心中，代代永流传。

2018 年，藤县龙母传说列入第七批自治区级非物质文化遗产代表性项目名录。

藤县龙母传说传承谱系

代别	姓名	性别	民族	学历	学艺时间（年）	传承方式
第一代	李七贤	男	汉	小学	无从考究	家族传承
	李楚浣	男	汉	私塾	无从考究	师徒传承
	彭桂英	女	汉	小学	1949	师徒传承
第二代	李炎明	男	汉	大专	1963	师徒传承
	李明远	男	汉	大专	1962	家族传承
	李先明	男	汉	中专	1979	师徒传承
第三代	李威霖	男	汉	大学	1999	家族传承
	李东海	男	汉	中专	1999	家族传承
	陈沛伟	男	汉	小学	1999	师徒传承

Legend of Loong Mother in Tengxian County

· Meng Tujin ·

Loong (Chinese dragon) is a mythical creature deeply embedded in the ancient myths and legends of China and East Asia. It serves as a symbol of auspice and represents one of the most significant cultural icons of the Chinese nation. The *Analytical Dictionary of Characters* describes the loong as "the leader of squamose animals, capable of traversing both dark and light realms, and able to transform in size and shape. It soars in the sky during the spring equinox and submerges underwater at the autumn equinox." The *Annals of the Five Emperors* recounts that after defeating Chiyou and the Yan Emperor, the Yellow Emperor toured his territories, "occupying Fushan", thereby unifying military symbols and establishing political alliances. He also integrated elements from the original totems of various tribes to create a new animal image—the loong.

This illustrates that the loong's imagery is profoundly rooted in the spirit and lineage of the Chinese nation.

In Tengxian County, historically known as Tengzhou, numerous relics symbolize the loong's significance.

A woman named Wen, born in Tengxian County, later earned the title of "Loong Mother". According to the *Annals of Tengxian County*, there is meticulous textual research regarding her birthplace, residence, and burial site. The records state: "According to historical documents, the Loong Mother was an immortal from the Qin Dynasty, known as Wen or Pu... Presently, when individuals examine the old records from the annals of Zhaoqing City in eastern Guangdong and the Xiao Tong Ancestral Temple in Yuecheng, they unanimously conclude that the Loong Mother hails from Tengxian County. Regardless of where she was raised, it is unequivocally verified that she is an immortal from Tengxian County. However, the location of her tomb in Yuecheng raises questions. Her father, named Tianrui, married a daughter from the Liang family in Yuecheng, and they had three daughters, one of whom was the Loong Mother... When she accompanied her mother to Yuecheng, she fell in love with the area and desired to settle there. After becoming familiar with the region, she discovered a stream where she found a stone egg. Upon hatching, it released five creatures resembling geckos, which were fond of water. Loong Mother nurtured them and released them into the river. Years later, they returned to visit their mother, appearing magnificent. Recognizing her sons' return, Loong Mother joyfully greeted them from a distance. When bidding farewell to her parents, she proclaimed, 'I will go to Yuecheng with my loongs, and thus rode her loong to the estuary at dusk...'" Following Loong Mother's death, a temple was erected in her honor, where the majority of wishes from the faithful are said to be granted, leading to a continual stream of worshippers even today.

The *Annals of Tengxian County* explicitly records the narrative of Loong Mother nurturing five loongs, affirming her origins in ancient Tengzhou. As the river goddess of the river civilization that flourished in ancient Tengzhou, Loong Mother remains a lasting symbol in the hearts of the people of Tengxian County.

Numerous sites in Tengxian County are linked to the life of Loong Mother, including the "Loong Alley Terrace", which is recognized as one of the eight scenic wonders of ancient Tengzhou, and the "Loong Neck", a well-known feature among the local populace. Additionally, the "Jinfeng Village, " where Loong Mother battled Taoist Priest Lai, and "Loong Mother Mountain", where she practiced Taoism, are significant locations. At the foot of Loong Mother Mountain lies a picturesque village surrounded by mountains and rivers, known as "Longteng", symbolizing the loong's flight.

Founded in the twelfth year of the Sui Dynasty (592 AD), Tengzhou derives its name from the Tengjiang River and Baiteng Mountain. Ancient Tengzhou boasts beautiful landscapes, and its millennia-long history has fostered the eight ancient wonders of the region, which include "Jian River with the Spring Tide", "The Autumn Wind Blowing Through Stone Wall", "The Autumn Scenery of Vegetation Falling in Duck Beach", "Loong Alley Terrace", "The Moon in Dong Mountain", "Sunny Day with Fog in Chi Canyon", "Gu Mountain Growing Verdant Vegetation", and "Wen Ridge Surrounded by Clouds". Loong Alley Terrace is located to the west of Xijiang River, where a loong alley stone lies submerged. It is said that this location is where Loong Mother raised five loongs that frolicked in the water. Prior to the completion of the Changzhou Water Conservancy Project, during dry autumn and winter months, the loong alley stone would be exposed. Loong Alley Terrace is also associated with a poignant legend involving Loong Mother's battle with Taoist Priest Lai to protect the people. According to this legend, Loong Mother treated the husband of Fengjie at the foot of Big Boundary Mountain, located near Lion Mountain. She instructed individuals to gather herbs at night. When an herb picker reached the summit of Dajie Mountain with a pine torch, he noticed stones moving toward Shihua Gorge, where a three-story stone perimeter was rapidly constructed on both sides, leaving only five minutes to close off the gorge. Finding this peculiar, he rushed back to inform Loong Mother. She realized that Taoist Priest Lai was blocking the gorge's entrance with stones from Lion Mountain, attempting to drown those trapped inside while monopolizing the gold mine in Jinfeng Village, which yielded ten kilograms of gold daily. To thwart Taoist Priest Lai's scheme, Loong Mother summoned Fengjie and others to ascend Dajie Mountain to learn the rooster's crow. She swiftly traversed the mountain using her magical abilities, returning to Shengxi Village to fetch a gold washing tray to divert the floodwaters. Upon hearing the rooster crow, Taoist Priest Lai mistook it for dawn and hurriedly ceased his magic, fleeing the scene. The stones that could not be positioned in time became five keel-shaped rocks in Shihua Gorge, where they now lie quietly. The inhabitants of the gorge were ultimately saved, although Fengjie's husband perished due to delayed treatment. In commemoration of Fengjie's heroic act in rescuing the people, the village she resided in was named Feng Village. The area where villagers commenced mining was designated Jinpo Village. Together, these two villages are referred to as Jinfeng Village, while the location where Loong Mother crossed the mountain's entrance is known as Longku Village, with the river at the exit called Loong Alley Terrace.

According to the legend, Loong Mother sought to cultivate immortality and learn Taoism through herbal collection and alchemy. She journeyed to Lion Mountain to pay homage to the Mother of Lion Mountain as her mentor, subsequently healing many sick villagers. As a result, she garnered a devoted following. One of the mountain ranges in the Lion Mountain series was subsequently named Loong Mother Mountain. Numerous artifacts associated with Loong Mother can be found in Loong Mother Mountain, including "Loong Mother Giving Sons", "Loong Mother's Holy Inkstone", "Loong Mother's Furnace", and "Loong Mother's Immortal Cultivation Rock". These relics are scattered throughout the mountain, each accompanied by the moral lessons imparted by Loong Mother.

Loong Mother raised five loongs, fostering a deep bond among them. As the loongs matured, they traced the river to the sea. The first emperor of the Qin Dynasty, a worshipper of the loong totem in search of the elixir of immortality, dispatched envoys bearing vast quantities of gold, silver, and jewels to Xiou, inviting Loong Mother to reside in the capital's palace. Unwilling to abandon her southern homeland, Loong Mother remained discontented aboard the official ship of the Qin envoy. Upon learning of her distress, the five loongs secretly shielded her. They summoned storms so that the Qin envoy's ship was thwarted by inclement weather, causing it to turn back to Wuzhou on four separate occasions. Realizing the protective actions of the five loongs, the Qin envoys were compelled to abandon their mission. Ultimately, the first emperor of the Qin Dynasty reluctantly permitted Loong Mother to return home. Demonstrating her commitment to her people, Loong Mother guided them in cultivating the land and managing waterways for their benefit. She passed away from exhaustion on the 15th day of the 8th lunar month in 211 BC. After her death, the five loongs mourned her loss, transforming into five Xiucai (ancient scholars) who donned mourning attire to oversee Loong Mother's funeral, honoring her as if they were her own sons. Following the funeral, the five loongs vigilantly guarded her tomb day and night, refusing to depart even after forty-nine days.

The legacy of Loong Mother continues to endure in Tengxian County's landscapes and in the collective memory of its people, establishing a lineage of cultural inheritance.

The Legend of Loong Mother in Tengxian County was included in the seventh batch of Guangxi's representative intangible cultural heritage items in 2018.

The Inheritance Pedigree of Loong Mother legend in Tengxian County

Generation	Name	Gender	Nationality	Education Background	Year of Craft Leanring	Means of Inheritance
First	Li Qixian	Male	Han	Primary school	Unknown	Family inheritance
First	Li Chuhuan	Male	Han	Old-style private school	Unknown	Apprenticeship
First	Peng Guiying	Female	Han	Primary school	1949	Apprenticeship
Second	Li Yanming	Male	Han	Junior college	1963	Apprenticeship
Second	Li Mingyuan	Male	Han	Junior college	1962	Family inheritance
Second	Li Xianming	Male	Han	Specialized secondary school	1979	Apprenticeship
Third	Li Weilin	Male	Han	College	1999	Family inheritance
Third	Li Donghai	Male	Han	Specialized secondary school	1999	Family inheritance
Third	Chen Peiwei	Male	Han	Primary school	1999	Apprenticeship

藤县太平米饼制作工艺

○ 李秋芳

中国劳动人民,最不缺乏的是勤劳和智慧,大到四大发明,小到地方小吃,无不显示着人们的聪明才智。藤县的太平米饼制作工艺就是如此。

藤县太平镇盛产粮食和蔗糖,比县内其他地方富庶,是商旅首选、兵家必争之地。特殊的地理位置和丰富的物产,还有高温潮湿的气候特点,是藤县太平米饼制作工艺得以诞生的重要原因。太平米饼制作工艺有着悠久的历史,可以追溯到东汉时期。当时战争频繁,北方来的士兵水土不服,伙房便用太平镇出产的糯米碾成粉,加上太平镇盛产的糖混合在一起做成烙饼,作为军粮。太平人的饮食一直是"饭稻羹鱼",见了烙饼,觉得很好吃,又可以储存,于是纷纷效仿。一方水土养一方人,藤县多数人受不了烙饼,吃了容易上火,于是改烙为蒸,并把炒花生和白糖等放入饼中做馅。

小小的米饼承载着几代人的记忆,深深触动着人们的味蕾。而美食的获得需要

藤县太平米饼制作工艺

长时间的辛苦劳作和耐心的等待，太平米饼的制作亦是如此。在农家，冬至一到，人们就开始了米饼制作的准备过程：把上佳的本地糯米炒到香气四溢、黄而不焦的时候，取出碾成粉末。然后找些青翠欲滴的较大的菜叶，层层叠叠地埋在糯米粉中，以此来润粉。这是关键的一个环节，糯米粉的润泽程度决定了米饼的好坏。上好的菜叶以最本真最直接的方式深埋到糯米粉中，与之朝夕相处，深度交流。人们需要经常观察粉的润泽程度，看看是否需要更换新鲜的菜叶。大概一个月后，菜叶慢慢地变黄变干了，糯米粉已卸下了满身的燥热，变得软软润润的，还增添了丝丝清香。

制饼的粉润好了，就找一个相宜的日子，一家人坐在一起，拿出锅碗瓢盆，还有印饼的工具——饼印。饼印分两部分，一部分是约1厘米高、直径4厘米的圈，以前是用竹片围成的，现在一般用合金直接制作成形。饼的形状、大小就靠这个圈了。另一部分是个小圆片，一面的中间竖着一根小小的棍子，

太平米饼制作过程组图 / 霍雨锋　摄

另一面上雕刻着"福""禄""寿""喜"这类寓意着美好的字眼。

开始和粉了，人们把白糖煮成浓浓稠稠的糖浆，和进等待已久的糯米粉中，不断地揉搓，直到它们不分彼此。这时的饼粉，黄黄的、松松软软的，静静地等待着与馅料的相逢。最原始最常用的馅料是花生米（炒香）、芝麻（炒香）和黄砂糖。如果喜欢吃肉，就事先用白糖腌制一粒粒肥膘，做成冰肉。

开始印饼了，在饼圈里面铺上一层润好的饼粉，放进馅料，再加一层粉，盖上饼印，双手大拇指摁着饼印，其余八指扶着饼圈，齐齐发力，整个饼圈在手下团团转。须臾之间，饼成，撤印，直径四厘米的精致米饼就出现在眼前了。

为了便于携带和收藏，还需要最后一道工序，那就是放进热气腾腾的锅中蒸一蒸，让各种食材尽情地释放出自己最本真的味道，交汇融合成为极致的美食。

"小饼如嚼月，中有酥与饴"是大文豪苏东坡在《留别廉守》中的诗句，也是对藤县太平米饼最好的诠释。甜是人类最简单最原始的美食体验，聪明的藤县太平人深谙此道。小小的米饼经过太平人巧手制作，甜而不腻，糯米粉入口即化，而花生和芝麻却越嚼越香。如果是加入了冰肉的米饼，一口咬下去，你已分不清白糖和肥肉了，它们已经是你中有我，我中有你了，却又倔强地保留着各自的那一份甜美甘醇。小小的米饼，外表看上去平淡无奇，但弥足珍贵的美食往往如此。如果苏东坡当时在藤县能够品尝到太平米饼的话，不仅会说"松如迁客老，酒似使君醇"，而且会加上"饼是太平香"吧。

饼的味道也是人情的味道，中国人善于用食物来缩短人与人之间的交往距离。饼做好了，左邻右舍都会共享喜悦。米饼是传统走亲访友的送礼佳品，是藤县太平镇群众必不可少的年货，于是自然而然地形成了过年亲戚来往必送米饼的习俗。

藤县太平米饼制作工艺遍布太平镇，与太平镇相邻的濛江

藤县太平米饼制作工艺

太平米饼饼印 / 欧伟文　摄

镇、和平镇、古龙镇、东荣镇、平福乡等乡镇群众因为与太平镇群众联姻，使这个米饼制作工艺逐渐传播开来，这些相邻乡镇的群众也模仿太平镇的做法制作米饼。每当临近过年，人们就开始用此方法做米饼，互相赠送，互相交流。据嘉庆二十一年（1816年）的《藤县志》记载："士大夫家设春饼春茶相邀曰贺春。"后来藤县太平米饼制作工艺逐渐辐射到较远的大黎镇以及藤县浔江以南的乡镇，继而传遍全县。

太平米饼越来越受人欢迎，需求量越来越大，朝雪米饼厂、汇香米饼厂、萃香米饼厂、来利食品厂、太平红日食品厂等厂家如雨后春笋般在太平镇冒出来。

创新往往是获得发展的前提。人们利用机器代替了手工制作中的碾米、煮糖浆、和粉、搓粉、印饼、蒸饼等几道工序，大大增加了产量。太平人的智慧是无穷的，人们为了更好地掌握炒糯米这道工序，就把小铁砂混进来同炒，让糯米快速而均匀熟透，而后用铁簸箕簸去小铁砂，留下金黄酥香的糯米粒。

制作好的太平米饼 / 霍雨锋 摄

虽然现在是机器时代，但人们并不愿意把所有的事情都交给机器，尤其是掺和了人们温情的润粉和印饼的过程。人们亲自动手，关注着饼粉的润泽度，享受着米饼在自己手下诞生的喜悦。

小小的米饼中，除了原来用白糖或黄砂糖、花生、芝麻、冰肉作馅料，太平镇的人们又依据各人不同的喜好，创造性地运用叉烧、肉松、椰蓉等作为馅料。米饼的外层，又分别用艾叶、紫薯、高粱等绿色食品和进糯米粉中，创造出艾叶米饼、紫薯米饼、高粱米饼等新品种。在众人的合力下，藤县太平米饼制作工艺日益成熟，太平米饼多次被评为广西名优特产。

太平米饼每一道制作工序都有技巧，时间、温度、比例都很讲究，稍有偏差，口感就天差地别。这些技巧，靠的是祖祖辈辈的口传心授，代代相传。

2020年，藤县太平米饼制作工艺列入第八批自治区级非物质文化遗产代表性项目名录。

藤县太平米饼制作工艺传承谱系

代别	姓名	性别	民族	学历	学艺时间（年）	传承方式
第一代	朱氏	女	汉	不详	无从考究	家族传承
第一代	黄兰英	女	汉	不详	无从考究	家族传承
第一代	潘丽珍	女	汉	不详	无从考究	家族传承
第二代	何秀芬	女	汉	小学	1960	家族传承
第二代	周润英	女	汉	不详	1940	家族传承
第二代	邱礼姬	女	汉	小学	1953	家族传承
第三代	黄德亮	男	汉	初中	1973	家族传承
第三代	梁锦芳	女	汉	初中	1977	家族传承
第三代	胡朝雪	女	汉	初中	1984	家族传承
第三代	黄自杰	男	汉	中专	1990	家族传承
第四代	黄舞国	男	汉	高中	2015	家族传承
第四代	杨琼珍	女	汉	高中	2016	师徒传承
第四代	陈飞羽	女	汉	小学	2011	家族传承

Taiping Rice Cake Production Craft in Tengxian County

· Li Qiufang ·

  The industriousness and ingenuity of the Chinese people are evident in everything from the Four Great Inventions to local delicacies. The Taiping rice cake from Tengxian County exemplifies this cultural heritage.

  Taiping Town, located in Tengxian County, is blessed with abundant grains and cane sugar, making it one of the wealthiest areas in both geographical and agricultural terms. The town's unique geography, coupled with its high temperature and humid climate, significantly contributes to the development of the Taiping rice cake production craft. The history of Taiping rice cake dates to the Eastern Han Dynasty. During this period of frequent warfare, soldiers from the north struggled to adapt to the local environment. Consequently, kitchens began to grind glutinous rice, produced in Taiping Town, into powder and mix it with locally abundant sugar to create pancakes as rations. The diet of the Taiping people consisted primarily of rice and fish, and upon tasting these pancakes, they found them delicious. Furthermore, the pancakes could be stored easily, leading the locals to adopt this culinary practice. However, due to the prevalence of inflammation caused by pancakes, the preparation method was modified to steaming, and fried peanuts and sugar were added as fillings.

  These small rice cakes carry the memories of generations and resonate with people's palates. The preparation of Taiping

藤县太平米饼制作工艺

rice cakes is a labor-intensive process that requires time and patience. In rural areas, the production begins with the arrival of the winter solstice. Locals fry high-quality glutinous rice until it becomes fragrant and golden but not burnt, then grind it into powder. They layer green mustard leaves within the glutinous rice powder to moisten it—a crucial step, as the degree of moistening directly affects the quality of the rice cake. The finely chopped mustard leaves remain deeply embedded in the powder, allowing them to infuse their flavor over time. About a month later, the mustard leaves gradually turn yellow and dry, while the glutinous rice flour becomes soft and moist, acquiring a subtle fragrance.

Once the cake powder has been sufficiently softened, a suitable day is chosen for the communal preparation. Participants gather with pots, pans, and cake-printing tools, which consist of two components: a ring, traditionally made of bamboo but now often crafted from alloy, measuring about one centimeter in height and four centimeters in diameter, and a small round piece featuring a central stick on one side and auspicious Chinese characters such as "*Fu*", "*Lu*", "*Shou*", and "*Xi*" carved on the other.

To mix the powder, white sugar is heated to create a thick syrup, which is then incorporated into the glutinous rice flour. The mixture is kneaded until thoroughly blended, resulting in a yellow, soft dough that awaits its filling. The initial fillings consist of fried peanuts, fried sesame seeds, and sugar. For those who prefer a savory option, sugar can be used to marinate fatty meat beforehand.

When it comes time to shape the cakes, a layer of cake powder is spread within the ring, followed by the filling, another layer of powder, and the cake print. Participants press down with their thumbs while supporting the ring with their other fingers, rotating the entire mold. Moments later, a delicate rice cake, approximately three to four centimeters in diameter, emerges.

To enhance portability and preserve freshness, the cakes are steamed, allowing the various ingredients to release their authentic flavors.

The poetic phrase, "Small cakes just like the moon, crisp and sweet, " from the renowned poet Su Dongpo, aptly describes the Taiping rice cake. Sweetness is the most fundamental aspect of human culinary experience, and the resourceful people of Taiping understand this well. Their expertly crafted small rice cakes are sweet but not overly rich. The glutinous rice flour melts in the mouth, while the peanuts and sesame contribute additional sweetness. When ice meat is added, the flavors harmonize seamlessly, masking the distinction between sugar and fat while preserving their individual essences. Though the small rice cakes may appear unassuming, they embody the principle that true delicacies often present themselves in simple forms. Had Su Dongpo tasted the Taiping rice cakes of his time, he might have added, "The cake in Taiping is fragrant, " to his praises of pine and wine.

The flavor of the rice cake extends beyond taste; it embodies human relationships. The Chinese culture often utilizes food to bridge social distances. When the cakes are cooked, neighbors share in the joy, making rice cakes a traditional gift when visiting friends and family. They are particularly essential during the New Year festivities in Taiping Town, fostering the custom of exchanging rice cakes with relatives during the Spring Festival.

The Taiping rice cake production craft is widespread throughout Taiping Town. People from neighboring areas such as Mengjiang Town, Heping Town, Gulong Town, Dongrong Town, and Pingfu Town have gradually adopted this tradition, often due to intermarriage with residents of Taiping. As the Chinese New Year approaches, families begin preparing rice cakes, sharing recipes and techniques with one another. According to the *Annals of Tengxian County* in the 21st year of Jiaqing period (1816 AD), "Literati families established spring cakes and spring tea to invite each other, an activity known as congratulating spring." Over time, the Taiping rice cake production craft has spread to distant Dali Town and areas south of the Xunjiang River in Tengxian County.

As the popularity of Taiping rice cakes continues to grow, demand has surged. Numerous manufacturers, including Chaoxue Rice Cake Factory, Huixiang Rice Cake Factory, Cuixiang Rice Cake Factory, Lai Li Food Factory, and Taiping Hongri Food Factory, have emerged in Taiping Town.

Innovation plays a vital role in this development. Modern machinery has replaced manual labor in various production processes such as rice milling, sugar cooking, powder mixing, kneading, cake printing, and steaming, significantly increasing output. The ingenuity of the Taiping people is boundless. For instance, to optimize the frying process, small iron sand is mixed with the rice, allowing it to cook quickly and evenly. After frying, the iron sand is winnowed away, leaving behind glutinous rice grains with a golden crisp flavor.

Despite living in an age dominated by machines, people remain committed to maintaining a personal touch in the cake-printing process, valuing the smoothness of the flour and the joy of crafting rice cakes by hand.

In addition to traditional fillings of white or yellow sugar, peanuts, sesame, and frozen meat, the residents of Taiping Town have creatively incorporated barbecued pork, minced meat, and coconut into their rice cakes to cater to diverse tastes. They also blend green ingredients such as wormwood, purple sweet potato, and sorghum into the glutinous rice flour, resulting in innovative varieties like wormwood cake, purple sweet potato cake, and sorghum cake. Through collective efforts, the Taiping rice cake production craft in Tengxian County has matured, earning recognition as a famous specialty of Guangxi.

The craft of Taiping rice cake production encompasses skillful techniques across every stage, emphasizing the importance of time, temperature, and proportion. Even minor deviations can result in significant differences in taste. These techniques have been passed down through generations, creating a rich legacy of craftsmanship.

The Taiping rice cake production craft in Tengxian County was included in the eighth batch of Guangxi intangible cultural heritage list in 2020.

藤县太平米饼制作工艺

The Inheritance Pedigree of Taiping Rice Cake Production Craft in Tengxian County

Generation	Name	Gender	Nationality	Education Background	Year of Craft Leanring	Means of Inheritance
First	Zhu Shi	Female	Han	Unknown	Unknown	Family inheritance
First	Huang Lanying	Female	Han	Unknown	Unknown	Family inheritance
First	Pan Lizhen	Female	Han	Unknown	Unknown	Family inheritance
Second	He Xiufen	Female	Han	Primary school	1960	Family inheritance
Second	Zhou Runying	Female	Han	Unknown	1940	Family inheritance
Second	Qiu Liji	Female	Han	Primary school	1953	Family inheritance
Third	Huang Deliang	Male	Han	Junior high school	1973	Family inheritance
Third	Liang Jinfang	Female	Han	Junior high school	1977	Family inheritance
Third	Hu Chaoxue	Female	Han	Junior high school	1984	Family inheritance
Third	Huang Zijie	Male	Han	Specialized secondary school	1990	Family inheritance
Fourth	Huang Wuguo	Male	Han	Senior high school	2015	Family inheritance
Fourth	Yang Qiongzhen	Female	Han	Senior high school	2016	Apprenticeship
Fourth	Chen Feiyu	Female	Han	Primary school	2011	Family inheritance

彩扎（藤县狮头）

○ 孙燕凤

彩扎（藤县狮头）是流传于广西藤县的一种民间工艺美术式样。中国舞狮分为南狮和北狮，藤县的彩扎狮头为南狮。南狮狮头分"刘备""关羽""张飞"三个角色，色彩鲜艳，具有强烈的视觉冲击力，通过不同的纹饰来展现人物的性格特征。其中黄色剑纹代表刘备的仁德，红色刀纹代表关羽的忠义，黑色矛纹代表张飞的英勇。不同角色的狮头用于不同场合的表演。随着时代的变化，狮头的角色逐渐模糊化，因其大块着色统称彩狮。

藤县狮头规格按大小区分为1～9号狮头，其中1～3号为成年人使用，通常重2.5～3公斤，8、9号狮头专供幼儿园小朋友用，其余狮头则是中小学教学活动使用。

彩扎狮头材料以竹篾为主，主要选用年份较久的毛竹、单竹、坭竹，经过破、修、浸、晾几道工序做成。

"破"就是将竹子破为各种规格的竹篾。用于底框的竹篾，选毛竹为佳，需破成厚度0.8～1厘米、宽2～3厘米的扁形长条篾，长度则以所制作的狮头型号而定。主体竹篾则选用单竹第一层，俗称竹青，统一破为厚约0.5厘米、宽约0.8厘米的扁长条篾和直径为0.5～0.8厘米的圆形长条篾。

将竹篾刮去竹青表层，用破篾刀修刮竹篾至顺滑、无刺。竹篾整体一致的形状，体现了工匠熟能生巧的"修"竹绝活。

接着把修好的竹篾分类捆绑，浸泡入石灰水中3天，以达到驱虫防蛀的效果。

然后取出浸泡好的竹篾解散铺开，放置在通风

彩扎（藤县狮头）

威武的狮头 / 何柏 摄

向阳处晾干水分，但忌烈日暴晒，以防竹篾过干变形断裂。

经过环环相扣、一丝不苟的几道工序，竹篾才可以正式使用，足见狮头扎作选料用料的严谨。

其他材料还有胶丝或麻丝、木棒、糨糊、白色纱纸、纱布、羊毛、兔毛，以及各种颜色的颜料、画笔，用于制作狮头的下巴、耳朵、眼睛、眼睑和绒毛、绒球、触须等。

彩扎（藤县狮头）分扎、扑、画、装四道工序，每道工序都需要技巧，靠匠人一双巧手和丰富的经验去完成。

首先是扎，即用竹篾扎成狮子头的模型。除特别部位用细铁丝扎牢固之外，其他均用纱纸搓成纸条（纸条只搓 $\frac{2}{3}$，$\frac{1}{3}$ 上糨糊），扎绑在每个竹篾的交接处，未搓部分纸条涂上糨糊贴在外，起到稳定、牢固的作用。

要使狮头形象好看，必须按部位尺寸要求去扎作，如 2 号狮头口径 45 厘米，3 号狮头口径 43 厘米，这些都有严格的规定。

其次是扑，扎成狮头模型后，将纱纸裁成 5 张 15 厘米 × 20 厘米大的纸张，涂上糨糊粘扑于狮头框架处，将狮头框架全部

扎狮头 / 何柏 摄

粘扑狮头 / 欧伟文 摄

彩扎（藤县狮头）

粘扑满。先用糨糊将薄如蝉翼的纱纸扫透，然后一张张覆盖到扎好的狮头上，一层纱纸风干后再扑一层，风干后又再扑一层纱纸，重复两到三次，就成了狮头白坯。但最后一次必须粘纱纸，以便绘画。

再次是画，也即给狮头白坯"写色"，这是狮头扎作重要的一步。狮头的颜值取决于画工，全凭画工一支巧笔。要求画工具有一定的美术功底，画工根据狮头"刘备""关羽""张飞"等角色在白坯上描上不同的图案，绘以不同的色彩、花纹。传统花纹有虎斑纹、如意纹、祥云纹、小刀纹、线纹等。如果是画彩狮，则根据画工的喜好画色、画纹，只要求大块着色，达到色彩鲜艳、浓烈、繁杂的效果。

由于狮头立体感强且面部表情丰富，画工落笔时要又准又稳，不能有半点偏差，非常考验画工的手艺。

最后是装。装相对简单些，就是对狮头进行最后的装饰，将狮头的下巴、耳朵、眼睛、眼睑装附上去，再装胶丝、毛料、绒球等饰物，丰富狮头的外观。

经过匠人一番精心的装饰后，彩扎狮头栩栩如生。

狮头绘画 / 何柏 摄

狮头装饰 / 梁斯瑜 摄

制作完成的狮头 / 杨定登　摄

　　藤县中等专业学校批量生产彩扎狮头。民间小作坊有太平镇太平街吴润生的家庭作坊，属家族传承，在20世纪八九十年代为鼎盛时期，每年都扎作四五十只狮头。这些都很好地传承了中华民族传统手工技艺——彩扎狮头。

　　2023年，彩扎（藤县狮头）列入第九批自治区级非物质文化遗产代表性项目名录。

彩扎（藤县狮头）代表性传承人

级别	姓名	性别	出生时间（年）	认定时间（年）
县级	张舒欣	女	1991	2023

Lion Head Colorful Tying Craft in Tengxian County

· Sun Yanfeng ·

The colorful tying craft of the lion head is a distinctive folk-art form prevalent in Tengxian County, Guangxi. Chinese lion dances are categorized into southern and northern styles, with the lion head tying craft in Tengxian County specifically associated with the southern lion. The southern lion heads are characterized by their vibrant colors, which create a strong visual impact. These lion heads often represent three historical figures: Liu Bei, Guan Yu, and Zhang Fei. Each character is depicted with distinct patterns: yellow sword stripes signify Liu Bei's benevolence; red knife stripes symbolize Guan Yu's loyalty; and black spear stripes denote Zhang Fei's bravery. The lion heads corresponding to these characters are used in various performances. Over time, the roles of the lion heads have become less defined, and they are now collectively referred to as "*Caishi*" (colored lions) due to their vivid coloration.

In Tengxian County, lion heads are categorized by size, ranging from numbers 1 to 9. Sizes 1 to 3 are designed for adults, typically weighing between 2.5 to 3 kilograms, while sizes 8 and 9 are intended for kindergarten children. The remaining sizes are used for educational purposes in primary and middle schools.

The primary material for crafting the lion head in Tengxian County is bamboo, specifically Mao, Dan, and Ni bamboo, known for their durability. Several procedures are involved in preparing the bamboo: breaking, fixing, soaking, and airing.

The "breaking" process involves cutting the bamboo into various

精美的狮头 / 何凯 摄

specifications. Mao bamboo is preferred for the base frame, which is fashioned into flat strips measuring 0.8 to 1 cm in thickness and 2 to 3 cm in width, with length varying according to the lion head design. The first layer utilizes Dan bamboo, commonly referred to as "Qing" bamboo. This bamboo skin is processed into strips approximately 0.5 cm thick and 0.8 cm wide, as well as circular strips with diameters ranging from 0.5 to 0.8 cm.

Subsequently, the bamboo strips are scraped to remove the outer skin, which is essential for achieving smooth surfaces. This step ensures that the bamboo strips are free of splinters and have a consistent shape, reflecting the skill and experience of the craftsman involved in the "fixing" stage.

After fixing, the bamboo strips are classified, bundled, and immersed in lime water for three days to render them insect-repellent and moth-proof.

Following this treatment, the soaked bamboo strips are laid out to dry in a well-ventilated area under sunlight. However, care must be taken to avoid excessive exposure to heat, which could cause the bamboo to dry out excessively and become deformed or brittle.

Upon completing these meticulous preparations, the bamboo strips are deemed suitable for use, demonstrating the rigor involved in material selection.

Additional materials required for the craft include rubber thread or hemp thread, sticks, adhesive, white gauze paper, colored pigments, brushes, and various components that form the lion's head, such as jaws, ears, eyes, and eyelids. Ornaments such as floss, pompons, wool, rabbit fur, and tentacles are also incorporated.

The lion head colorful tying craft in Tengxian County comprises four main procedures: tying, coating, painting, and fitting. Each procedure demands specific skills and relies on the craftsmanship and extensive experience of the artisans.

The first step, tying, involves assembling the bamboo sticks into a lion head model. Special components are secured with fine iron wire, while other sections are bound using strips of gauze paper, with one-third of the strip coated in paste. The uncovered sections are treated with adhesive for added stability.

To ensure a proper fit, the tying process adheres to specific size requirements. For instance, the No.2 lion head has a diameter of 45 cm, while the No.3 lion head measures 43 cm. These dimensions are strictly regulated.

The second step, coating, involves cutting the yarn paper into five pieces measuring 15 cm × 20 cm, which are then coated with paste and applied to the lion head frame. A layer of gauze paper, as thin as a cicada's wing, is applied over the tied lion head, and after each layer air-dries, another layer is added. This process is repeated two or three times until the white base of the lion head is completed. During the final application, yarn paper is glued on to facilitate easier painting.

The third procedure, painting, involves applying color to the white base of the lion's head. This critical step determines the aesthetic quality of the lion head. The painter must possess artistic skills to create various patterns on the white base, corresponding to the roles of the lion heads, such as Liu Bei, Guan Yu, and Zhang Fei. Each lion is adorned with unique colors and patterns. The process begins with a white background, followed by intricate patterns. Traditional designs include tiger stripes, ruyi motifs, auspicious clouds, knife stripes, and line stripes. For colored lions, the painter applies large areas of color according to their preferences, aiming for a vibrant and complex visual effect.

Due to the three-dimensional nature of the lion head and its expressive features, the painter must hold the brush steadily and accurately, presenting a significant challenge that tests the artisan's skill and precision.

The final step, fitting, involves attaching the chin, ears, eyes, and eyelids of the lion head, along with incorporating rubber threads, wool, pompoms, and decorative elements to enhance the lion's appearance.

With careful embellishments, the colorful lion heads come to life, exuding

狮头绘画 / 何锦奋　摄

彩扎（藤县狮头）

vibrancy.

Tengxian County's specialized secondary school produces numerous colored lions, while small family workshops, such as Wu Runsheng's workshop on Taiping Street in Taiping Town, carry on the tradition. During the 1980s, this craft reached its peak, with an annual production of 40 to 50 lion heads, exemplifying the successful inheritance of this traditional Chinese handicraft.

In 2023, the lion head colorful tying craft in Tengxian County was included in the ninth batch of Wuzhou intangible cultural heritage representative items.

The Representative Inheritors of Lion Head Colorful Tying Craft in Tengxian County

Level	Name	Gender	Year of Birth	Time of Certification
County	Zhang Shuxin	Female	1991	2023

采茶歌

○ 曾春凤

采茶歌中的茶公和茶娘 / 苏向　摄

采茶歌，也叫"采茶""茶歌"，其起源没有史料记载，属于民间音乐，它有自己的舞台，并辅以道具，伴以乐器，演绎古今传奇。

古藤州属百越之地，处于西江流域的浔江之畔，较早受到中原文化熏陶。在明末清初时期，民族歌舞音乐在各族人民中有较大发展，说唱音乐更是异彩纷呈，藤县采茶歌就是在这个时期流传起来的。

藤县因浔江贯穿而过，一水分隔形成藤南和藤北两大片区，但浔江并非难以跨越的银河，民间的风土人情、风俗习惯、文化艺术，乃至俗语、俚语不会因"盈盈一水间"而不大相同。因此，采茶歌先在藤县南部岭景、象棋、金鸡、藤州等乡镇的农村兴起、传播，很快，歌声飘过浔江，飘过蒙江，飘过大楼江，飘进了藤县北部的濛江、太平、古龙等乡镇的千家万户。人们耳濡目染，深深被这种易于表达心声的民间音乐吸引。

采茶歌

清末以来，藤县采茶歌流传更为广泛。在春节或婚嫁等喜庆的日子，民间采茶歌手相互对唱，增添喜庆气氛。到了20世纪五六十年代，藤县塘步、太平、濛江、古龙等乡镇的广大农村掀起更大一波唱采茶歌的热潮。各村成立采茶队，把采茶歌搬上舞台，并和本村及周边村寨的采茶歌手对唱，相互切磋技艺、交流心得。上演曲目有传统题材的《肖永伦》《孟姜女》等，现代题材的《十二月采茶歌》等。平时，民间歌手在田间地头、村场、树下都可以随口即兴吟唱。

采茶歌一般由两人或多人组成，多数为茶公和茶娘两人对唱。茶公、茶娘相当于京剧中的主角小生和花旦。茶公穿着讲究，黑色的唐装显得儒雅正统；茶娘也着黑色唐装，但以斜襟区分性别。

采茶歌的道具比较简单，除了茶公和茶娘腰扎的彩带，值得一提的是他们手握的纸扇。扇子在中国有着深厚的文化内涵，进入戏曲似乎顺理成章。简简单单一把纸扇，被人握在腕中挥洒自如，时而扬波翻浪，时而消暑送凉，时而"犹抱琵琶半遮面"，达到扇人合一之境界，给观众以视觉上的感染力和震撼力，为采茶歌大大增添了魅力。

茶公、茶娘对唱采茶歌时，辅以简单的台步和动作，无论是抬膝挺腰的跳步、脚尖叠着脚跟的碎步，还是左摇右摆的十字步，均须依照歌词的内容情节表演到位，肢体语言让采茶歌表达的内容或情感更加形象丰富。肢体传情，音乐表意。音乐音乐，有音就有乐。采茶歌的伴奏乐器主要是二胡、秦琴，并配以锣鼓伴奏和过场。二胡即二弦胡琴，起源于唐朝。二胡具有"四美"：音色天成之美，风格独特之美，生活情感交融之美，意境天然之美。而采茶歌的唱词大都不事雕琢，取之于生活，流传于藤县民间，因而二胡和采茶歌的呼应、配合，恰恰是"高山流水遇知音"。

采茶歌用藤县方言传唱，唱词多用诙谐的民间语言，大量采用比喻、夸张、双关手法，而且句式押韵，唱起来朗朗上口，情感丰富，具有浓郁的地方色彩。"多啊才李白佢做果啊超群，天啊上谪仙嘟降凡尘，学富五车藏啊腹内，才啊高八啊斗非凡人。非啊是天公佢做来注定，一啊切在于嘟辛与勤，十载寒窗不啊怕苦，只啊望他啊朝步青云。"这首《十载寒窗步青云》，唱词中的

"啊""嘟""佢""做果""做来",相当于《诗经》《离骚》中的语气助词"兮",如"巧笑倩兮,美目盼兮""路漫漫其修远兮,吾将上下而求索"。这些助词,用在唱词中既有对称美、音乐美,又有缓冲语速、加强语气的作用,藤县方言叫"话邓"。此外,采茶歌唱词去掉语气助词后,类似于七言古诗,每一句都必须押韵,韵律整齐,朗朗上口。

采茶歌涵盖了丰富的形式和内容,它是文学、音乐、舞蹈、美术等多种艺术元素组成的有机整体。采茶歌旋律是徵调或五声音阶,偶有变宫出现,以级进为主,曲调平稳、方整,多在慢速到稍快的中速之间,长于抒情,具有浓郁的生活气息和民歌小调色彩。采茶歌唱腔淳朴清新,悠扬动人,韵味绵长,特别是方言抑扬顿挫的穿插,更显亲切感人、情景交融。

随着文化艺术等娱乐的多样化,采茶歌的演唱群众多以中老年人为主,他们一般都是在茶余饭后或劳作闲时演唱,形成队伍的演出现在鲜为人知。

2010年,采茶歌列入第二批市级非物质文化遗产代表性项目名录。

采茶歌传承谱系

代别	姓名	性别	民族	学艺时间（年）	传承方式
第一代	莫家其	男	汉	无从考究	师徒传承
第二代	周柱超	男	汉	无从考究	师徒传承
	饶桂清	女	汉	1961	师徒传承
	钟家成	男	汉	1972	师徒传承
	周雅清	男	汉	1977	师徒传承
第三代	莫柱松	男	汉	1980	师徒传承
	莫志英	女	汉	1980	师徒传承
第四代	陈绪寅	男	汉	1986	师徒传承
	李华琼	女	汉	1987	师徒传承
	李伟霞	女	汉	1990	师徒传承
	李建梅	女	汉	1992	师徒传承

Tea–Picking Song

· *Zeng Chunfeng* ·

The tea-picking song in Tengxian County, also known as "tea picking" or "tea song", lacks historical records regarding its origins. It is classified as folk music and is characterized by performances that interpret ancient and modern legends, often accompanied by props and musical instruments.

Historically, the region of ancient Tengzhou is part of the Baiyue area, situated along the Xunjiang River within the Xijiang River Basin. This region has been influenced by Central Plains culture earlier than many others. During the late Ming and early Qing dynasties, folk songs and dances flourished among various ethnic groups, and rap music spread in diverse forms. The tea-picking songs in Tengxian County gained popularity during this period.

The Xunjiang River traverses Tengxian County, dividing it into two areas known as Tengnan and Tengbei. However, the river does not create a cultural divide; folk customs, traditional practices, and colloquial expressions remain interconnected. Consequently, tea-picking songs first emerged and spread in rural areas surrounding Lingjing, Xiangqi, Jinji, and Tengzhou towns in southern Tengxian County. Soon, these songs crossed the Xijiang River, the Mengjiang River, and the Dalou River, influencing many households in the northern towns of Mengjiang, Taiping, and Gulong. This folk music captivates audiences due to its straightforward expression of deep emotions.

Since the late Qing Dynasty, the tea-picking songs of Tengxian

采茶歌演员排练 / 何锦奋　摄

County have enjoyed a broader dissemination. On festive occasions, such as the Spring Festival or weddings, folk tea-song singers perform together to enhance the celebratory atmosphere. By the 1950s and 1960s, a significant resurgence of tea-picking song performances occurred across the rural areas, including towns and villages such as Tangbu, Taiping, Mengjiang, and Gulong. Villages established tea-picking teams that showcased these songs on stage, often singing duets with tea-picking singers from their villages and neighboring communities. Additionally, performers exchanged skills and ideas. Traditional performances include pieces like "*Xiao Yonglun*" (a representative work of Niuniang opera from Cenxi) and "*Meng Jiangnv*" (one of the four great love legends of ancient China), while modern themes include "*Tea-Picking Songs in December*" (a Guangxi folk song). During leisure time, folk singers often improvise in fields, villages, or under trees.

　　Tea-picking song performances typically involve two or more singers, most commonly duets between a male and female singer,

采茶歌

analogous to the main roles of Sheng and Dan in Beijing opera. The male singer, dressed elegantly in a black Tang suit, contrasts with the female singer, who dons a black Tang dress; the distinct lapel styles signify their genders.

The props used in tea-picking songs are relatively simple. Besides the ribbons tied around the waists of the male and female singers, the paper fan they hold is significant. Fans carry profound cultural connotations in China, making their inclusion in performances seem natural. A simple paper fan is often held at the wrist and manipulated gracefully, sometimes resembling rising waves, a gentle summer breeze, or evoking the imagery of "her face was still half hidden behind a pipa".

When the male and female singers perform the tea-picking song together, they incorporate simple movements and steps, such as jumping with raised knees, folding their heels, or swaying side to side, which align with the lyrical content and narrative of the songs. These movements enhance the emotional expression of the songs. Overall, body language conveys feelings, while music conveys meaning. Tea-picking songs are primarily accompanied by traditional Chinese instruments such as the erhu (a two-stringed bowed instrument) and the Qinqin (a national musical instrument), complemented by gongs and drums to create dynamic transitions. The erhu, originating from the Tang dynasty, possesses "four beauties": its authentic timbre, unique style, emotional depth, and natural artistic conception. Most lyrics in tea-picking songs are derived from real-life experiences rather than fabricated, circulating within the folk community of Tengxian County. The interplay between the erhu and tea-picking songs mirrors the sentiment expressed in the saying, "A confidant alone has a keen ear for idyllic melodies".

The tea-picking songs of Tengxian County are sung in dialect, often featuring humorous folk language that incorporates metaphors, exaggerations, and puns. The strong local style lends

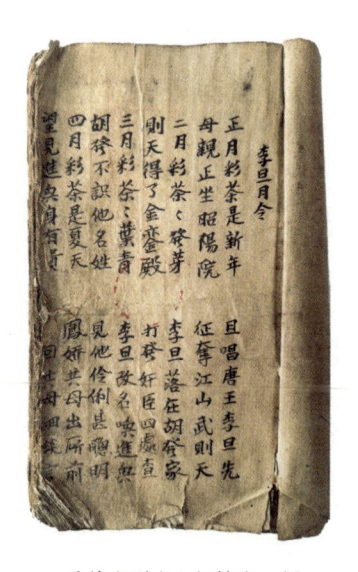

采茶戏剧本 / 何锦奋 摄

itself to rhyming patterns, making the songs catchy and vibrant. An example of this can be seen in the lyrics: "The gifted Li Bai (a renowned Tang dynasty poet) is outstanding; he is a celestial being descended to earth. A man of many talents, he is not an ordinary person. His success is not mere chance; it is the result of his hard work. He studied diligently for ten years, aspiring to reach the pinnacle." These lines are drawn from *Pursuing a Meteoric Rise through Ten Years of Hard Study* (a representative work of tea-picking songs). Words such as "*a*", "*du*", "*qu*", "*zuo guo*" and "*zuo lai*" serve as tonal auxiliary words akin to those in *The Book of Songs* and *Li Sao*, exemplified by lines like "Beautiful face, smile truly beautiful; bright eyes, truly charming" and "the road ahead will be long, and our climb will be steep". The rhythm is primarily driven by a steady tempo, with melodic variations that balance symmetry and rhythm, while also serving to moderate the pace of the lyrics and enhance their tonal qualities. The local dialect of Tengxian County is referred to as "*Hua Deng*". When modal particles are omitted, the lyrics of tea-picking songs resemble seven-character ancient poems, with each line adhering to a neat rhyme scheme that enhances their memorability.

Tea-picking songs encompass a rich variety of forms and content, representing an integrated whole composed of literature, music, dance, and art. The melodies are primarily based on fine-tuning or five-tone scales, occasionally transitioning to Gong mode (which focuses on emotional expression). The singing style is characterized as simple yet fresh, melodious, and moving. The interplay of dialect and cadence conveys warmth and emotional resonance, illustrating the connection between human feelings and the environment.

With diversified entertainment options, the performance of tea-picking songs has largely been dominated by middle-aged and elderly individuals, who typically sing during leisure moments or after tea. Organized performances have become increasingly rare.

In 2010, the tea-picking song was listed in the second batch of Wuzhou intangible cultural heritage items.

采茶歌

The Inheritance Pedigree of Tea-picking Song

Generation	Name	Gender	Nationality	Education Background	Year of Craft Leanring
First	Mo Jiaqi	Male	Han	Unknown	Apprenticeship
Second	Zhou Zhuchao	Male	Han	Unknown	Apprenticeship
Second	Rao Guiqing	Female	Han	1961	Apprenticeship
Second	Zhong Jiacheng	Male	Han	1972	Apprenticeship
Second	Zhou Yaqing	Male	Han	1977	Apprenticeship
Third	Mo Zhusong	Male	Han	1980	Apprenticeship
Third	Mo Zhiying	Female	Han	1980	Apprenticeship
Fourth	Chen Xuyin	Male	Han	1986	Apprenticeship
Fourth	Li Huaqiong	Female	Han	1987	Apprenticeship
Fourth	Li Weixia	Female	Han	1990	Apprenticeship
Fourth	Li Jianmei	Female	Han	1992	Apprenticeship

同心米粉制作工艺

○ 甘丽云

"民以食为天,食以粉为先。"在广西,米粉交响曲的声音层次丰富。米粉飘动的蒸汽,是诗意里的烟火气。每一个有同心米粉的早晨,都是有灵魂的。

米粉的起源

同心镇地处藤县东南部,在一个小盆地的中心位置,这里田地连片,当地人习惯把成片的田地叫"田垌"。境内丘陵起伏,峰岭连绵,雨量充沛,支支汊汊的河在自然流动中滋养着100多平方公里的生灵,浸润着一万多亩的良田。"水光潋滟晴方好,山色空蒙雨亦奇。"无论晴或雨,同心镇都能给人一种闲适感。阳光是温柔和安静的,雨也是那么的美,柔柔的、迷蒙的,又有着浓浓的温情。

同心米粉主产于同心镇的同心村一带,故称同心米粉。一方水土养一方米,米粉好不好吃,一个非常重要的因素在于大米的好坏。"好水好田出好米,十里稻花香百里。"同心镇的田垌里,风吹稻浪的景象,就是米粉最初的孕育。

春耕、夏耘、秋收、冬藏,历经自然的过程,一粒粒饱满的大米变得香气怡人。勤劳手巧的同心镇人民,没有辜负这天赐好米,无论是以前口粮紧缺的年代,还是现在粮食富足的新时代,都能妥妥地把它加工成为优质米粉,在不同的时代丰盈着人们对吃的梦想。

诱人的米粉 / 李莎莎 摄

米粉的制作

　　同心米粉制作技艺是劳动人民长期生活实践的智慧结晶。制作同心米粉使用的米必须要用隔年的粘米，配以清澈甘甜的山涧泉水，经科学方法和传统工艺精制而成。同心米粉以其粉嫩滑，油丝白净，汤清不浊，入口爽脆细嫩的特点而久负盛名。整个生产过程有多道工序，主要包括选米泡洗、打浆、炊粉、晒粉、切粉、晾干、捆扎包装等。

　　第一道工序：选米泡洗。有经验的传承人，会选用早造粘米。早造粘米生长期短，一般为80～120天，米吸水率大，糊化后体积大，特别适合做米粉。把米淘洗后，浸泡30～40小时。想要做出优质的米粉，具体浸泡时间也要根据季节的不同有所调整。

　　第二道工序：打浆。打浆前有个小技巧，要在浸泡好的大米里添加熟饭，熟饭的比例也会决定米粉的质量与口感，大约百分之七的比例，即100公斤大米添加7公斤熟饭。季节不同所需比例也不尽相同，大米与熟饭调和，这样打浆做出来的米粉更加嫩滑，有韧性，有滋味，还有回甘，这是同心米粉的独特之处。

　　第三道工序：炊粉。"炊"是藤县方言，指隔水蒸。用一只直径一米左右的圆形平底大簸箕，把打好的米浆均匀铺洒在簸箕上，把簸箕放到烧开水的大锅上，盖上盖子，利用蒸汽蒸煮两分钟左右。这个火候也是要根据经验把控，火候不够粉不熟，火候过了粉糊粘簸箕。

第四道工序：晒粉。把蒸熟的粉张从簸箕上划脱下来，平铺在竹箅上，每箅三张或四张粉。放到太阳光下暴晒。晒场上一排一排的圆形粉张，远远看去像一排一排的明月，甚是壮观。

第五道工序：切粉。圆粉张晒得七八成干，就要收起来，一张一张地过水堆叠好，过水也是视季节不同用的水温不同，待粉张回软了，用双手适量沾点米粉专用的油均匀涂抹上去，确保每处地方都能沾到油，再折叠成像毛巾一样的长条状，均匀切丝。

第六道工序：晾干。把粉丝整齐排放在竹箅上，用另一块竹箅盖上，插上篾条夹紧，像做三明治一样。10月后可以放在阴凉的地方自然晾干，而农历正月到五月期间必须在48小时内晒干，否则会变质发霉。

第七道工序：捆扎包装。用染了红色的薄竹篾片把粉丝捆扎，每扎50克，再用保鲜袋封装，入箱。这时的米粉呈半透明的润泽虾肉色，条细匀称，美观、油亮、小巧、别致。

为了保证生态米粉原汁原味，同心米粉在加工过程中不添加任何添加剂、防腐剂和其他淀粉，是纯绿色无公害食品。

米粉的发展

同心米粉的制作，不仅能带给当地农民经济上的收益，还能在满足人们生活需要的同时，提升文化品位。

20世纪60年代中后期，米粉加工小作坊已经初露头角；到了70年代，米粉成为集体生产队的副业，同心镇有米粉加

同心米粉制作工艺

晒粉张 / 欧伟文 摄

工小作坊 100 多家，年产量 600 多吨；80 年代，有米粉加工小作坊 150 多家，年产量 1100 吨；90 年代，有米粉加工小作坊 200 多家，年产量 1800 多吨。进入 21 世纪后，米粉加工小作坊慢慢减少，取而代之的是拥有先进生产设备的中小型企业，年产量超 3000 吨。同心米粉多由经销商运至各地销售，以广西和广东两地为主。

2021 年，在同心镇开发区举办了第一届同心米粉美食节，煮米粉、炒米粉、米粉糕、米粉卷、炸粉丝、米饼酥等 37 种美食吸引全县 3300 多人投票，获得广西广播电视台的重点报道，同心米粉的知名度和影响力都得到了进一步提升，推动了同心米粉加工集约化、规模化、品牌化发展。

2010 年，同心米粉制作工艺列入第二批市级非物质文化遗产代表性项目名录。

同心米粉制作工艺传承谱系

代别	姓名	性别	出生时间（年）	学艺时间（年）
第一代	周品强	男	不详	无从考究
第二代	李培珍	男	1938	1960
第二代	周振强	男	1942	1962
第三代	周恒生	男	1955	1976
第三代	李锦评	男	1955	1980
第三代	周剑生	男	1966	1990
第三代	周来林	男	1969	1995
第四代	周伟华	男	1977	1997
第四代	周伟广	男	1978	1998
第四代	李耀孟	男	1977	2000

The Craft of Making Tongxin Rice Noodles

· *Gan Liyun* ·

"Food is the priority of the people, and rice noodles are paramount." In Guangxi, rice noodles compose a symphony rich in sound layers. The rising steam of freshly cooked rice noodles embodies the beauty of life in poetic form. Each morning, the aroma of Tongxin rice noodles resonates with the essence of the soul.

The Origin of Rice Noodles

Tongxin Town is situated in the southeastern part of Tengxian County, at the center of a small basin densely populated with fields, which locals affectionately refer to as "Tiandong". The region's rolling hills, peaks, and mountains, along with its abundant rainfall and nourishing rivers, support over one hundred square kilometers of life across more than ten thousand acres of fertile land. "The weather is clear, the mountains shrouded in mist, and the rain is exquisite." Regardless of whether it is sunny or rainy, Tongxin Town imparts a sense of leisure. The sun casts a gentle warmth, while the rain creates a beautiful, smooth, and misty ambiance that envelops the town in comfort.

Tongxin rice noodles are primarily produced in Tongxin Village within Tongxin Town, which is how they acquired their name. The quality of the rice, determined by its growing environment, is crucial for the noodles' flavor. "Good water and fertile fields produce good rice; the ten miles of flowers can perfume a hundred miles." The sight of wind caressing the waves of rice in "Tiandong" signifies the birth of rice flour.

The cycle of spring ploughing, summer cultivation, autumn harvest, and winter storage culminates in a delightful fragrance as the rice matures. The industrious and skilled residents of Tongxin Town honor the bountiful harvests bestowed by nature. Whether in the past, when rations were scarce, or in the present era of abundant grains, they consistently transform quality rice into high-quality noodles, enriching the local community's culinary experience.

The Production of Rice Noodles

The craft of producing Tongxin rice noodles is the result of the long-term practices of local artisans. The rice used for making these noodles must be sticky rice sourced every other year, combined with pure, clear spring water from the mountain streams in Tongxin Town, and refined through a blend of scientific methods and traditional processes. Tongxin rice noodles are renowned for their smooth, clear, and crisp texture. The entire production process comprises over ten steps, including selecting, soaking, washing, beating, steaming, drying, cutting, and bundling the noodles.

The first step involves selecting, soaking, and washing the rice. Experienced artisans choose early-season sticky rice, which has a short growth period of generally 80 to 120 days and possesses excellent water absorption qualities, resulting in a substantial volume after gelatinization, making it particularly suitable for rice flour production. After washing the rice, it is soaked for approximately 30 to 40 hours, with the soaking time adjusted according to seasonal needs to ensure high-

同心米粉及配菜 / 霍雨锋　摄

quality noodles.

The second step is beating the rice into a thick liquid. An important tip is to add cooked rice to the raw rice before beating. The proportion of the cooked rice significantly influences the quality and taste of the final noodles, with the recommended proportion being approximately 7%, meaning that for every 100 kilogram of raw rice, 7 kilogram of cooked rice is added. This ratio may vary by season. The resulting combination yields the unique smoothness, toughness, taste, and sweetness characteristic of Tongxin rice noodles.

The third step involves steaming the rice flour. In the local dialect of Tengxian County, the term "*chui*" refers to steaming over water. A large, circular, flat dustpan, approximately one meter in diameter, is used to spread the rice pulp evenly. This dustpan is then placed atop a large pot of boiling water, covered, and steamed for about two minutes. The control of heat is crucial; insufficient heat results in raw noodles, while excessive heat leads to burning.

The fourth step is drying the rice flour. After steaming, the rice sheets are removed from the dustpan, arranged on bamboo racks with three to four pieces per rack, and sun-dried. A row of round pink slices in the sun resembles a series of bright moons, creating a stunning visual.

The fifth step is cutting the noodles. Once the rice sheets are nearly dry, they are collected, individually watered, and stacked. The washing temperature of the rice sheets varies by season. When the sheets become soft, they are lightly coated with a specific amount of oil and then folded like a towel before being cut into shreds.

The sixth step involves drying the noodles. The cut noodles are arranged neatly on bamboo strips, covered with another strip, and tied together with thin bamboo clamps, resembling a sandwich. They can then be placed in a cool area to dry naturally after October. However, during the first lunar month to the fifth lunar month, they must dry within 48 hours to prevent spoilage.

同心米粉切丝 / 霍雨锋 摄

捆扎好的同心米粉 / 欧伟文 摄

The seventh step is bundling and packaging the noodles with thin, red-dyed bamboo strips. Each bundle contains 50 grams and is placed in a fresh bag before being boxed. At this stage, the rice noodles have a translucent, moist, shrimp-like color, characterized by a delicate and symmetrical appearance.

To preserve the original flavor of ecological rice noodles, Tongxin rice noodles are made from pure, pollution-free ingredients, with no additives, preservatives, or starch added during processing.

The Development of Rice Noodles

The traditional rice noodle production craft in Tongxin Town not only generates economic benefits for local farmers but also enriches cultural heritage while fulfilling the community's culinary needs.

In the late 1960s, small rice noodle processing workshops began to emerge. By the 1970s, rice noodle production became a sideline for collective production teams. At that time, over 100 small workshops operated in Tongxin Town, yielding more than 600 tons annually. The 1980s saw the number of processing workshops increase to over 150, with an annual output of 1,100 tons. By the 1990s, more than 200 workshops produced over 1,800 tons annually. In the 21st century, smaller workshops gradually decreased, giving way to small and medium-sized enterprises equipped with advanced production technology, resulting in an annual output exceeding 3,000 tons. Tongxin rice noodles are primarily distributed to various locations by dealers, mainly within Guangxi and Guangdong provinces.

In 2021, the first Tongxin Rice Noodle Festival was held, featuring 37 varieties of dishes, including boiled rice noodles, fried rice noodles, rice noodle cakes, rice noodle rolls, and fried glass noodles, which garnered over 3,300 votes countywide and received significant attention from Guangxi Radio and Television. The popularity and influence of Tongxin rice noodles were further amplified, promoting intensive, large-scale, and branded development in the processing sector.

In 2010, the craft of making Tongxin rice noodles was included in the second batch of Wuzhou's intangible cultural heritage list.

The Inheritance Pedigree of Making Tongxin Rice Noodles

Generation	Name	Gender	Birth Time	Year of Craft Leanring
First	Zhou Pinqiang	Male	Unknown	Unknown
Second	Li Peizhen	Male	1938	1960
	Zhou Zhenqiang	Male	1942	1962
Third	Zhou Hengsheng	Male	1955	1976
	Li Jinping	Male	1955	1980
	Zhou Jiansheng	Male	1966	1990
	Zhou Lailin	Male	1969	1995
Fourth	Zhou Weihua	Male	1977	1997
	Zhou Weiguang	Male	1978	1998
	Li Yaomeng	Male	1977	2000

藤县元宵歌

○ 苏海

歌起源于村野民间，是谓民歌、山歌。藤县元宵歌起源于何时已不可考，但历史悠久。藤县南部的岭景、象棋、新庆等乡镇在每年农历正月初二至十五的晚上都会唱元宵歌，颇有"元宵歌声起，村人怨夜短"的滋味。藤县元宵歌广为流行，历代相传，至今还有个别的村庄在传唱。

藤县元宵歌是用藤县白话方言以唱的形式猜谜对歌。元宵歌只猜物谜，不同于其他山歌猜字谜、物谜都有。村民都是日出而作，日落而息，在白天事先约定，待晚饭及天黑后进行对歌。元宵歌都是在晚上进行，白天一般唱山歌居多。唱元宵歌的地方选在村中隔着百米左右的田垌或江河两边，相隔一定的距离是为了避免泄密，不让对方听到己方讨论谜语的声音。人员多是自由组合，数量不等，也有商量分组的。元宵歌没有专门的服饰，没有乐器伴奏，没有台步舞美，唱歌者都是日常的穿戴，开口而歌，顺应而答，这边唱来那边和。唱歌者都是村中有文化、思维敏捷、反应快又有好唱腔的人。其余的都是帮站台助阵凑热闹者。有活动的村子往往也会吸引邻近的村民过来参与，热闹非凡，人声此起彼伏，笑声连连，划破夜空，好不开怀。

藤县元宵歌

原生态歌曲《元宵歌》表演 / 霍雨锋 摄

元宵歌一般分为开歌邀约、订立规则、猜谜斗歌、歌罢送别四个环节。

开歌邀约

第一次开口邀请黄先生。

甲：啰兄，

请请你姓黄的老先（啰又）生。

今晚（你嘟）正是元（嘟）宵节啰兄，

同众喜庆（嘟）倾（又啰）倾。

第二次邀请。

甲：玻璃（嘟）写帖我（嘟又）镜（取敬音）（嘟）请你（啰兄），

敬请姓黄你只老先（啰又）生。

以前同众都饮（嘟）饮笑啰兄，

为何今晚你咁无（啰又）情。

第三次邀请。

甲：单帖写来我又双（嘟）帖请，

我继续请请你姓黄个老先（啰又）生。

今晚正是元（嘟）宵节啰兄，

几大你（啰）都要来同倾（又啰）倾。

元宵歌的开场是尤其讲究礼节的，开声邀约对方时，要三请对方，这是一种礼数，省不了。第一次是"请"，第二次是"敬请"加了一点点埋怨"为何今晚你咁无（啰又）情"，第三次提高了诚意"单帖写来我又双（嘟）帖请"，再加上决心"几大你（啰）都要来同倾（又啰）倾"。三迎三请后对方才会开口回歌：

藤县元宵歌

乙：那（嘟）就是啰兄，
　　大家都来同你倾（又啰）倾。
　　今晚正是元（嘟）宵节啰兄，
　　大家唱到只二三（啰又）更。

甲：顺（嘟）从你啰兄，
　　顺从歌台你（嘟）顺从（啰又）兄。
　　既然又大家咁（嘟）高兴啰兄，
　　经经要唱到只二三（啰又）更。

乙：老（嘟）先又生啰兄，
　　大家就订定条约又讲分（啰又）明。
　　你作斩竹我（嘟）作斩就木啰兄，
　　大家就搭起只大歌（啰又）棚。

至此，邀约成功。

订立规则

甲：那（嘟）就是啰兄，
　　大家就搭起只大歌（啰又）棚。
　　同众就讲古要哞（啰又）蜡，
　　无抓无捉侬冇（啰又）倾。

乙：那（嘟）就是啰兄，
　　无抓无捉冇想（啰又）倾。
　　有抓有捉侬就讲啰兄，
　　大家就搭起只大歌（啰又）棚。

甲：成（嘟）应你啰兄，
　　订了歌台就要讲定啰兄。
　　无抓无捉不想（啰又）倾。
　　有竹要讲祝三姐啰兄，

　　　　有铁要讲铁拐李（啰又）兄。
　　乙：有木要讲穆（嘟）桂英啰兄，
　　　　有水要讲壬癸水（啰又）兄。

　　元宵歌规则的订立，就是在出谜面时双方要共同遵守的准则。元宵歌的谜面都是一些实物，如有竹要讲祝英台，有铁要讲铁拐李，有木要讲穆桂英，有水要讲壬癸水，有铜要讲吕洞宾，有铝要讲吕无忌，有火要讲火丙丁等。规则的用词，大都采用古代名人的名字，也有采用一些常用术语的，取其音用其意，一语双关，形象生动，幽默诙谐。

猜谜斗歌

　　甲：闲话讲多会（嘟）重赘啰兄，
　　　　那你打物是真（啰又）情。
　　　　浅浅物儿你放（嘟）只过啰兄，
　　　　等我同班得来（啰又）倾。
　　乙：那你（嘟）息静就听啰兄，
　　　　你哋息静就听歌（啰又）声。
　　　　小小物儿放（嘟）只过啰兄，
　　　　等你同班就得来又（啰又）倾：
　　　　麻姑连线真（嘟）后生啰兄，
　　　　铁拐加钩排列（啰又）成。
　　　　祝英偷情又（嘟）来伴啰兄，
　　　　单人双手（嘟）冇时（啰又）停。
　　甲：老师考试我又背睇啰兄，
　　　　背睇你物儿你成（啰）冇（啰）又成。
　　　　冇着之时冇着紧啰兄，

藤县元宵歌

　　　　　　一一二二我背分（啰又）明：
　　　　　　麻姑连线真（嘟）后生啰兄，
　　　　　　铁拐加钩排列（啰又）成。
　　　　　　祝英偷情又（嘟）来伴啰兄，
　　　　　　单人双手（嘟）冇时（啰又）停。
　　乙：听都到了啰兄，
　　　　　　我只古皮你嘀声就（啰）灵。
　　　　　　万望你先生就修悠谂啰兄，
　　　　　　你谂去谂来怕就会嘀声就成。
　　甲：先生你（嘟）真是老先生啰兄，
　　　　　　你只古皮又确是（啰又）成。
　　　　　　总是我边人都颓又拙啰兄，
　　　　　　冇有一只读书（啰又）生。
　　　　　　你只古皮我实难古啰兄，
　　　　　　怕要肚脏都谂翻（啰又）倾。
　　乙：你赚（嘟）得讲啰兄，
　　　　　　你边（嘟）尽是读书（啰又）生。
　　　　　　我只物儿（嘟）冇密贴啰兄，
　　　　　　你详齐四句就分（啰又）明。

　　元宵歌的猜谜斗歌，一般以四句作为一个唱段，唱到激动之时也会在对方唱两句后，抢唱两句，也有连唱六句八句的。但出谜面约定就是四句，不可多或少。元宵歌斗歌是双方各出一个谜语互相竞猜，猜中为赢，猜不对的可以请求对方作点提示，直至猜中后，双方继续新一轮竞猜。

　　假如乙方猜不到，就会请求甲方给出提示。

　　乙：先生你（嘟）确是老先生啰兄，
　　　　　　你只古皮我实冇（啰又）明。

还望先生开（嘟）条路啰兄，

开条大路等我（啰又）行。

你只物儿何（嘟）处有啰兄，

几轻几重要报分（啰又）明。

或是我见过或冇见过啰兄，

请你先生要回（啰又）声。

甲：古只物儿你（嘟）见过啰兄，

五斤打上百斤打转是真（啰又）情。

日日趁圩你都会见啰兄，

家家户户（嘟）放在门（啰又）庭。

经对方提示后，如果还猜不中，可以再次请求提示，直至猜中；如果歌会结束还猜不中，那就要带着谜面回家，待明天晚上再来斗歌了。如此这样，元宵歌从农历正月初二一直唱到十五，方罢歌台。等待来年元宵至，万水千山放歌声。

元宵歌的斗歌，输方如果一时猜不出，总会想退出斗歌。可赢方会抓住不放，取笑一番才会罢休。输方唱：

乙：我冇唱了我冇唱了啰兄，

柴刀斧头出尽都劈冇（啰又）惊。

我边一帮睇牛（嘟）佬啰兄，

冇有一只（嘟）读书（啰又）生。

还望先生多（嘟）原谅啰兄，

今晚元宵系咁（啰又）倾。

甲：水推竹排我留紧（嘟）你啰兄，

留住歌台留住（啰又）兄。

要你唱番二（嘟）三只啰兄，

大家方可转家（啰又）庭。

这样留住了对方，再唱上三两段方可结束。

歌罢送别

乙：先生你（嘟）真是老先生啰兄，
　　今晚元宵（嘟）怕是咁（啰又）倾。
　　既然深更夜（嘟）又静啰兄，
　　有心就明晚再来（啰又）倾。

甲：风吹竹表顺（嘟）从你啰兄，
　　我顺从歌台我（嘟）顺从（啰又）兄。
　　明晚既然贪（嘟）高兴啰兄，
　　侬队大家（嘟）再来（啰又）倾。

甲：送又送你啰兄，
　　送送歌台又送送（啰又）兄。
　　抽高脚步你慢慢转啰兄，
　　抽高脚步转家（啰又）庭。

乙：祝你工作多顺利啰兄，
　　保你禄位得高（啰又）升。
　　年年考试得第一啰兄，
　　清华大学有你（啰又）名。

元宵歌对歌一般是唱到子夜时分，因为明天又要农耕劳作。时间一到，欢歌相送，再次邀约，等待明晚，再续前话。唱罢，各自回家休息。

元宵歌作为一种传统音乐，来源于民间，启迪于自然，根植于村野，经久存续。作为乡间文化，方言俚语通俗易懂，歌词来源于生活，灵活搭配，合辙押韵，韵律优美，朗朗上口，引经据典，隽言妙语，一语双关，妙趣横生。元宵歌承载历史风俗，传达民情民意，寄托美好愿望。

2014年，藤县元宵歌列入第三批市级非物质文化遗产代表性项目名录。

藤县元宵歌传承谱系

代别	姓名	性别	民族	学历	学艺时间（年）	传承方式
第一代	莫国南	男	汉	私塾	无从考究	师徒传承
	陈聚欢	男	汉	私塾	无从考究	师徒传承
第二代	陈聚家	男	汉	私塾	1945	师徒传承
	杨岳良	男	汉	私塾	1946	师徒传承
	陈聚容	男	汉	私塾	1950	师徒传承
第三代	杨寿昌	男	汉	初中	1962	师徒传承
	陈远宏	男	汉	高中	1950	师徒传承
	杨德超	男	汉	小学	1947	师徒传承
	杨盛昌	男	汉	初中	1965	师徒传承

Lantern Festival Song in Tengxian County

· Su Hai ·

The lantern festival song is a traditional folk song originating from the villages of Tengxian County, though its exact beginnings are unknown. Its rich history is evidenced by its ongoing popularity, particularly in the southern townships of Lingjing, Xiangqi, and Xinqing, where villagers sing it from the second day to the fifteenth day of the first lunar calendar. During this period, villagers often lament, "the night is so short." The lantern festival song has been passed down through generations, with many villages continuing to perform it today.

The lantern festival songs in Tengxian County are riddle-guessing songs sung in the local dialect. Unlike other folk songs, which may incorporate both objects and riddles, the riddles in the lantern festival songs are exclusively related to objects. Villagers typically rise at sunrise and rest at sunset; they agree in advance to sing together after dinner and after dark. While lantern songs are performed at night, folk songs are sung during the day. The performance locations are approximately 100 meters on either side of farmland or river that runs through the village, maintaining a distance to prevent the leakage of information and to ensure that discussions of riddles remain confidential. Participants are generally free to organize themselves into varying group sizes and can also discuss how to form groups. There are no special costumes, musical accompaniment, or choreographed dances; villagers wear their everyday attire, singing freely and responding to one another. The singers are typically well-educated, quick-thinking, responsive individuals who take pleasure in singing. Notably, skilled singers from neighboring villages often join in, creating a lively atmosphere filled with rising voices and joyful laughter that fills the night sky.

The lantern festival songs are typically divided into four parts: invitation, rule establishment, riddle-guessing, and farewell.

Songs for Invitation

For example, the first invitation:

A: Luo xiong (meaning "my friend"), you are invited, Mr. Huang. Tonight is the Lantern Festival, let us enjoy chatting together during this joyous occasion.

The second invitation:

A: Luo xiong, I write this invitation with glass to respectfully request your presence. Last time, we laughed and drank together, but why do you refuse my invitation tonight?

The third invitation:

A: I'll send the third invitation after the second is written. I continue to invite you, Mr. Huang. Tonight is the Lantern Festival, and you must join us to discuss the wonders of the world.

The opening of the lantern song is particularly important for establishing etiquette. Singers must invite one another three times, which is a formalized gesture of politeness that cannot be omitted. The first invitation serves as a polite request; the second adds a hint of complaint, and the third expresses sincerity and determination. Only after these three exchanges can the singing commence. After the invitations, the conversation continues:

B: Luo xiong, of course! Everyone is here to talk to you about life. Tonight is the Lantern Festival, and we will sing until the second or third night.

A: Luo xiong, I comply with your wishes. We will sing until two or three o'clock!

B: Luo xiong, let's make a clear agreement. You gather bamboo, and I'll gather wood, so we can build a grand stage for our singing.

Thus, the invitation is successful.

Songs for Establishing Rules

A: That's it, luo xiong. Let's set up a grand stage for singing. We will beat the drums and gongs together with the crowd. It cannot be done without proper preparation.

B: That's right, luo xiong. Preparation is key. We are good brothers negotiating our plans. Let's establish the rules.

A: I promise you, Luo xiong, we need to agree on a song stage. I can't proceed without preparation. If you have bamboo, we should discuss Zhu San Jie. If you have iron, we should mention Tie Guai, luo xiong.

B: And for wood, we can discuss Mu Guiying. If there is water, let's talk about Ren Gui Shui.

The rules of the lantern festival song are established, serving as guidelines that both parties must follow when presenting riddles. The riddles often pertain to tangible objects, referencing historical figures or elements, such as bamboo representing Zhu Yingtai, iron representing Tie Guai Li, wood representing Mu Guiying, water representing Ren Gui Shui, copper representing Lyv Dongbin, aluminum representing Lyv Wuji, and fire representing Huo Bing Ding. The wording of the riddles frequently employs names of ancient celebrities and incorporates common expressions that are pun-like in nature, characterized by vivid imagery, humor, and wit.

Riddle Guessing and Singing Competition

A: There's plenty of gossip, luo xiong. Let's play a game of riddle-guessing, Luo xiong. Let's see if you can figure out the riddle I have in mind. We can discuss the heavens and the earth together.

B: Please, listen quietly, luo xiong. You can listen to my song peacefully. Let's play a game of riddle-guessing, luo xiong. We'll talk about the heavens and the earth. Magu threads the needle, luo xiong. The iron crutch and the hook are paired once more. Zhu Ying partners in love. A single person works tirelessly with both hands.

A: I memorized this for the teacher's exam. Let's see if my memorization helps. Don't worry if you can't guess, luo xiong. I'll recite the riddle clearly: Magu threads the needle, luo xiong. The iron crutch and the hook are paired once more. Zhu Ying is a partner in love, luo xiong. A single person works tirelessly with both hands.

B: I've heard it all, luo xiong. You'll understand the drum beating inside me (meaning the riddle I'm posing). I hope you take your time to think about the answer.

A: You are very learned, luo xiong. Your riddle is truly difficult. We are a humble group, luo xiong. None of us are scholars. Your riddle is so challenging that even if I tried turning it over in my mind, I'm afraid I still wouldn't solve it.

B: You are being modest, luo xiong. Your companions are all well-read. My puzzle isn't difficult, luo xiong. You will understand it in just four lines.

During the Lantern Festival, riddle-guessing songs are typically sung in four lines. When excitement builds, however, one side may sing two lines after the other has sung its two, and occasionally, people become so animated they sing six or eight lines in a row. However, the standard remains four lines—no more, no less. The riddles are posed through song, and the winner is the one who correctly solves the most riddles. The one who struggles can request hints from the other party until they successfully guess the answer.

If Party B cannot guess the riddle, they will request a hint from Party A:

B: You are indeed a learned scholar, luo xiong. I truly cannot solve your puzzle. Please, show me the way, luo xiong. Where does your puzzle's answer lie? Is it something light or heavy, or perhaps something I've seen before?

A: You've seen it, luo xiong. It weighs between five and hundreds of *jin*. You see it every time you go to the market, luo xiong. Every household keeps it at their doorstep.

If even after the hint, the answer remains unclear, Party B may continue requesting more clues until they finally guess correctly. Should the answer remain elusive until the song ends, the guesser must take the unanswered riddle home and return the next evening for another round of competition. This tradition continues from the second day of the lunar New Year until the fifteenth, with the sounds of songs echoing through the mountains and rivers.

In these lantern festival song competitions, the losing side may attempt to withdraw from the game when stumped. However, the winning party often insists on prolonging the contest, urging the others to continue. The losing side may sing:

B: I won't sing anymore, luo xiong. I cannot guess the answer. We are all simple cowherds, luo xiong. None of us are scholars. Please forgive us, luo xiong. Let's just have a pleasant chat tonight.

A: I won't let you leave just yet, luo xiong. I want you to stay and sing two or three more rounds, luo xiong. Then we can all go home. In this way, we can bid farewell after a few more verses.

When it is time to part ways, the songs shift to ones of farewell:

B: You truly are a learned man, luo xiong. Let's stop here for tonight's Lantern Festival. It's getting late, luo xiong. Let's continue tomorrow with sincere hearts.

A: The wind stirs the bamboo, and I listen to you, luo xiong. I follow the song to heed your wishes. Tomorrow night, we will all gather joyfully to sing again, luo xiong, and continue our conversation about heaven and earth.

A: Then, I'll bid you farewell, luo xiong. Let us part with a farewell song, my brother. Take your time heading home, luo xiong. Walk carefully as you return.

B: I wish you success in your work, luo xiong. May you rise to great heights. May you excel in your exams each year. May all your endeavors prosper.

Lantern festival song competitions typically continue until midnight, as the next day's farming duties await. When the time comes, farewell songs are sung, and participants invite each other to meet again the following night, renewing their bond through song. After singing, they each head home to rest.

As a form of traditional music, lantern festival songs originate from folk customs, drawing inspiration from nature and deeply rooted in rural life. These songs, simple and easy to understand, reflect the lives of the villagers. With their flexible structure, harmonious rhyme, and references to classical stories, they remain engaging and meaningful. Lantern festival songs not only preserve historical traditions but also convey the feelings and aspirations of the people, offering prayers for good fortune.

In 2014, the lantern festival song was listed in the third batch of representative items of Wuzhou municipal intangible cultural heritage.

藤县元宵歌

The Inheritance Pedigree of Lantern Songs in Tengxian County

Generation	Name	Gender	Nationality	Education Background	Year of Craft Leanring	Means of Inheritance
First	Mo Guonan	Male	Han	Old-style private school	Unknown	Apprenticeship
First	Chen Juhuan	Male	Han	Old-style private school	Unknown	Apprenticeship
Second	Chen Jujia	Male	Han	Old-style private school	1945	Apprenticeship
Second	Yang Yueliang	Male	Han	Old-style private school	1946	Apprenticeship
Second	Chen Jurong	Male	Han	Old-style private school	1950	Apprenticeship
Third	Yang Shouchang	Male	Han	Junior high school	1962	Apprenticeship
Third	Chen Yuanhong	Male	Han	Senior high school	1950	Apprenticeship
Third	Yang Dechao	Male	Han	Primary school	1947	Apprenticeship
Third	Yang Shengchang	Male	Han	Junior high school	1965	Apprenticeship

藤县袁崇焕故事

○ 周雄

袁崇焕（1584—1630），是明末崇祯元年（1628年）兵部尚书兼右副都御史，督师蓟、辽、登莱、天津等处军务，明末抗击后金的主将。

明朝时，袁崇焕祖父袁西堂自粤东到广西梧州府苍梧县戎圩做生意。嘉靖初年，袁西堂见梧州府藤县山川毓秀，遂由广东东莞迁至藤县白马圩莲塘村（今藤县天平镇新马村）。袁崇焕就出生在藤县天平镇新马村。传说袁崇焕出生时，村里莲花井中有一朵莲花盛开，鲜艳夺目。

万历三十四年（1606年），22岁的袁崇焕在广西贡院考取了举人。年纪轻轻就中举，袁崇焕自然由衷高兴，作了《秋闱赏月》诗表达欣喜心情：

战罢文场笔阵收，客途不觉过中秋。
月明银汉三千界，歌碎金风十二楼。
竹叶喜添豪士志，桂花香插少年头。
嫦娥必定知人意，不钥蟾宫任我游。

袁崇焕雕像／欧伟文 摄

袁家亦农亦商，但袁崇焕却有读书上进求得功名、光宗耀祖报效社稷的远大志向。青少年时期的袁崇焕喜欢同好友谈天说地，纵论山川形胜、兵戈战阵之事，还在家乡河滩上纵马操刀习武。科考要熟读儒家经典，袁崇焕学习儒家文化，领会儒家爱国亲民理念，受到农民勤劳质朴、商人灵活机变和儒家修身治国三种文化的熏陶滋养，一步一步走上报国为民之路。

在古代考取举人难，中进士更难。袁崇焕持续奋发读书，但参加会试却屡考不中。从举人到考取进士经历了13年，在此期间他没有气馁而是愈挫愈勇，更加努力积极进取。

"苦心人，天不负。"万历四十七年（1619年），35岁的袁崇焕终于进士及第。

这一年，中国历史上发生了一件大事：明朝同后金展开萨尔浒之战，明军大败，后金军大胜。当时，袁崇焕关心国事、边事，在京城听到辽东战败的消息，他既喜亦忧——喜的是自己高中进士，忧的是明军大败局势严峻。

袁崇焕中进士后因朝廷未有官缺，于是领命荣归故里候任。他离京时，专门拜访奉诏来京议事的遵义副总兵陈策。对这位身经百战、功名显赫的同乡老前辈，袁崇焕挥笔写下《南还别陈翼所总戎》赠别诗，表达了深深的敬意，抒发了随时准备为国效命、建功立业的远大理想与抱负。

万历四十八年（1620年）初，袁崇焕受任福建邵武知县，在任上为官3年，勤于政事，清正廉洁，尽心为民，关注辽东，常与习辽事者相见谈兵。咸丰五年（1855年）《邵武县志》记载：袁崇焕在邵武任上"明决有胆略，尽心民事，冤抑无不伸。素矫捷有力，尝出救火，著靴上墙屋，如履平地。后以边才荐，累官辽东经略"。

天启二年（1622年）正月，袁崇焕到京师朝觐接受朝廷考核。御史侯恂上奏："见朝觐邵武县知县袁崇焕，英风伟略，不妨破格留用。"天启帝采纳侯恂建议，授袁崇焕为兵部职方司主事（正六品）。

袁崇焕到任后无心升官发财，只念社稷安危，在京食不甘味夜不安寝，没有和任何人打招呼，不顾豺狼虎豹出没，单骑到山海关外考察军情。回京师后，石破天惊地独自攘臂请行："予我军马钱谷，我一人足守此！"

当时，京师各官员言及辽事皆畏缩不敢任。而袁崇焕敢挑重担，胆略过人，以文官出身，却敢于请缨带兵上阵。于是，朝廷又破格提拔袁崇焕为山东按察司佥事（正五品）、山海监军，并发给他帑银20万两，用于招募兵士。

任新职后袁崇焕上《擢佥事监军方略疏》，一扫文臣武将普遍存在的悲观恐惧情绪，力请练兵选将，整械造船，固守山海，远图恢复。

袁崇焕先驻山海关，又被任命为宁前兵备佥事。他力主在山海关外二百里的宁远（今辽宁省兴城市）筑城坚守护卫严关，屏障关内捍卫京师，积蓄力量以图大举。在督领筑城过程中，袁崇焕勤于职守，做事扎实细致、雷厉风行，又善于团结将士，工程进展迅速，形成了明军以宁远为中心的防御体系。

天启四年（1624年），宁远防线营筑完工，成为抵御后金南犯的关外一座重镇。总计恢复被后金侵扰的五城二十堡，垦田5000余顷，兵民已达10万。袁崇焕"关外守关，主守而后战""以辽土养辽人，以辽人守辽土；且战且守，且筑且屯；守为正著，战为奇著，和为旁著；以实不以虚，以渐不以骤"的守辽战略逐渐形成。

天启六年（1626年）正月二十三日，后金大汗努尔哈赤率6万大军，号称20万，连陷松山、塔山等8座城堡后扑向宁远。辽东经略高第素不知兵事且胆怯无能，放弃了营造多年的军事防线，撤兵守山海关。袁崇焕上疏抗争，决心身卧宁远，说："我宁前道也！官此，当死此，我必不去！"他还"刺血为书，激以忠义，为之下拜，将士咸请效死"，同军民誓死守宁远孤城。努尔哈赤诱降袁崇焕遭严词拒绝。后金兵攻城前仆后继，冒死凿破城墙大洞三四处。在危急关头，袁崇焕身先士卒不幸负伤，仍"自裂战袍，裹左伤处，战益力；将卒愧，厉奋争先，相翼蔽城"。战至二十六日，明军不断发射西洋大炮，努尔哈赤受炮伤大败，遭到起兵48年来最严重的惨败，伤口感染一个月后郁郁而终。

闻报宁远大捷，京师士庶空巷相庆。宁远大捷打破了后金军不可战胜的神话，袁崇焕等刚建立的关（山海关）宁（宁远）防线经受住了考验，对明朝官心、军心、民心有巨大的振奋作用。

天启七年（1627年）五月六日，后金皇太极为报丧父之仇，亲率6万大军功打锦州。袁崇焕得报立即部署军备，亲自驻守宁远。

十一日，皇太极直趋锦州。守城大将赵率教与之议和，以拖延时间探听虚实，守待援军。双方激战、议和交替进行。锦州被困，袁崇焕派总兵满桂增援锦州，又派出奇兵进逼扰敌。

皇太极的后金援兵从沈阳来到锦州后，分一部凿三道壕沟围困锦州，自己率领官兵数万转而攻打宁远。袁崇焕固守宁远，除"凭坚城以用大炮"外，还列兵布阵城外，同

惟此幽兰寄亦乐　清风流水咏其怀

袁崇焕书法 / 欧伟文 摄

后金兵争锋,并亲临城堞指挥,凭堞大呼激励将士,命从城上以"红夷大炮"等火器齐力攻打。宁远激战之时,锦州守军打开城门攻向后金军大营,使皇太极在宁、锦先后受敌,不得不从宁远撤军转攻锦州。围困数日,明军凭坚城,用大炮据守。后金军久攻不下,伤不少于二三千人,马断草,兵缺粮。皇太极无可奈何只得下令撤军。

崇祯二年(1629年)十月二日,皇太极亲率 10 万大军避开袁崇焕驻守的关宁锦防线,绕道蒙古大漠进逼北京。袁崇焕闻之迅速调集兵力勤王。崇祯得知,下旨各镇援兵统归袁崇焕指挥,并进袁崇焕太子太保,服、俸从一品。十一月四日,袁崇焕一心事君,勤王心切竟不顾朝廷用兵禁忌,亲率 9000 铁骑直抵北京广渠门外,露宿扎营,驻卫京城外。二十日,后金军兵临北京城下,袁崇焕横刀跃马,在矢林镞雨、马颈相交中与后金军决战,护身铁甲多处中箭。辽军将士迎敌浴血奋战一天,取得广渠门之捷。二十七日,袁崇焕又与皇太极激战于左安门,打得后金军慌忙撤出南海子。袁崇焕取得了保卫京师大捷。

藤县袁崇焕故事

袁崇焕手植榕 / 欧伟文 摄

新马村袁崇焕故居遗址 / 欧伟文　摄

　　皇太极无奈施行"反间计"。崇祯中计以"议饷"为名召袁崇焕等入宫，以"通虏谋叛"罪将袁崇焕入狱。阉党余孽趁机图谋翻案，竟五次上疏："请杀袁崇焕！"

　　崇祯三年（1630年）八月十六日，崇祯下令以磔刑在北京西市杀害袁崇焕。袁崇焕临刑前作《临刑口占》云：

　　　　一生事业总成空，
　　　　半世功名在梦中。
　　　　死后不愁无勇将，
　　　　忠魂依旧守辽东。

　　一代忠臣袁崇焕凛然赴死，时年46岁。传说，袁崇焕死后村里的莲花井中，有一朵莲花盛开了七七四十九日才凋谢。

　　"节比文山，冤同武穆"，这是后人对袁崇焕的评价，这一冤案直至清初修书时才真相大白。清乾隆帝被袁崇焕的英雄气概所感动，特意为袁崇焕平反。后朝皇帝为自己祖上推翻的前朝大臣平反，这在历史上是极其少见的。

袁崇焕是中国古代战争史上著名的以少胜多的军事家之一。袁崇焕故事在藤县广为传播，代代流传。

2016年，藤县袁崇焕故事列入第四批市级非物质文化遗产代表性项目名录。

袁崇焕故事传承谱系

代别	姓名	性别	民族	学历	学艺时间（年）	传承方式
第一代	袁顺舟	男	汉	不详	无从考究	师徒传承
	何家达	男	汉	不详	无从考究	家族传承
	何文达	男	汉	不详	无从考究	家族传承
第二代	何绍光	男	汉	高中	1972	家族传承
	何胜华	男	汉	初中	1958	家族传承
	何福华	男	汉	高中	1966	家族传承
第三代	何勇光	男	汉	初中	1992	家族传承
	袁叙堂	男	汉	高中	1975	家族传承
	韦潍	男	汉	高中	1989	师徒传承
	何维松	男	汉	高中	1989	家族传承

The Story of Yuan Chonghuan in Tengxian County

· Zhou Xiong ·

Yuan Chonghuan (1584 – 1630 AD) served as the chief military officer of the Ministry of War during the first year of the Chongzhen period in the late Ming Dynasty (1628 AD). He oversaw military affairs in the regions of Ji, Liao, Lai, and Tianjin, and he played a crucial role in combating the Later Jin on both political and military fronts during this tumultuous period.

In the Ming Dynasty, Yuan Xitang, the grandfather of Yuan Chonghuan, engaged in trade from eastern Guangdong to Rongxu in Cangwu County, Wuzhou Prefecture, Guangxi. In the early years of the Jiajing period, Yuan Xitang was enchanted by the scenic beauty of Wuzhou Prefecture and subsequently relocated from Dongguan City in Guangdong to Liantang Village of Baima Fair, now known as Xinma Village in Taiping Town, Tengxian County. Legend has it that a magnificent lotus flower bloomed in the village's lotus well at the time of Yuan Chonghuan's birth.

In the thirty-fourth year of Wanli period (1606 AD), at the age of twenty-two, Yuan Chonghuan was admitted to the Gongyuan of Guangxi as a meritorious scholar. Filled with joy at his early success, he composed a poem *The Autumn and the Moon* to express his delight: "Having finished the exam, I unexpectedly encounter the Mid-Autumn Festival along the way. The moon shines brightly in the distance, as the autumn wind blows and everyone dances to celebrate. I am filled with ambition on my journey home, hoping to succeed in the examination. Chang'e, the moon goddess, must know my desires; may she open the moon palace for me to revel within it."

The Yuan family engaged in farming and trade, yet Yuan Chonghuan harbored lofty ambitions for education, aspiring to achieve fame and serve his country. As a youth, he enjoyed discussing mountains, rivers, and warfare with friends, often practicing martial arts on the riverbank in his hometown. The Confucian classics were essential for success in the imperial examinations, and Yuan Chonghuan diligently studied Confucian culture, understanding the values of patriotism and social responsibility. Influenced by the hardworking ethos of farmers, the adaptability of merchants, and the principles of Confucian self-cultivation and governance, he gradually embarked on a path dedicated to serving his country and its people.

During the era of imperial examinations, passing these rigorous tests was exceedingly difficult. Despite repeated failures, Yuan Chonghuan remained undeterred; his determination only grew stronger.

"Where there is a will, there is a way." In the forty-seventh year of Wanli period (1619 AD), at the age of thirty-six, he persevered through hardship and finally became a scholar.

That same year marked a significant event in Chinese history: The Battle of Saerhu, where the Ming forces faced defeat against the Later Jin. Yuan Chonghuan, deeply invested in state and border affairs, felt a mix of elation over his academic achievements and concern for the dire situation following the Ming army's defeat.

After becoming a scholar, Yuan Chonghuan was ordered to return to his hometown due to a lack of official vacancies. Before departing Beijing, he paid a special visit to General Chen Ce, the deputy general of Zunyi, who was in the capital for discussions. To express his profound respect for this seasoned veteran, Yuan Chonghuan composed a poem *Farewell to General Chen on the Way South*, indicating his aspiration to emulate the spirit of the old general and his commitment to serving the country.

In the early part of the forty-eighth year of Wanli period (1620 AD), Yuan Chonghuan was appointed governor of Shaowu County in Fujian Province, where he served for three years. He was diligent in government affairs, fought against corruption, and dedicated himself to the welfare of the people. He remained attentive to developments in Liaodong, frequently engaging in discussions about military matters with Liao officials. According to the *Annals of Shaowu County*, during his tenure, "Yuan Chonghuan exhibited remarkable courage, civic dedication, and a commitment to justice. He was respected and influential. He once fearlessly handled a fire, climbing the walls of a building as if traversing solid ground. His exemplary service led to his recommendation for the position of Liaodong official."

In the first month of the second year of Tianqi period, Yuan Chonghuan traveled to the capital to accept the imperial examination. The imperial censor Hou Xun submitted a memorial to the throne, advocating for Yuan Chonghuan's exceptional talents as governor of Shaowu County. In response, Emperor Tianqi adopted the suggestions of Hou Xun and others, appointing Yuan Chonghuan to the Ministry of War as a sixth-rank official.

Following this promotion, Yuan Chonghuan displayed little interest in personal advancement, focusing instead on the security of the state. He remained restless in the capital, refraining from communication with others. Undeterred by the threats posed by wolves, tigers, and leopards, he undertook inspections of military conditions at Shanhai Pass, a crucial juncture where the Ming Great Wall met the sea in present-day Hebei Province. Upon returning to the capital, he requested, "Provide me with troops, funds, and provisions; I can guard this area alone!"

At that time, many officials in the capital were reluctant to engage with Liaodong affairs. However, Yuan Chonghuan possessed a strong sense of duty to his country and was willing to take risks and shoulder heavy responsibilities. Despite being a civil official by background, he volunteered to lead troops into battle. Consequently, the court promoted him to chief inspector of Shandong, a fifth-rank official, and superintendent of Shanhai Pass, providing him with 200,000 silver coins for recruiting soldiers.

In his new position, Yuan Chonghuan submitted memorials to the throne entitled *The Strategy of Promoting Qianshi* and the inspector in the army, aiming to alleviate the widespread fear and pessimism among civil and military officials.

Yuan Chonghuan first defended Shanhai Pass and was appointed as the Qianshi of the Ningqian Army. He advocated for the construction of city walls and moats in Ningyuan (present-day Xingcheng City in Liaoning Province), located 200 miles outside Shanhai Pass, to strengthen defenses and secure the area. By fortifying the capital within the barrier pass, he accumulated strength to plan a significant offensive. Throughout the construction process, Yuan Chonghuan worked diligently, demonstrating meticulous attention to detail. His vigorous discipline and resolute actions helped him unite the soldiers, resulting in rapid progress on the project. The Ming army thus established a defensive system centered on Ningyuan.

By the fourth year of Tianqi period (1624 AD), the Ningyuan defense line was completed, becoming a crucial outpost against the Later Jin's southern incursions. Five cities and twenty fortresses previously disturbed by the Jin dynasty were restored, and over 5,000 fields were reclaimed. The total population of soldiers and civilians reached 100,000. Yuan Chonghuan's strategic ideas began to take shape:

"Defend the pass outside the gate, focus on fortification, and engage in battle only when necessary, " "Nourish the Liao people with Liao soil and defend them with the same, " "Fight and defend together, " "Build and stockpile resources simultaneously, " and "Prioritize defense while employing wisdom in warfare." He emphasized the importance of practicality over abstraction and advocated for patience over impulsiveness. These principles constituted effective strategies for defending Liaodong.

On the 23rd day of the first lunar month in the sixth year of Tianqi period (1626 AD), Nurhachi, the Khan of the Later Jin, led an army of 60,000 troops—reported as 200,000—to capture eight castles, including Songshan and Tashan, before attacking Ningyuan. The commander of Liaodong Gaodi, lacking awareness of military strategy, was timid and incompetent, ultimately abandoning the years of military fortifications and retreating to guard Shanhai Pass. Yuan Chonghuan, however, resolved to defend Ningyuan at all costs, declaring, "I serve as an official here, and I shall die here without retreating!" He also "stabbed his blood onto a document to pledge his loyalty, prompting the soldiers to salute him and express their willingness to follow his orders." He vowed to guard the isolated city of Ningyuan with both the army and the local populace. When Nurhachi attempted to seduce Yuan Chonghuan, his efforts were met with staunch refusal. The Later Jin forces launched repeated assaults on the city, risking their lives to breach three or four significant gaps in the wall. At a critical moment, Yuan Chonghuan led the defense, despite sustaining injuries. He persevered, even tearing his robe to bandage his wound while continuing to participate in the fighting. His resolve inspired both the general and the soldiers, who were determined to protect the city. On the 26th day of the siege, the Ming army fired western artillery, wounding Nurhachi, who suffered one of the most severe defeats in his years of warfare. His injury became infected, leading to his death a month later.

Hearing the news of Ningyuan's victory, the capital's people celebrated everywhere. The victory at Ningyuan broke the "myth" of invinciblability of the later Jin Army, tested the defense line of Shanhai Pass and Ningyuan which had just been established by Yuan Chonghuan, and had a great exciting effect on the heart of officials, soldiers and people of the Ming Dynasty.

On the sixth day of the fifth lunar month in the seventh year of Tianqi period (1627 AD), Khan Huangtaiji of the Later Jin, seeking to avenge his father's death, led 60,000 troops to attack Jinzhou. In response, Yuan Chonghuan immediately mobilized his forces and personally took command at Ningyuan.

By the 11th day, Huangtaiji's forces reached Jinzhou. Zhao Shuaijiao, the city's defending general, negotiated for a temporary peace to buy time for reinforcements. The two sides engaged in both negotiations and battle. As Jinzhou came under siege, Yuan Chonghuan dispatched General Mangui to reinforce the city and sent elite troops to harass the enemy.

After receiving reinforcements from Shenyang, Huangtaiji's forces intensified the siege by digging three trenches around Jinzhou. He then led tens of thousands of soldiers to assault Ningyuan. Yuan Chonghuan staunchly defended Ningyuan, employing cannon fire and positioning troops outside the city to engage the Later Jin forces. He personally commanded the defense from the battlements, encouraging his soldiers and ordering them to use firearms, including "red cannons", in the defense. While Ningyuan faced fierce fighting, the garrison at Jinzhou launched a surprise attack on the Later Jin camp, forcing Huangtaiji to withdraw from Ningyuan

藤县袁崇焕故事

新马村袁崇焕故里的莲花墩 / 欧伟文 摄

and focus his efforts on Jinzhou. Despite days of siege, the Ming forces, using artillery, held the city. The Later Jin troops, unable to breach the defenses, suffered significant casualties—losing no fewer than two or three thousand men. Shortages of grass for their horses and food for their soldiers further weakened Huangtaiji's army, ultimately forcing him to retreat.

On the second day of the tenth luner month in the second year of Chongzhen period (1629 AD), Huangtaiji led 100,000 troops in a maneuver that bypassed the Guanningjin defensive line manned by Yuan Chonghuan, circumventing through the Mongolian desert to advance on Beijing. Yuan Chonghuan swiftly mobilized his troops to protect the capital. Emperor Chongzhen, upon learning of the situation, dispatched reinforcements and promoted Yuan Chonghuan to "*Taizitaibao*" (Tutor of the Crown Prince), granting him the privileges and salary of a first-rank official. On the forth day of the eleventh luner month, sensing the urgency, Yuan Chonghuan led 9,000 cavalries to Guangqu Gate in Beijing, defying imperial protocol regarding the deployment of troops. His forces camped in the open. On the 20th day of the eleventh luner month, when the Later Jin army reached the city, Yuan

Chonghuan led his forces into battle. During the engagement, he was struck by multiple arrows. Despite his injuries, Yuan Chonghuan's troops fought fiercely throughout the day, securing a victory at Guangqu Gate. On the 27th day of the eleven luner month, he engaged Huangtaiji's forces again at Zuoan Gate, forcing the Later Jin to hastily retreat from Nanhaizi. Yuan Chonghuan achieved a significant victory in the defense of the capital.

Huangtaiji, unable to breach Beijing, sought to exploit internal strife. He spread rumors of treachery, implying that Yuan Chonghuan had secretly colluded with the enemy. Emperor Chongzhen, swayed by these allegations, summoned Yuan Chonghuan under the pretense of discussing his salary but instead accused him of treason. Yuan Chonghuan was imprisoned on charges of betrayal. The eunuch faction, seizing the opportunity, lobbied five times for his execution, petitioning: "Please execute Yuan Chonghuan!"

On the sixteenth day of the eight lunar month, in the third year of Chongzhen period (1630 AD), Emperor Chongzhen ordered Yuan Chonghuan's execution by dismemberment in the Western Market of Beijing. Before his death, Yuan Chonghuan lamented, "My life's work has been in vain; my half-life of fame was but a dream. Fear not the absence of a heroic general after my death; my loyal spirit will still guard Liaodong."

Yuan Chonghuan, a loyal and unjustly condemned minister, died at the age of 46. Legend has it that after his death, a lotus flower bloomed in a village well and flourished for forty-nine days before withering.

Later generations compared Yuan Chonghuan's noble character to that of Wen Tianxiang and the injustice he suffered to that of Yue Fei. The truth of his wrongful execution was only revealed at the beginning of the Qing Dynasty. Emperor Qianlong, moved by Yuan's heroic spirit, officially exonerated him—a rare event in Chinese history.

Yuan Chonghuan remains one of the most celebrated military strategists in ancient Chinese history, renowned for his victories despite overwhelming odds. His story, widely circulated in Tengxian County, has been passed down through generations.

In 2016, the story of Yuan Chonghuan in Tengxian County was included in the fourth batch of Wuzhou municipal intangible cultural heritage list.

The Inheritance Pedigree of the Story of Yuan Chonghuan in Tengxian County

Generation	Name	Gender	Nationality	Education Background	Year of Craft Leanring	Means of Inheritance
First	Yuan Shunzhou	Male	Han	Unknown	Unknown	Apprenticeship
	He Jiada	Male	Han	Unknown	Unknown	Family inheritance
	He Wenda	Male	Han	Unknown	Unknown	Family inheritance
Second	He Shaoguang	Male	Han	Senior high school	1972	Family inheritance
	He Shenghua	Male	Han	Junior high school	1958	Family inheritance
	He Fuhua	Male	Han	Senior high school	1966	Family inheritance
Third	He Yongguang	Male	Han	Junior high school	1992	Family inheritance
	Yuan Xutang	Male	Han	Senior high school	1975	Family inheritance
	Wei Wei	Male	Han	Senior high school	1989	Apprenticeship
	He Weisong	Male	Han	Senior high school	1989	Family inheritance

藤县鱼生制作工艺

○ 林 源

"食不厌精,脍不厌细","脍"是指切得很薄的肉或鱼片。我国很多地方都有吃生鱼片的传统饮食习俗,藤县叫吃鱼生。我们大抵可以作这样一个猜测,从原始社会先民们吃生鱼生肉到煮熟了再吃的历史进程中,由于吃生鱼有特别的鲜味,因而吃鱼生这个饮食习俗就保留了下来。

我国史料记载吃鱼生最早可追溯到周宣王五年(前823年),从出土的青铜器"兮甲盘"上的铭文可以看到,当年周师于彭衙(今陕西白水县内)迎击狁狁,凯旋而归。大将尹吉甫私宴张仲及其他友人,主菜是烧甲鱼和生鲤鱼片。《诗经·小雅·六月》记载了这件事:"吉甫燕喜,既多受祉。来归自镐,我行永久。饮御诸友,炰鳖脍鲤。侯谁在矣,张仲孝友。"

历代诗词里边有不少描写"鱼脍"的佳句。曹植《名都篇》有"脍鲤臇胎虾,炮鳖炙熊蹯"。李白有诗题目为《酬中都小吏携斗酒双鱼于逆旅见赠》。王维《洛阳女儿行》有"侍女金盘脍鲤鱼"。白居易《轻肥》有"脍切天池鳞"。陆游《幽居》有"鱼脍槎头美"。郁达夫《留别三首》有"此行不为鲈鱼脍"。

藤县鱼生有其独具特色的吃法,这种不知起于何时世代流传的饮食习俗,主要分布在新庆镇、天

制作好的鱼生 / 欧伟文 摄

藤县鱼生制作工艺

平镇、藤州镇及周边相邻村落，以新庆镇最为兴盛。新庆镇有传统的"鱼生节"，每年农历七月十日至十四日，人们清早起床，下塘用鱼罾罾鱼，将活蹦乱跳的草鱼制作成鱼生，端到祠堂祭拜祖先，祈求年年有余，然后呼朋唤友聚餐小酌，祝岁岁平安。

制作藤县鱼生，有选鱼、备料、片鱼、拌鱼四大主要工序，四大主要工序里又有若干道小工序，环环相扣，甚为讲究。制作鱼生必须用专用的刀案和碗碟，并且要对所有器具高温消毒，确保干净卫生。

选鱼。做鱼生要用活鱼，选用无污染的山塘鱼或河鱼，以草鱼、赤眼鲮为主，也用鲢鱼、青竹鱼、罗非鱼、塘角鱼、黄鳝等。新庆镇、天平镇等地，属岭南丘陵地区，山水丰美，人们喜欢在山冲田边挖塘，引山泉水养四大家鱼，喂草料，鱼肉鲜嫩无腥味。

备料。做鱼生的配料，有盐、姜、米醋、米酒、白糖、酱油、洋葱、蒜米、紫苏、辣椒、芝麻、粉丝、黄豆、花生仁、花生油（茶油也可）。黄豆、粉丝都要慢火炒酥，把黄豆擂成粉，把粉丝切成小段。花生要用红衣花生仁，慢火炒酥，擂碎，但不能成粉，要成粗细不一的粒状才有嚼头，齿颊留香。鱼生的佐食，是米粉。用清水把米粉煮到刚熟，捞起沥水拌适量花生油，放在簸箕里铺开晾着，防止打结黏团。

片鱼。这是一道最考技艺的工序，分放血、去鳞、起鱼肉、起鱼皮、切鱼片五道小工序。放血，把水盆放在水龙头下方，开着长流水，把鱼尾巴一刀砍去，放鱼进盆里，待鱼血流干，再把鱼抓起来从头到尾顺向捋几次，直到鱼血完全放尽。去鳞，把鱼鳞刮光，并撬去鱼鳃，用刀背在已去鳞的鱼身从头到尾轻轻刮去表皮渍液。这是鱼皮去腥的小窍门，有经验的厨师才懂。起鱼肉，把鱼侧身平放在案板上，在鱼鳃边骨肉相接处深切一刀，再在鱼背骨肉相接处，从头到尾划拉一刀，刀口顺势把半边鱼肉整条切下，另一边鱼身肉用同样方法切下。起鱼皮，把鱼肉条铺在案板上，皮朝上，在鱼肉条上方用刀开个口使皮肉分离，然后一手捏肉，一手捏皮，用力一撕，再把鱼肉摊放在簸箕里收水。鱼皮切成条块，用沸水焯熟备用。切鱼片，把整条鱼肉平铺在案板上，从头到尾斜切成片，每片大约三毫米厚，然后把鱼片分散铺在簸箕上晾置十来分钟。

拌鱼。这是一道最讲经验的工序，鱼生是否好吃，全在这里。放鱼片进盆里，把提前泡过生姜片的米醋倒进去，快速均匀搅拌鱼片，再把醋水滤掉。根据经验和口味需要，放盐、姜丝、米醋、米酒、白糖、酱油、洋葱丝、蒜米、紫苏丝、辣椒粒、花生油等，把鱼与配料拌匀，滤出汁液备用。把拌好的鱼生上碟，撒上芝麻、粉丝段、黄豆粉、花生仁碎，上桌。滤出的汁液，可用来凉拌米粉。

藤县鱼生鲜、嫩，滋味丰富，别具特色，很受欢迎。紫苏能杀菌去腥，炒花生、黄豆能中和鱼生的寒凉。简单的搭配却完美演绎了中国美食的博大精深。

2016年，藤县鱼生制作工艺列入第四批市级非物质文化遗产代表性项目名录。

藤县鱼生制作工艺传承谱系

代别	姓名	性别	民族	学历	学艺时间（年）	传承方式
第一代	吴凤济	男	汉	私塾	无从考究	家族传承
第二代	吴永庚	男	汉	私塾	无从考究	家族传承
第三代	吴绍良	男	汉	小学	1938	家族传承
第三代	张光尉	男	汉	小学	1932	家族传承
第四代	吴其新	男	汉	小学	1960	家族传承
第四代	张传化	男	汉	小学	1952	家族传承
第四代	麦普壬	男	汉	初中	1970	家族传承
第四代	李世宁	男	汉	小学	1980	师徒传承
第五代	吴先弟	男	汉	小学	1982	家族传承
第五代	张万昌	男	汉	高中	1985	家族传承
第五代	孙远文	男	汉	初中	1991	师徒传承
第六代	吴绪劲	男	汉	初中	2014	家族传承
第六代	陆家胜	男	汉	初中	2014	师徒传承
第六代	唐灿烘	男	汉	初中	2014	师徒传承
第六代	黄永华	男	汉	初中	2014	师徒传承

The Craft of Making Yusheng in Tengxian County

· Lin Yuan ·

The saying goes, "The more exquisite the food, the better; the finer the slice, the better." In this context, "slice" refers to thin fish or meat. In various regions of China, there exists a traditional dietary custom of consuming raw fish. In Tengxian County, this practice is known as "Yusheng". (The term specifically refers to the fillet of river fish and is recognized as part of China's intangible cultural heritage, distinct from Japanese seafood sashimi.) This custom likely evolved from a primitive stage when our ancestors consumed raw fish and meat, which was eventually replaced by cooking due to the unique taste of raw fish, thus preserving the Yusheng eating habit.

Historical records of raw fish consumption in China can be traced back to the fifth year of Emperor Xuan's reign during the Zhou Dynasty (823 BC). Inscriptions on a bronze vessel known as the "*xi jia dish*" reveal that during the Zhou army's campaign against the Xianyun (formerly known as the Xiongnu tribe) at Pengyu (present-day Baishui County, Shaanxi Province), General Yin Jifu hosted a banquet for Zhangzhong and his friends, serving stewed soft-shelled turtle and sliced carp. *The Book of Songs* states: "Jifu was entertained with joy, receiving many gifts from the king. Returning home from Gaojing (the capital of the Zhou Dynasty), after a long time, fill your glass with wine to honor your friends; steamed turtle and sliced carp are delicious. Who else is at the feast? Filial friend Zhangzhong was also present."

Numerous notable Chinese literary works depict Yusheng. Cao Zhi, in his *Famous Capital Chapters*, wrote, "Finely cut carp, cooked shrimp, stir-fried turtle, barbecue bear's paws." Li Bai authored a poem titled "*I wrote this poem as a token of my appreciation to a small official in Zhongdu who visited me at the inn with a bucket of wine and two fish*". Wang Wei's poem *Luoyang Ladies*

Tour features "The maid had a golden plate of finely cooked carp." Bai Juyi's poem *Light Fat* describes "fine cut fish, tasting fresh and tender." Lu You's poem *Seclusion* mentions "The slice of meat with Parabramis pekinensis is very fat." Yu Dafu in his *Farewell Poem* declares, "I'm not here for the bass."

In Tengxian County, Yusheng is characterized by its unique eating customs, passed down through generations. This tradition is primarily observed in Xinqing Town, Tianping Town, Tengzhou Town, and neighboring villages, with Xinqing Town being the most renowned. Xinqing hosts a traditional "Yusheng Festival" each year from the 10th to the 14th day of the seventh lunar month. During this festival, locals rise early to catch fish with forks and prepare Yusheng using live grass carp. They then take the dish to their ancestral temples to honor their ancestors and pray for an abundant harvest.

The making of Yusheng in Tengxian County involves four main processes: fish selection, ingredients reparation, fish slicing, and mixing. Additionally, there are several intricate procedures that are interconnected and precise. Yusheng must be prepared using a special knife and dish, both of which must be disinfected at high temperatures to ensure sanitation.

First, choosing the fish is crucial. Only live fish should be used, specifically selecting unpolluted mountain pond or river fish. Grass carp and red-eye dace are the primary fish, while silver carp, green bamboo fish, tilapia, pond horn fish, and yellow eel are also acceptable. The Lingnan hilly region, encompassing Xinqing, Tianping, and surrounding areas, is known for its vibrant mountains and rivers. Residents often dig ponds near the mountains and fields to raise these fish in mountain spring water, feeding them grass to ensure the fish

制作鱼生的配料 / 欧伟文 摄

are fresh and tender, free from any unpleasant odors.

Second, preparation of ingredients is essential. The ingredients for Yusheng include salt, ginger, rice vinegar, rice wine, sugar, soy sauce, onion, garlic, perilla, chili, sesame, vermicelli, soybeans, peanuts, and either peanut or tea oil. Beans and rice vermicelli should be fried slowly over low heat. The beans should be ground into a fine powder, and the rice vermicelli should be rubbed into small grains. Peanuts must be fried until crisp, ensuring they maintain a chewable texture rather than turning to powder. This preserves their aroma. The rice noodles should be boiled in clean water until just cooked, then drained and mixed with an appropriate amount of peanut oil to prevent them from clumping together as they dry.

Third, slicing the fish is the most technical aspect of the process, which involves five steps: bloodletting, scaling, fish lifting, filleting, slicing the fish. Bloodletting involves placing the fish in a basin under a gentle water flow. After cutting off the fish's tail, the fish is placed in the basin where it will naturally bleed out. Once the blood has drained, the fish is stroked from head to tail multiple times to ensure all blood is expelled. Scaling entails scraping off the scales and removing the gills. For skinning the fish, the back of the knife is used to gently scrape off any remaining skin stains, a technique known only to experienced chefs, helping to eliminate fishy odors. Filleting involves placing the fish on a chopping board on its side, making a deep cut where the flesh meets the bone at the gills, and then making a cut from head to tail along the spine. Both sides of the fish are treated in the same manner. Skinning involves placing the fish skin-side up, using a knife to separate the skin while pulling it away with the other hand. The skin is then cut

炒制鱼生配料 / 欧伟文　摄

切鱼片 / 欧伟文　摄

into strips, blanched in boiling water, and set aside. Finally, slicing the fish means cutting it at an angle from head to tail into pieces approximately 3 millimeters thick, which are then spread on a dustpan to dry for over 10 minutes.

Fourth, mixing the fish is one of the most experiential steps in the process. The quality of Yusheng hinges on this stage. The fillets are placed in a bowl, and rice vinegar, previously infused with ginger slices, is poured over them. The fillets are stirred quickly and evenly, and the vinegar is then strained. Depending on personal preference and experience, salt, ginger, rice vinegar, rice wine, sugar, soy sauce, onion, garlic, shredded perilla, pepper, and peanut oil are added. The mixture is strained again for use later. Finally, the mixed fish is plated and garnished with sesame seeds, rice vermicelli, soybean powder, and peanut kernels, ready to serve. The strained juice from earlier can be used with the rice noodles.

Yusheng from Tengxian County is characterized by its fresh and tender fish, delivering a rich and unique flavor that appeals to people of all ages. Perilla serves to eliminate bacteria and prevent liver fluke. Fried peanuts and soybeans help neutralize the coolness of Yusheng, while the simple combination of ingredients beautifully illustrates the breadth and depth of Chinese cuisine.

In 2016, the making of Yusheng in Tengxian County was included in the fourth batch of Wuzhou Municipal Intangible Cultural Heritage list.

The Inheritance Pedigree of Making Yusheng in Tengxian County

Generation	Name	Gender	Nationality	Education Background	Year of Craft Leanring	Means of Inheritance
First	Wu Fengji	Male	Han	Old-style private school	Unknown	Family inheritance
Second	Wu Yonggeng	Male	Han	Old-style private school	Unknown	Family inheritance
Third	Wu Shaoliang	Male	Han	Primary school	1938	Family inheritance
Third	Zhang Guangwei	Male	Han	Primary school	1932	Family inheritance
Fourth	Wu Qixin	Male	Han	Primary school	1960	Family inheritance
Fourth	Zhang Chuanhua	Male	Han	Primary school	1952	Family inheritance
Fourth	Mai Puren	Male	Han	Junior high school	1970	Family inheritance
Fourth	Li Shining	Male	Han	Primary school	1980	Apprenticeship
Fifth	Wu Xiandi	Male	Han	Primary school	1982	Family inheritance
Fifth	Zhang Wanchang	Male	Han	Senior high school	1985	Family inheritance
Fifth	Sun Yuanwen	Male	Han	Junior high school	1991	Apprenticeship
Sixth	Wu Xujin	Male	Han	Junior high school	2014	Family inheritance
Sixth	Lu Jiasheng	Male	Han	Junior high school	2014	Apprenticeship
Sixth	Tang Canhong	Male	Han	Junior high school	2014	Apprenticeship
Sixth	Huang Yonghua	Male	Han	Junior high school	2014	Apprenticeship

龙母出巡

○ 郑彬昌

藤县,古称藤州,是龙母的故里。龙母文化流传千百年,龙母出巡是其中重要的组成内容。

藤县地处西江流域,境内河流纵横,民众依水而生。为了生存,人们一直与恶劣的自然环境作抗争,产生了众多的传奇人物,龙母就是其中之一。

传说龙母是广西藤县人,一天,她在西江河边拾到一个巨蛋,拿回家孵出了五条小龙,她把五个龙子养大,因而人们称她为龙母。龙母有着非凡的本事,能耕能织,能渔能牧,能预知风雨,能医治百病,能消灾解祸,能保境安民,为百姓造福。龙母去世后,人们为了纪念这位有德于民、有功于国的女中英杰,便为她立庙,岁岁祭祀。

西江流域都修建有龙母庙,当地有祭祀龙母的习俗。龙母出巡是龙母祭祀中一项重要的活动,除了表达念念不忘龙母的恩泽,同时还有祈求风调雨顺、国泰民安之意。龙母出巡这一民俗一直流传于整个西江流域。

藤县作为龙母故乡,龙母出巡是龙母诞活动的重头戏,也是最隆重的仪式。藤县龙母出巡一般每三年举办一次。在农历五月初七晚,先由四名品行优秀的妇女为龙母神像进行沐浴更衣,更换新的服饰。到了第二天(初八)早上,要举行请龙母仪式,然后请出龙母,进入出巡方阵。

龙母出巡方阵很讲究也很隆重,方阵依次由牌匾、彩旗队、花车、龙母神像、龙狮、八音锣鼓队等组成,八音锣鼓队后是数十乃至百多人的出巡队伍。队伍由村中德高望重的人员组成,仪仗整齐威严,气势热烈壮观。

龙母出巡

龙母出巡/欧伟文 摄

藤县龙母出巡时，会沿着藤县各大街道社区路线行进，每到一处街道（村小组）都会举办简单的祭拜仪式，先由龙和狮围着神台绕香案舞动两圈，然后开始燃香祭拜。其间，道公会在一旁唱祈福歌、跳祈福舞，祈祷龙母保佑一方民众，善男信女拜祭龙母，并进行放生仪式，祈求健康顺利、风调雨顺、国泰民安。

藤县龙母出巡属于民俗活动，龙母被塑造成人们心目中的偶像，寄寓着人们追求幸福吉祥的愿望，已经成为一种民间信仰。这种信仰在西江流域经历了两千多年的传承，已深入人心，具有永恒的魅力。

2016年，龙母出巡列入第四批市级非物质文化遗产代表性项目名录。

龙母出巡传承谱系

代别	姓名	性别	民族	学历	学艺时间（年）	传承方式
第一代	龙帮芬	女	汉	不详	无从考究	师徒传承
第一代	唐宏坤	男	汉	小学	1993	师徒传承
第一代	黄凤贞	女	汉	不详	无从考究	师徒传承
第二代	唐孔文	男	汉	初中	2000	师徒传承
第二代	唐石松	男	汉	小学	2008	师徒传承
第二代	秦金泉	男	汉	小学	2008	师徒传承
第二代	莫彩群	女	汉	不详	2008	师徒传承
第三代	梁雪群	女	汉	小学	2008	师徒传承
第三代	梁群英	女	汉	小学	2010	师徒传承
第三代	霍秀芳	女	汉	小学	2012	师徒传承

龙母出巡 / 霍雨锋 摄

龙母出巡队伍 / 欧伟文 摄

Loong Mother Parade

· Zheng Binchang ·

Tengxian County, historically known as Tengzhou, is known as the hometown of the Loong Mother. The culture surrounding the Loong Mother has been transmitted for thousands of years, and the Loong Mother parade is a significant aspect of this tradition.

Situated in the Xijiang River Basin, Tengxian County features a network of rivers that sustain its inhabitants. To survive in this challenging natural environment, the local people have created numerous legends, including the story of the Loong Mother.

According to the legend, the Loong Mother originated in Tengxian County, Guangxi. As a teenager, she discovered a giant egg by the Xijiang River, which she took home and eventually hatched into five little loongs. She raised these loongs to adulthood, earning her the title of Loong Mother. Renowned for her extraordinary abilities—such as ploughing, weaving, fishing, herding, weather forecasting, curing ailments, eliminating disasters, protecting the country, and benefiting the people—she became a revered figure. Following her death, the community built a temple in her honor, where annual sacrifices are made to commemorate this virtuous heroine who contributed to the well-being of the people and the nation.

Numerous temples dedicated to the Loong Mother exist throughout the Xijiang River Basin, where the custom of offering sacrifices takes place annually. The Loong Mother parade is one of the key activities associated with these sacrifices, expressing gratitude to the beloved Loong Mother while also praying for favorable weather, peace, and prosperity. The patrol symbolizes health and well-being for the year ahead, and the folk custom has spread widely throughout the Xijiang River Basin.

As the birthplace of the Loong Mother, Tengxian County's Loong Mother parade is a highlight of the Loong Mother's birthday celebrations and represents the most solemn of ceremonies. This event is typically held every three years. On the seventh night of the fifth lunar month, four gentlewomen bathe the Loong Mother statue, dress it in clean clothing, and replace its loong robes. A ceremony to invite the Loong Mother takes place on the morning of the eighth day, during which she is welcomed into the patrol procession.

The Loong Mother parade procession is characterized by its grandeur and meticulous organization. It includes decorative plaques, a colorful flag team, festooned vehicles, the Loong Mother statue, loong lions, and a team of musicians playing eight-tone gongs and drums. Following the performance of the gongs and drums, dozens, or even hundreds, of parade teams, comprising esteemed members of the village, join the procession, creating an impressive and majestic atmosphere.

Locals support the procession as it passes. Each street or village group hosts a simple worship ceremony during the parade. Initially, the loong and lion dance teams circle the incense table twice before burning incense in worship. During this time, the *Daogong* (the officiating clergy) sings a blessing song and performs a dance, praying for the Loong Mother's blessings upon the people. All attendees offer their reverence to the Loong Mother and participate in a release ceremony, praying for health, well-being, good weather for crops, peace, and prosperity.

The Loong Mother parade in Tengxian County is a folk activity that embodies the spirit of the Loong Mother, passed down orally through generations and solidified as an idol in the hearts of the people. This belief, which has endured for over 2,000 years in the Xijiang River Basin, remains deeply ingrained in the local culture, exuding timeless charm.

In 2016, the Loong Mother parade was officially included in the fourth batch of Wuzhou municipal intangible cultural heritage list.

The Inheritance Pedigree of Loong Mother Parade in Tengxian County

Generation	Name	Gender	Nationality	Education Background	Year of Craft Leanring	Means of Inheritance
First	Long Bangfen	Female	Han	Unknown	Unknown	Apprenticeship
First	Tang Hongkun	Male	Han	Primary school	1993	Apprenticeship
First	Huang Fengzhen	Female	Han	Unknown	Unknown	Apprenticeship
Second	Tang Kongwen	Male	Han	Junior high school	2000	Apprenticeship
Second	Tang Shisong	Male	Han	Primary school	2008	Apprenticeship
Second	Qin Jinquan	Male	Han	Primary school	2008	Apprenticeship
Second	Mo Caiqun	Female	Han	Unknown	2008	Apprenticeship
Third	Liang Xuequn	Female	Han	Primary school	2008	Apprenticeship
Third	Liang Qunying	Female	Han	Primary school	2010	Apprenticeship
Third	Huo Xiufang	Female	Han	Primary school	2012	Apprenticeship

古藤州传说

○ 王飞

民国时期的古藤州城门 / 何锦奋 翻拍自《藤州史话》第一辑

藤县，据考古推断距今已有一万多年的历史，古称藤州。

相传一万年前，北流河与西江交汇处，有两个村庄，一个东村，一个西村，中间隔着北流河。东村东靠独山和东山，独山在村前把水口，防止北流河水的冲犯；东山有古庙，庙里供奉舜帝。舜帝南巡时曾到藤州治水有功，后崩于苍梧之野，时人遂立庙供奉。据传此庙甚是灵验，有求必应，求风得风，求雨得雨，香火鼎盛，故而西村的人逢年过节总得过江祭拜。西村西靠鸡谷山，山前有池曰南湖，湖水深不见底，常年清澈，甘甜可口，据传能医百病，一般的皮肤病、肠胃病或是大热症，只要用此湖水熬药，便能一剂见效，药到病除。于是，东村的人也常常过来取水。

但是，两村却苦于一河之隔，湍急的北流河水使得两个村落之间的交流十分困难。由于当时的造船技术十分落后，只靠竹排或木艇往来，所以常常会发生沉溺事故。于是，两村的人经过合议，决定在那年的二月二日宰牛杀羊，一起到东山舜庙举行祭拜大典，以求风调雨顺、五谷丰登、过江顺风顺水、一年四季平安。说来也奇怪，这天人们忽然发现从庙前地里长出一条紫藤，紫藤越长越长、越长越粗，很快就长到河边，飞架在河面上，一直延伸至对岸。紫藤不断汲取着河水的养分，主干变得越来越粗，足有成年男子张开双臂的宽度，两旁的枝蔓也变得交错相连，恰好长成了两道栏杆。据《藤县志》记载："藤巨三丈围，枝叶蔓生，占地数亩许，其大堪称千古罕有。"人们尝试从上面走过对岸，没想到安全极了，从此这条巨大的紫藤就成了两村交流的桥梁。

但是有一天，两个村子之间因为一点小事起了争执，随着矛盾加剧，双方甚至大打出手，刀剑相向。西村人渐渐抵挡不住，仓皇地从古藤上逃回村子。为了防止东村人攻上来，他们挥刀砍断了古藤，就在古藤断裂的一刹那，突然一声巨响，一道金光"嗖"的一声往东北方向飞去，随即电闪雷鸣，大雨倾盆而下，天地失色，日月无光。

当两村人从慌乱中清醒时，河面望去已空无一物，紫藤消失得无影无踪，就像从未现世那般，没留下一点痕迹。

西村人意识到自己触犯了神灵，已犯下弥天大罪，于是把武器沉到河底，双手合十，跪求上苍的宽恕。东村人也伤心地哭了起来。

但上天并未宽恕他们，大雨连续下了一个多月，凶猛的洪水淹没了两岸无数庄稼和房屋，一时间满目疮痍。

一天晚上，两村中最德高望重的智日老叟做了一个梦，在梦中，他看见一个身材魁梧的男子，手持红光闪闪的宝剑，脚踩白色祥云，从东北上空袅袅飞来。第二天，老者站在河边的一块巨石上向两村人讲述了这个梦境，并说这是上天的指示。

两村族长听罢，当即割破中指，滴血为誓：谁找到这把宝剑，退了洪水就拜他为王！

东村有一个叫智亥的青年，拜别了相依为命的母亲后，独自踏上了寻找红光宝剑的征程。一路上他杀死了许多嗜血如命的猛兽，几经波折，历经千辛万苦，终于找到了宝剑的所在地。但有一条巨蛇在旁守护着宝剑，那蛇向他张开了血盆大口，露出了两颗黑得发亮的硕大毒牙。智亥并无退缩之意，随即一冲而上与它大战了七天七夜，直至天昏地暗，日月无光，终于打死了巨蛇，夺得宝剑。

智亥拿着这柄宝剑回到了村里，把宝剑沉入河底，镇住这条横行霸道的水龙，止住了滔滔洪水。但那紫藤已不复存在，两岸人民往来只能像从前那样以竹排和木艇过河。

随着商品流通、贸易往来、人际交流越来越频繁，当时的那种依靠步行和渡船、竹排的交通方式以及手提、肩扛、头顶的运输方式已很难适应社会发展的需要，于是交通运输设施的兴建与运输工具的制造便应运而生。一河两岸的

《攀藤过江》罗汉任绘 / 何锦奋 摄

古藤州传说

人民在智亥的带领下，在原来紫藤过江的河面上建起了浮桥，将船只和竹排首尾相连，从山上采伐来许多藤蔓，做成缆索，将舟体紧密锚定。从此，两地之间的往来更加密切，也带动了附近的三村十六峒。两村逐渐建成了街圩。为了纪念紫藤，东村改名为"感义村"，西村改名为"永平村"，将浮桥称为"藤舟"，将两村合称为"藤州"。从此，藤州人在这块土地上繁衍生息，藤州这个名字也一代代传了下来。这就是关于古藤州的传说。

2016 年，古藤州传说列入第四批市级非物质文化遗产代表性项目名录。

古藤州传说传承谱系

代别	姓名	性别	民族	学历	学艺时间（年）	传承方式
第一代	李七贤	男	汉	私塾	无从考究	家族传承
	霍云	男	汉	高中	无从考究	师徒传承
	区朝坤	男	汉	初中	1947	家族传承
第二代	李明远	男	汉	高中	1955	家族传承
	卢延任	男	汉	高中	1966	师徒传承
	陆功裕	男	汉	专科	1955	师徒传承
	区家志	男	汉	初中	1960	家族传承
第三代	李威林	男	汉	高中	1990	家族传承
	吴华	男	汉	初中	1969	师徒传承
	区添	男	汉	中职	2009	家族传承

The Legend of Ancient Tengzhou

· Wang Fei ·

Tengxian County, which boasts a history spanning over 10,000 years according to archaeological findings, was known as Tengzhou in ancient times.

Legend has it that 10,000 years ago, two villages existed at the confluence of the Beiliu River and the Xijiang River: East Village and West Village, separated by the Beiliu River. East Village was situated adjacent to Du Mountain and East Mountain, which served as a natural barrier against the northward-flowing river. An ancient temple dedicated to Emperor Shun was located on East Mountain. According to legend, when Emperor Shun undertook a southern expedition to control flooding, he visited Tengzhou and subsequently passed away in a place called Cangwu. As a result, the local people constructed temples to honor Emperor Shun. It is said that this temple possessed remarkable efficacy, responding to the wishes of the faithful. Consequently, residents of West Village would often cross the river to pay their respects during festivals. West Village was located near Jigu Mountain, with a pool known as Nan Lake situated at the foot of the mountain. This lake, deep and clear year-round, was renowned for its sweet and refreshing water, believed to cure various ailments, including skin diseases, gastrointestinal issues, and fevers. Residents of East Village frequently traveled to Nan Lake to collect its water for medicinal purposes.

However, the rushing Beiliu River created significant challenges for communication between the two villages. At that time, shipbuilding technology was rudimentary, relying solely on bamboo rafts and wooden boats, leading to frequent drowning accidents. To address these difficulties, the villagers decided to hold a worship ceremony at the Shun Temple on the second day of the second lunar month, slaughtering cattle and sheep to pray for favorable weather, abundant harvests, and safe river crossings throughout the year. Strangely,

古藤州传说

on that day, the villagers discovered a wisteria vine sprouting in the field in front of the temple. This wisteria grew rapidly, soon spanning the river and reaching the opposite bank. Absorbing nutrients from the river, its trunk thickened to the width of an adult man's outstretched arms. The intertwining branches and vines formed railings on either side. According to the *Chronicles of Tengxian County*, "The vines reached about ten meters in height, with sprawling branches and leaves covering several acres, a remarkable sight for its time." Villagers soon found that they could walk safely across the wisteria, which became a vital bridge connecting the two communities.

One day, however, a trivial dispute escalated into a major conflict between the villages. As tensions grew, a violent confrontation erupted, prompting the villagers of West Village to flee back across the wisteria in panic. To prevent an attack from East Village, they cut the wisteria with swords. At the moment the vine was severed, a loud noise erupted, and a golden light shot toward the northeast. Thunder and lightning followed, unleashing a torrential downpour. The world darkened, obscuring the sun and moon.

When the villagers emerged from their panic, they found that the wisteria had vanished without a trace, as if it had never existed.

Realizing their grievous mistake and the offense to the gods, the West Village villagers cast their weapons into the river, kneeling in prayer for forgiveness. The villagers of East Village wept in sorrow.

Despite their pleas, the gods did not forgive them. Rain fell relentlessly for over a month, resulting in catastrophic floods that devastated countless crops and homes on both banks of the river.

One night, the most respected elder in both villages, named Zhi Ri, had a prophetic dream. In his vision, he saw a burly man wielding a red-glittering sword, flying on auspicious clouds from the northeast. The next day, Zhi Ri recounted his dream to the villagers, declaring it a divine message. Inspired by this revelation, the village patriarchs swore an oath with their blood: whoever found the sword would be crowned king after the floodwaters receded.

In East Village, a young man named Zhi Hai bid farewell to his mother, embarking on a quest to find the red-glittering sword. Along the way, he battled numerous ferocious beasts, overcoming various trials and hardships until he finally located the sword's

刻有"藤城"二字的古城墙 / 何锦奋 摄

resting place. However, a serpent guarded the sword. When the serpent opened its maw, revealing two enormous, glistening black fangs, Zhi Hai did not falter. He engaged the creature in combat for seven days and nights until, engulfed in darkness, he ultimately defeated the serpent and claimed the sword.

Upon returning to his village with the sword, Zhi Hai cast it into the river to subdue the rampant water and control the raging floods. However, the wisteria was gone, and the inhabitants of both banks were left to rely on bamboo rafts and wooden boats for river crossings once more.

As trade and communication increased between the two villages, the existing means of transportation became inadequate. Consequently, the construction of transportation infrastructure and the creation of new tools became necessary. Under Zhi Hai's guidance, the villagers built a pontoon bridge at the former location of the wisteria. Boats and bamboo rafts were aligned end to end, and many vines were cut from the mountains to serve as cables, securing the vessels. This development significantly enhanced communication between the two communities and stimulated trade with three nearby villages and sixteen *dong* (localities akin to villages). The two villages gradually evolved into a bustling marketplace. In memory of the wisteria, East Village was renamed Ganyi Village, and West Village became Yongping Village. The pontoon bridge was designated as "boat of vine", and the two villages collectively came to be known as Tengzhou. Thus, Tengzhou flourished on this land, and its name has been passed down through generations.

In 2016, it was included in the fourth batch of Wuzhou Municipal Intangible Cultural Heritage list.

古藤州传说

The Inheritance Pedigree of Ancient Tengzhou Legend in Tengxian County

Generation	Name	Gender	Nationality	Education Background	Year of Craft Leanring	Means of Inheritance
First	Li Qixian	Male	Han	Old-style private school	Unknown	Family inheritance
	Huo Yun	Male	Han	Senior high school	Unknown	Apprenticeship
	Ou Chaokun	Male	Han	Junior high school	1947	Family inheritance
Second	Li Mingyuan	Male	Han	Senior high school	1955	Family inheritance
	Lu Yanren	Male	Han	Senior high school	1966	Apprenticeship
	Lu Gongyu	Male	Han	Junior college	1955	Apprenticeship
	Ou Jiazhi	Male	Han	Junior high school	1960	Family inheritance
Third	Li Weilin	Male	Han	Senior high school	1990	Family inheritance
	Wu Hua	Male	Han	Junior high school	1969	Apprenticeship
	Ou Tian	Male	Han	Secondary vacational school	2009	Family inheritance

藤县道家村传说

○ 李燕霞

道家村在藤县象棋镇，坐落在北流河边，山环水绕，竹木青葱，是一个被山拥抱被水亲厚的美丽山村，国家 AAAA 级旅游景区石表山就坐落在村中。优越的地理环境和丰厚的自然资源共同铸就了这里的生态与文明、人文与历史，使得这里山水锦绣，气象万千。

这里民俗丰富，物产丰饶，牛歌戏、元宵歌、水上船歌这些流传千年的生态歌谣仍在传唱；软枝沙田柚、野生红菌、米酒等土特产早已名声在外。这里历史悠久，人文荟萃，村中尚存司署衙门、观音阁、敕封大王庙、窦家司牌坊、粤东会馆等多处古建筑遗址。现在，石表山上仍可见汉唐时期的古寨门、古石墙、古石井，村中仍可见隋唐时的护城河、唐代的古码头、清代的福隆庄……

关于道家村，有很多传说，这些传说里，有口传的民间文学成分，也夹杂有书传的真实史料。各

种生动的叙述，也自然地让道家村变得生动起来。

相传古时，滔滔的北流河水在天地间蜿蜒湍流，穿山过寨，在流经一个三江水口的村寨时，因此地地势平缓，两边山峰高兀，自然地形成了一个盆地。经过长年累月的水流冲击，在干旱时，这里便形成了一大片一大片连绵的大沙滩，沙质细腻，颜色亮黄，甚是奇特，寨子的人啧啧称奇，这里便也成了人们眼里的圣地。

后来，有一位须眉皆白的老人来到寨子。此人长发飘飘，一顶草笠一把宝剑，一副仙风道骨的模样。他径直往河岸边一座陡峭的山峰走去，人们也不知道他怎么登上了那座陡峭的山峰。一番极目远眺之后，他挥剑刻石，一气呵成刻就了一篇赞扬此地风水的铭文，并最终把此山命名为石表山，山下边的这个寨子命名为"道家村"。

还有一说，传说"道家"这一称谓，最早来源于"窦家"。相传东汉建武十八年（42年），由于交趾郡女子征侧和她的妹妹征贰一起举兵造反，光武帝刘秀就派大将马援率

道家村的石表山田园风光 / 许旭芒　摄

道家村石表山景区 / 黎志军　摄

两万多人的军团前去平定。当他们来到道家村时，刚好遇到山洪暴发，江河横溢，被困了一个多月，无法继续发兵前进。马援见滞留时日太长，恐怕有负皇命，心里很着急。有一天，当他一个人独自到河边察看洪水时，拿在手上的《道德经》竟然失手掉到河里了。这一掉不要紧，没想到原来洪波滚滚的江水竟然一下子平息了下来。马援大喜，马上挥师溯流而上，径往交趾，一举平定了二征的叛乱。当马援带着队伍得胜归来又路经道家村时，听到山民们唱的山歌，又感慨先前的伏波际遇，忍不住感慨一声："到家矣！"刚好又有个渔人将捞得的《道

德经》送来奉还给他，马援更是称奇，于是，就以得道之家赐以当地"道家"之名。谁知当地人会错了意，以为他是感慨当时借窦家居兵，而且，当地刚好有"窦"姓人，所以，就错听为"窦家"了。此后，"窦家"的名称就流传了下来。

到唐初时，当地人窦始在石表山上自封为王，叫窦家土司，当地因此又叫窦家寨。到唐天宝年间（742—756），皇帝敕封窦圣为司官叫窦家司，窦家的名声就更加响亮了。到了明朝的时候，窦家司又经曾、梁、谢各姓人继署司官、巡司，但仍称窦家司。到清光绪年间（1875—1908），窦家寨的后人杨道留学日本，又参加孙中山同盟会后，接受了新思想，于民国初期任融安县县长时，认为窦家的"窦"已失去意义，"窦家"已成为历史，应改称"道家"，并报请当时政府备案，自此，"道家"便沿用至今。

两个传说里，都有村人们朴素的想象，但后一个传说的后半部分，已经把村庄的史实融进去了。道家村因为正处于思罗河与北流河交汇处，地理位置得天独厚，所以，从隋唐起，历代均设驿站，传递皇帝政令，接待来往官员。当时，从京城到南方交趾、雷州、廉州、高琼等边远地方赴任或贬谪的官员，都经长江入湘江，过漓水，到苍梧，溯浔江，到藤县，入绣江，经此地至北流。正因为这里环境优美，资源丰富，地理位置得天独厚，特别是得益于北流河这条"水上丝绸之路"，使得当地曾一度非常辉煌。这里帆桨往来如梭，船歌响遏行云，人文荟萃，成为商品集散地，也成为中原文化南移的一个交融点。明清时期，粤东客商在此经商者达二三十家，街上店铺林立，还有司衙、学堂、旅店、酒楼、会馆、作坊等，一派繁荣景象。就在新中国成立前，这里还常年有100多条船停靠在码头沿岸，附近镇、村的人都羡慕地称这里为"小南洋"。

很多名人学士经过这里，都留下了诗词墨宝。其中，最为人称道的是明朝大学士解缙所作的《窦家寨》：

> 窦家寨前朝雨晴，
> 思罗江内水初生。
> 杨梅果熟春欲暮，
> 豆蔻花开鸠乱鸣。

道家村福隆庄 / 欧伟文　摄

道家村之名也因了这些历史、传说和诗词愈加丰满起来。

2016年，藤县道家村传说列入第四批市级非物质文化遗产代表性项目名录。

藤县道家村传说传承谱系

代别	姓名	性别	民族	学历	学艺时间（年）	传承方式
第一代	杨象桂	男	汉	私塾	无从考究	师徒传承
第一代	王大成	男	汉	私塾	无从考究	师徒传承
第二代	杨象森	男	汉	初中	1950	师徒传承
第二代	杨德勇	男	汉	初中	1965	师徒传承
第二代	杨象新	男	汉	初中	1972	师徒传承
第二代	杨伟东	男	汉	初中	1978	师徒传承
第二代	杨松	男	汉	初中	1997	师徒传承
第三代	杨业军	男	汉	高中	1998	师徒传承
第三代	杨伟崇	男	汉	高中	1998	师徒传承
第三代	杨幸东	男	汉	高中	2000	师徒传承

The Legend of Daojia Village in Tengxian County

· Li Yanxia ·

Daojia Village is situated in Xiangqi Town, alongside the Beiliu River, enveloped by mountains and water, characterized by lush bamboo and trees. It is a picturesque mountain village, celebrated for its natural beauty. Within the village lies the national 4A-level scenic area known as the Shibiao Mountain Leisure and Tourism Scenic Area. The exceptional geographic environment and abundant natural resources contribute to the ecological richness, cultural heritage, and historical significance of this locale, making it a place of stunning landscapes and favorable climate.

The village is steeped in folklore and abundant in local products. Ecological songs that have been passed down for thousands of years, including ox-song opera, Lantern Festival songs, and boat songs, continue to be sung. Additionally, local specialties such as soft-stemmed Shatian pomelo, wild red mushrooms, and mijiu (rice liquor) have gained renown. Daojia Village boasts a long history and rich cultural heritage, with numerous ancient architectural sites still extant, including the official office of the Secretary, the Guanyin Pavilion, the Royal Palace of the Great King, Doujia Temple, and the Guangdong East Association Hall. Notable remnants from the Tang and Han dynasties, such as the ancient gate of the stockaed village, ancient stone walls, and wells, can still be seen on Shibiao Mountain. Furthermore, the moat from the Sui and Tang dynasties, an ancient wharf from the Tang dynasty, and the Fulong Zhuang from the Qing dynasty are still present in the village.

藤县道家村传说

福隆庄 / 欧伟文 摄

Despite its small size, Daojia Village has a rich narrative. Numerous legends abound, blending oral folklore with historical facts and vivid narratives that breathe life into Daojia Village.

According to legend, in ancient times, the torrent of the Beiliu River wound tumultuously through the landscape, cascading down from the mountains surrounding the village. The river converged at the mouths of three rivers, where the gentle terrain and towering peaks on either side naturally formed a plateau. Over years of erosion, a large continuous beach emerged during droughts, characterized by its unusually bright yellow sand. The villagers revered this beach, and it became a sacred site in the eyes of the local population.

Later, an elderly man with white hair and beard arrived in the stockaded village. This man, dressed in a straw hat and long hair, exuded an immortal aura, carrying a sword. He ascended a steep peak on the riverbank in a manner unknown to the villagers. After surveying the area, he wielded his sword to carve an inscription into a stone, extolling the Feng Shui of the location. He ultimately named the mountain Shibiao Mountain and designated the village below it as "Daojia Village".

Another legend suggests that the name Daojia originated from the "Dou family". According to this account, in the 18th year of the Jianwu period of the Eastern Han Dynasty (42 AD), a woman named Zheng Ce and her sister, Zheng Er, from Jiaozhi County led a rebellion. In response, Emperor Liu Xiu dispatched General Ma Yuan with an army of over 20,000 soldiers to quell the insurrection. Upon reaching Daojia, Ma Yuan encountered severe flash floods that trapped his troops for more than a month, preventing further advancement. Concerned about the prolonged delay and the potential violation of the emperor's orders, Ma Yuan grew anxious. One day, while inspecting the floodwaters alone, he accidentally dropped the *The Classic of the Virtue of the Tao* into the river. Miraculously, this event caused the raging river to calm instantly.

Overjoyed, Ma Yuan directed his troops upstream toward Jiaozhi, successfully suppressing the rebellion. Upon returning victorious and passing through the Tao family territory, he heard the mountain folk singing songs and lamenting past struggles. Unable to contain his emotions, he exclaimed, "Homecoming!" Coincidentally, a fisherman returned the *The Classic of the Virtue of the Tao* to him, leaving Ma Yuan astonished. He subsequently named the village "Daojia" in recognition of Taoist enlightenment. However, the local population misinterpreted this as a lamentation requesting assistance from the "Dou soldiers", given that some locals bore the surname "Dou". Thus, the "Dao" was misunderstood as "Dou", leading to the enduring use of the Dou family name.

By the early Tang Dynasty, a local figure named Dou Shi proclaimed himself king (ruler of Doujia) and established the region known as Doujiazhai. During the Tianbao period (742 - 756 AD) of the Tang Dynasty, the emperor appointed Dou Sheng as the official overseeing a division named Doujia, further enhancing the village's reputation. By the Ming Dynasty, the Doujia Division had evolved into a governing or patrol department, managed by individuals of various surnames, yet retained its original designation. During the Guangxu period (1875 - 1908 AD) of the Qing Dynasty, Yang Dao, a member of the Dou family, studied in Japan, joined the United League of China found by Sun Yat-sen. He embraced new ideas, and later became the governor of Rong'an County in the early Republic of China. He believed the term "Dou" in "Doujia" had lost its original meaning and petitioned the government to change it to "Daojia". Since then, "Daojia" has been used to this day.

Both legends reflect the simple imagination of the village people, yet the latter part of the narrative undoubtedly incorporates historical facts related to the village. Due to its strategic location at the confluence of the Siluo River and Beiliu River, Daojia has served as a post station since the Sui and Tang dynasties, facilitating the transmission of imperial decrees and accommodating incoming and outgoing officials. Officials journeying from the capital to remote regions, such as Jiaozhi, Leizhou, Lianzhou, and Gaoqiong for appointments or demotions, would navigate the Yangtze River, cross the Lijiang River, travel to Cangwu, trace the Xunjiang River, proceed to Tengxian County, enter the Xiujiang River, and finally reach Beiliu River via Daojia. The village's beautiful environment and abundant resources, coupled with its advantageous position—especially as a hub along the "Water Silk Road" of the Beiliu River—contributed to the Dou family's former prominence. The area buzzed with activity, as sails and oars moved like shuttles and boat songs echoed across the waters. The village became a commodity distribution center and a melting pot for Central Plains culture migrating southward. During the Ming and Qing dynasties, as many as 20 to 30 merchants from eastern Guangdong conducted business here, leading to bustling streets lined with shops, as well as offices, schools, inns, restaurants, halls, and workshops. Before the founding of the People's Republic of China, more than 100 boats were docked along the wharf, and people from neighboring towns and villages affectionately referred to this place as "Little Nanyang", with "Nanyang" being an old term for Southeast Asia.

Many celebrated individuals and scholars passed through Daojia Village, leaving behind poems and literary treasures. Among them, the most renowned is "*Doujiazhai*", composed by Xie Jin, a prominent scholar of the Ming Dynasty: "The morning rain clears in Doujiazhai, while the waters of Siluo River arise anew. The ripe waxberry heralds spring's twilight, while turtledoves sing amidst cardamom blooms."

The name of Daojia Village is enriched by this tapestry of prosperity, history, legends, and poetry.

In 2016, the legend of Daojia Village was included in the fourth batch of Wuzhou municipal intangible cultural heritage list.

The Inheritance Pedigree of Daojia Village Legend in Tengxian County

Generation	Name	Gender	Nationality	Education Background	Year of Craft Leanring	Means of Inheritance
First	Yang Xianggui	Male	Han	Old-style private school	Unknown	Apprenticeship
First	Wang Dacheng	Male	Han	Old-style private school	Unknown	Apprenticeship
First	Yang Xiangsen	Male	Han	Junior high school	1950	Apprenticeship
Second	Yang Deyong	Male	Han	Junior high school	1965	Apprenticeship
Second	Yang Xiangxin	Male	Han	Junior high school	1972	Apprenticeship
Second	Yang Weidong	Male	Han	Junior high school	1978	Apprenticeship
Second	Yang Song	Male	Han	Junior high school	1997	Apprenticeship
Third	Yang Yejun	Male	Han	Senior high school	1998	Apprenticeship
Third	Yang Weichong	Male	Han	Senior high school	1998	Apprenticeship
Third	Yang Xingdong	Male	Han	Senior high school	2000	Apprenticeship

藤县神仙脚迹传说

○ 吴献凤

神仙留下的脚迹 / 杨定登　摄

　　藤县神仙脚迹传说源于梁山伯和祝英台的故事，藤县人确信他们来过藤县，并留下了足迹。在神仙脚迹的山下有英台庙，英台庙清朝已有，后被毁，1996年重建，与江对面谷山脚下的梁山伯庙隔江相望，烟火相招，朝夕相守。《梁山伯与祝英台》（简称梁祝传说）与《白蛇传》《孟姜女》《牛郎织女》并称中国古代四大民间传说。其中，梁祝传说是我国最具辐射力的口头传承艺术，也是在世界上产生广泛影响的中国民间传说。梁祝传说在民间流传已有1600多年，可谓是家喻户晓。神仙脚迹传说沿袭了梁祝传说，也可以说是梁祝传说的续集。当地流传着祝英台为当地民众造福的故事，她的形象由此变得高大起来。

　　神仙脚迹的来历有多种版本，流传最广泛的有两种。其中一种是传说祝英台女扮男装去读书，跟梁山伯成为朋友。后来女扮男装的事情败露，古代女子是不允许读书的，于是书院把祝英台赶走。梁山伯跟祝英台一起离开书院，顺江而下，来到藤州，并在西江中间一个叫航州的地方停下来，继续读书。

有一天，西江突发洪水，梁山伯和祝英台跟着逃难的人躲在岸边的高山上，因此留下了脚迹。

另一个版本是这样的：

当年祝英台为梁山伯殉情化蝶之后，她的动人故事感动了上天，玉皇大帝为了表彰她对爱情的专一，特许她位列仙班，封为传粉仙子，掌管天上花园的花粉传播。

有一年王母娘娘发下请帖，请三界诸佛、各路神仙到瑶池开蟠桃大会。在蟠桃大会上，英台看见天蓬元帅和嫦娥仙子在私下里亲热，触景生情，动了凡心，勾起了她对山伯的思念。于是英台偷偷溜出南天门，驾起祥云，四处寻山伯去了。

英台来到了藤州，见此地山清水秀，人杰地灵，遂按下云头，住了下来，且一住就是好几年。其间，百姓有什么苦心事多向英台倾诉、求教。英台也乐于为他们解难、完愿，和这里的人民结下了深厚的情谊。

再说蟠桃大会结束之后，各路神仙各归本位。此时，王母娘娘发现不见了传粉仙子，于是命千里眼出南天门看个究竟，得知传粉仙子已在藤州住下，即命吕洞宾下界捉拿。

吕洞宾来到藤州，落下云头，站在山巅之上，要传粉仙子即时随其回天廷复命。可英台已经爱上了这个地方，不愿再回到天上，和吕洞宾顶撞起来。两人言来语去，惹得吕洞宾大怒，大脚一跺，地动山摇，山崩地裂，巨石纷纷滚下，堵塞了半边河道（现在英台庙下可以见到滚下的大石，使浔江在此形成差不多90°的急转弯）。英台为了不给当地人民带来更多的灾难，只好和吕洞宾回到了天上。

现在屹立在山巅之上的大石，传说就是吕洞宾跺烂的，脚迹也是他的。

当地人民为了纪念祝英台，在她上天的地方建了个英台庙，如果有什么心愿，到英台庙跟英台讲讲，大多都能如愿以偿。

神仙脚迹 / 杨定登　摄

2016 年，藤县神仙脚迹传说列入第四批市级非物质文化遗产代表性项目名录。

藤县神仙脚迹传说传承谱系

代别	姓名	性别	民族	学历	学艺时间（年）	传承方式
第一代	李七贤	男	汉	私塾	无从考究	家族传承
	霍云	男	汉	高中	无从考究	师徒传承
第二代	李明远	男	汉	高中	1955	家族传承
	卢延任	男	汉	高中	1966	师徒传承
	陈焕英	男	汉	本科	1971	师徒传承
第三代	李威林	男	汉	高中	1990	家族传承
	吴华	男	汉	初中	1989	师徒传承

The Legend of the Fairy Footprints in Tengxian County

· Wu Xianfeng ·

The legend of the fairy footprints in Tengxian County is rooted in the story of Liang Shanbo and Zhu Yingtai, one of the four great folk love stories of ancient China, also known as *The Love Eterne*. According to local belief, these two lovers visited Tengxian County and left their footprints behind. At the foot of the so-called "immortal trace" lies Yingtai Temple, which dates back to the Qing Dynasty. After its destruction, the temple was rebuilt in 1996 and is situated across the river from Liang Shanbo Temple. These two temples attract visitors and stand in proximity to one another day and night. The tale of Liang Shanbo and Zhu Yingtai, along with *The Legend of the White Snake*, *Meng Jiangnv's Tale*, and *The Cowherd and the Weaver Girl*, comprise the four prominent folklores of ancient China. Among them, the story of Liang Shanbo and Zhu Yingtai is the most influential in terms of oral inheritance in China and has gained significant recognition worldwide. This love story has captivated audiences for over 1,600 years. The legend of the fairy footprints serves as a sequel to the story of Liang Shanbo and Zhu Yingtai, inheriting its narrative structure while enhancing the local perception of Zhu Yingtai as a noble character who benefits the community.

There are multiple versions regarding the origin of the fairy footprints, two of which are particularly well-known. The first version recounts how Zhu Yingtai disguised herself as a man to pursue her studies and formed a friendship with Liang Shanbo. However, her true identity as a woman was eventually discovered, as women were prohibited from receiving an education in ancient times. Consequently, the academy expelled Zhu Yingtai. After leaving the academy together, Liang Shanbo and Zhu Yingtai traveled to Tengzhou along the river. They subsequently stayed in a place called Hangzhou, located midway along the West River, with plans to continue their studies. One day, a sudden flood struck the West River, forcing Liang Shanbo and Zhu Yingtai to seek refuge on a high hill near the riverbank, leaving their footprints behind.

The second version of the legend unfolds as follows:

After Zhu Yingtai died for the love of Liang Shanbo, her story resonated with the heavens. In recognition of her devotion, the Emperor Jade granted her the rank of a fairy pollinator, responsible for pollen transmission in the heavenly garden.

One year, the Mother Goddess of the Heavens summoned all the Buddhas and gods from the Three Realms to a celestial peach conference at the abode of the Fairy Mother Goddess. During the gathering, Zhu Yingtai observed the Tianpeng Marshal and Chang'e fairy in an intimate moment. This sight stirred her emotions and ignited memories of her love for Liang Shanbo, compelling her to sneak out of the South Gate and ride on auspicious clouds in search of him.

Zhu Yingtai arrived in Tengzhou, captivated by its beautiful mountains and rivers. Enchanted by the area's outstanding people and ideal location, she settled there for several years. During her stay, the locals frequently sought her assistance during times of difficulty, and she willingly helped them fulfill their wishes. This generosity fostered a profound bond between Zhu Yingtai and the community.

When the peach banquet concluded, the gods returned to their respective realms. At this time, the fairy pollinator was found to be missing. The Mother Goddess dispatched the "Eye of Thousands of Miles" (a deity believed to possess the ability to see clearly from great distances) to investigate. Upon discovering that the pollinator fairy had made her home in Tengzhou, she sent Lyv Dongbin to retrieve Zhu Yingtai.

Lyv Dongbin descended from the clouds to Tengzhou, standing atop a mountain. He called out loudly, demanding that Zhu Yingtai return to heaven immediately. However, Zhu Yingtai had grown fond of her earthly home and refused to go back. Their argument escalated, angering Lyv Dongbin, who stomped his feet in frustration, causing tremors that shook the mountains and cracked the ground. Massive stones tumbled down, blocking half of the river (today, one can still see these stones near Yingtai Temple, which has caused the Xun River to form a nearly 90-degree turn). To spare the village and its people from disaster, Zhu Yingtai ultimately agreed to return to heaven with Lyv Dongbin.

The large stone that now stands atop the mountain bears the footprints of Lyv Dongbin.

To honor Zhu Yingtai, the local people constructed Yingtai Temple at her heavenly residence. It is said that if one makes a wish at Yingtai Temple and converses with Zhu Yingtai, most wishes will be granted.

In 2016, the legend of the fairy footprints was included in the fourth batch of Wuzhou municipal intangible cultural heritage list.

The Inheritance Pedigree of Fairy Footprints Legend in Tengxian County

Generation	Name	Gender	Nationality	Education Background	Year of Craft Leanring	Means of Inheritance
First	Li Qixian	Male	Han	Old-style private school	Unknown	Family inheritance
	Huo Yun	Male	Han	Senior high school	Unknown	Apprenticeship
Second	Li Mingyuan	Male	Han	Senior high school	1955	Family inheritance
	Lu Yanren	Male	Han	Senior high school	1966	Apprenticeship
	Chen Huanying	Male	Han	Bachelor	1971	Apprenticeship
Third	Li Weilin	Male	Han	Senior high school	1990	Family inheritance
	Wu Hua	Male	Han	Junior high school	1989	Apprenticeship

藤县思罗河传说

○ 李燕霞

思罗河发源于容县的大容山，上游叫泗罗河，入藤县境内后叫思罗河，河水清澈舒缓，经无数山峦、村庄，一路蜿蜒，最后在道家村注入北流河。

关于思罗河的传说有很多，其中流传最广的有两个。一说思罗河古时叫皇家河，是玉皇大帝和七仙女下凡到人间的地方，也是后来诸神下凡登天之地，更是方士登临石表山夜观天象必经之地。

因是皇家河，这条河流便有它的灵动与韵致。这是一条温婉的河，水流平缓，河道弯曲迂回，河面不太宽也不太窄，最窄处30多米，最宽处也就100多米，既不显得空旷也不显得逼仄。水也不特别深，最浅处竹排几乎可以擦着河底的沙子滑过，伸伸手，就可以掬起一捧水，捧起一捧沙。河的前半段主要是河流与田园风光的结合，后半段则是河流与丹霞地貌的结合。悠长的河面会因远近深浅和天色的不同，幻化出不同的色彩，或浅蓝，或深翠，或鹅黄……

河里鱼虾肥硕，味道鲜美。河面上经常停泊着大量的疍家船，这些疍民们日夜与皇家河相伴，傍水而居，皇家河也无私地供养着他们。皇家河上一户疍家有个女儿，小名阿罗，年方二八，长得貌美如花，十里八乡出了名的俊俏，引得许多媒人竞相而来。谁知有一天，阿罗上岸的时候被附近对她垂涎已久的山大王掳去了，从此阿罗的父母便日夜思念他们的女儿，经常在皇家河上声声呼唤阿罗。后来，人们便把这条河改叫思罗河，原来的名字就渐渐没有人叫了。

还有一说是相传在公元1407年，明朝翰林学士解缙到广西任职期间，因惊诧古藤州美景，便与藤

美丽的思罗河/欧伟文 摄

州好友傅惟宗沿绣江往南一路上溯，至窦家寨，见这方村落一片叠翠，热闹非凡，可谓是风景别样，于是决定上岸走走。此时只见村中绿树成荫，杨梅果熟，鸡犬相闻，商铺林立，村人皆好客，见之都热情吆喝招呼。解缙边走边感慨，心底甚是喜欢。解缙和傅惟宗在村中游一圈，又吃了一顿美味的农家菜后，上船继续前行。

就在两人到码头跨上船只之时，解缙突然眼前一亮，见到思罗河口正在上行的一艘疍家船上，立着一位俊俏的女子，粉红的脸蛋，新月似的眉。那模样神似在京城曾经暗恋自己，不满父母包办而以死抗婚的曹姑娘，解缙一时间不由得看呆了。这时，那位俊俏的疍家女似乎也看到了张口呆立的解缙，掩面一笑，然后坐下来，一边织网一边低头哼唱起地方小曲。歌声唯美空灵，婉转动人，引得解缙跟随而去。

一路上，解缙顾不上欣赏两岸的旖旎风光和阵阵鸟叫，至思罗河中段的仙女把水口处，终于追了上来，可是又碍于自己

思罗河小景 / 何锦奋　摄

的身份不便鲁莽开口。好友傅惟宗把一切看在眼里，便以有要事须与船工商量为由来到那女子的船上。傅惟宗从那船回来后，便在解缙耳边如此这般地耳语了一番，说得解缙不断摇头，不胜感慨。原来，这名正处在豆蔻年华的女子姓罗，因还未出嫁，依照疍家的习俗不能随便跟陌生男子搭话相见。

　　事已至此，加上天色已晚，解缙只得带着落寞的心情和傅惟宗回到窦家寨投宿，一夜辗转难眠。次日一早，他们便冒着山雨匆匆坐上开往藤州的船只。船至绣水江心之际，却是山雨骤停，阳光明媚，使得窦家寨处在一片云蒸霞蔚之中。向来放歌山水美景的解缙，也被眼前仙境般的图画吸引住了，再看村寨边的思罗河，正是春潮涌动、新水初生之时，与山寨交相辉映，阳光下，像是新绿中的片片桃花盛开。那不是昨夜自己魂牵梦萦的地方吗？寨子、朝雨、阳光、春潮、村内的杨梅、江中的鸟声、豆蔻年华的罗姑娘、昨夜的辗转难眠……一切一切，全在心头翻滚、激荡。解缙于是忍不住即兴吟诗一首："窦家寨前朝雨晴，思罗江内水初生。杨梅果熟春欲暮，豆蔻花开鸠乱鸣。"后来，这首诗留了下来，思罗河的名称也因此流传下来。

对于两种传说，村民们因着朴素的情怀，更喜欢的是第一种，仙女、皇家河……想想都令人向往。而文人们则更喜欢第二种，因为那里既有历史的真实，又有才子佳人的想象，还有对爱情的向往。而不管哪种，表达的都是一种对美好的向往和追求！

2016年，藤县思罗河传说列入第四批市级非物质文化遗产代表性项目名录。

藤县思罗河传说传承谱系

代别	姓名	性别	民族	学历	学艺时间（年）	传承方式
第一代	杨象桂	男	汉	私塾	无从考究	师徒传承
	王大成	男	汉	私塾	无从考究	师徒传承
	杨象森	男	汉	初中	1950	师徒传承
第二代	彭进龙	男	汉	高中	1973	师徒传承
	杨象新	男	汉	初中	1972	师徒传承
	杨伟东	男	汉	初中	1978	师徒传承
	杨松	男	汉	初中	1997	师徒传承
第三代	杨业军	男	汉	高中	1998	师徒传承
	杨伟崇	男	汉	高中	1998	师徒传承
	杨幸东	男	汉	高中	2000	师徒传承

The Legend of Siluo River in Tengxian County

· Li Yanxia ·

The Siluo River originates from Darong Mountain in Rongxian County. In its upper reaches, it is known as Siluo River; however, upon entering Tengxian County, it retains the name Siluo River. The river flows gently and clearly, winding through countless mountains and villages before ultimately merging with the Beiliu River at Daojia Village.

Numerous legends surround Siluo River, with two being particularly prominent. The first legend states that the Siluo River was once referred to as the Royal River, the site where the Jade Emperor and the Seven Fairies descended to Earth. It was also believed to be a place where the gods returned to heaven and where alchemists observed the night sky from Shibiao Mountain.

The Royal River, characterized by its dynamic charm, flows gently with a graceful meander. The river is neither too large nor too small, with its narrowest point measuring approximately 30 meters in width and its widest point exceeding 100 meters. This gives it an inviting appearance, avoiding extremes of emptiness or constriction. The water is generally shallow, with bamboo shoots nearly brushing the sandy bottom. One can easily scoop up handfuls of water or sand. The river's upper reaches are primarily defined by a harmonious blend of riverine and pastoral scenery, while the lower reaches showcase stunning Danxia landforms. The river's surface displays various colors, from light blue to deep green to golden yellow, influenced by factors such as depth, distance, and the sky's hue.

The river abounds with fish and shrimp, known for their delicious taste. Numerous boat-dwelling families make their homes along its banks, living in close companionship with the Royal River. The river generously provides for these families. Among them is a family with a daughter nicknamed A Luo, who is 16 years old and renowned for her beauty, drawing suitors from far and wide. However, one fateful day, A Luo was taken by the nearby King of the Mountain while she was ashore. Since that day, her parents have mourned their daughter, often calling her name along the banks of the Royal River. In time, the river's name was changed to Siluo River, and the original name faded from common use.

Another legend recounts an event from 1407 AD when Xie Jin traveled to Guangxi as an advisor. Captivated by the beauty of ancient Tengxian County, he and his friend Fu Weizong journeyed south along the Xiujiang River to Doujiazhai, where they found the village alive with vibrant greenery, offering a unique landscape. They decided to disembark and explore. Upon entering the village, they were greeted by hospitable locals and were charmed by the sight of green trees, ripe plums, and the sounds of dogs and chickens. After enjoying a delightful farm-to-table meal, Xie Jin and Fu Weizong boarded their boat again to continue their journey.

Unexpectedly, as they were about to depart from the dock, Xie Jin's gaze fell upon a boat at the mouth of the Siluo River. On it stood a beautiful woman with a delicate complexion and moon-like eyebrows. At that moment, Xie Jin was reminded of a girl named Cao from the capital who had once harbored unrequited feelings for him and, in her despair over an arranged marriage, had tragically passed away. Captivated, Xie Jin could not help but stare. The lovely boat-dwelling woman, noticing his astonishment, smiled and resumed her task of weaving a net while humming a local tune. Her ethereal song enchanted Xie Jin, compelling him to follow her.

Along the way, Xie Jin became oblivious to the charming scenery and the melodious calls of birds. He finally caught up with the woman at the midpoint of the Siluo River. Due to his status, direct conversation with her was not appropriate. Thankfully, Fu Weizong, observant and resourceful, suggested they board the woman's boat to discuss something important. After returning from the boat, Fu whispered to Xie Jin, who was overwhelmed with emotion, that the woman was named Luo and had yet to marry, thereby following the customs of her people, which prohibited her from conversing with strange men.

Faced with this revelation and the day's late hour, Xie Jin returned to the Doujiazhai with a heavy heart. He struggled to sleep throughout the night. The next morning, they braved the mountain rain and hastily boarded their boat to Tengzhou. Upon reaching the heart of the Xiushui River, they were met with a sudden cessation of rain and a brilliant sunshine that enveloped Doujiazhai in mist. Xie Jin, known for his poetic praise of nature, was entranced by the fairy-like scene before him. He turned to gaze at the village along the Siluo River, where the spring tide surged, reflecting the sunlight in a manner reminiscent of peach blossoms in bloom. "Is this not the place that haunted my dreams last night?" Xie Jin pondered. The cottage, morning rain, sunshine, spring tide, plum trees, bird songs, and the mysterious young lady—all of these images stirred within his mind. Unable to contain his feelings, Xie Jin spontaneously composed a poem: "The morning rain clears in Doujiazhai, the waters of Siluo River arise anew. The ripe waxberry heralds spring's twilight, while turtledoves sing amidst cardamom blooms." This poem endured, and the name of Siluo River became immortalized.

Among the two legends, villagers tend to favor the first due to its simplistic charm, embracing the fairy tale of the Royal River and the warmth it evokes. In contrast, literati are more inclined toward the latter, as it intertwines historical reality, imaginative artistry, and longing for love. Regardless of preference, both legends express a universal yearning and pursuit of beauty.

In 2016, the legend of Siluo River was included in the fourth batch of Wuzhou municipal intangible cultural heritage list.

思罗河里的铜钟石 / 许旭芒　摄

静美的思罗河 / 许旭芒　摄

The Inheritance Pedigree of Siluo River Legend in Tengxian County

Generation	Name	Gender	Nationality	Education Background	Year of Craft Leanring	Means of Inheritance
First	Yang Xianggui	Male	Han	Old-style private school	Unknown	Apprenticeship
First	Wang Dacheng	Male	Han	Old-style private school	Unknown	Apprenticeship
First	Yang Xiangsen	Male	Han	Junior high school	1950	Apprenticeship
Second	Peng Jinlong	Male	Han	Senior high school	1973	Apprenticeship
Second	Yang Xiangxin	Male	Han	Junior high school	1972	Apprenticeship
Second	Yang Weidong	Male	Han	Junior high school	1978	Apprenticeship
Second	Yang Song	Male	Han	Junior high school	1997	Apprenticeship
Third	Yang Yejun	Male	Han	Senior high school	1998	Apprenticeship
Third	Yang Weichong	Male	Han	Senior high school	1998	Apprenticeship
Third	Yang Xingdong	Male	Han	Senior high school	2000	Apprenticeship

藤县咸酸菜制作工艺

○ 罗金霞

"酸"是人类烹饪史上最古老的口味,《尚书·说命下》中记载"若作和羹,尔惟盐梅",其中的梅就是酸梅果,在文中作为调味品出现。中国人自古就爱吃酸,人间五味,酸甜苦辣咸,将酸妥妥地排在首位。藤县咸酸菜色泽黄亮,酸脆可口,风味独特,把五味的首尾都占了,颇受人们的喜爱。

一方水土,一方食俗。秦以前,藤县属百越,为多部落聚居地,饮食文化具有多民族的色彩,与经济文化已较发达的中原地区相比,饮食相对简单。至秦统一中国,藤县属南海郡辖地,中原与岭南的文化、经济交往渐多。受中原饮食文化的熏陶、影响,饮食逐渐精细。再加上藤县境内河流密布,有西江干流和北流河穿县而过,在水路交通为王的古代,藤县又是"水上丝绸之路"的必经地,于是,南北饮食文化在藤县不断交会,后经汉历晋至明清,藤县人创造出具有藤县特色的食物制作技艺,形成丰富多彩的藤县饮食文化。藤县咸酸菜制作工艺便是其中的一种。

在中国,酸菜制作工艺最早有文字记载的,可以追溯到几千年前的西周时期,《周礼》中记载:馈食之豆,其实葵菹。根据东汉许慎《说文解字》解释:菹,酢菜也。酢今作醋字,有变酸的意思,所以菹指的应该就是今天的酸菜。而《诗经》中也曾这样写道:"中田有庐,疆场有瓜。是剥是菹,献之皇

咸酸菜坛 / 欧伟文 摄

藤县咸酸菜制作工艺

制作咸酸菜的芥菜 / 欧伟文　摄

祖。"而《释名》中对"菹"的解释更为透彻,"菹,阻也,生酿之,遂使阻于寒温之间,不得烂也"。"生酿之"指的是将新鲜的白菜或芥菜,直接制作成鲜美的酸菜。而"遂使阻于寒温之间,不得烂也",则是说在腌制酸菜的时候,一定要将其放在隔寒、热之地,这样腌制出来的酸菜才不会腐烂,口感特别酸爽、清脆。藤县居民历来有做咸酸菜的习惯,藤县咸酸菜制作工艺是古代人民创造发明保存食物的方法之一,它不仅使食物能长时间保存,也为饮食文化增添了多样化的选择。藤县咸酸菜的制作,也像《释名》中介绍的酸菜制作方法一样——生酿之。

地处亚热带季风气候地区的藤县是典型的农业大县,温润的气候为作物的生长提供了条件,尤其适合芥菜的生长。这为藤县咸酸菜的制作提供了充足的原料。每年的秋冬季,最适宜腌制咸酸菜的翠玉似的新鲜潮州芥菜上市了。农户就会把吃不完的芥菜拿来腌制成咸酸菜,留着自己吃或者出售。

藤县咸酸菜的制作工艺极为讲究。先要把芥菜从地里整棵收割回来,再人工挑选,去除黄叶,然后清洗干净,晾在阳光下去除水分,晒至微皱。菜上不能残留一滴水珠,不然后续工序都白费劲。接下来，就得开始腌制了。先给芥菜均匀地涂上盐和黄姜粉，盐是咸酸菜入味的重要成分，黄姜粉则是使咸酸菜色泽黄亮的关键，这两者必须比例合适，不能过多或过少，还得确保每棵芥菜都涂抹上，方能制作出味道适中的咸酸菜，要不然咸酸菜过咸或过淡、颜色灰暗，都不能称为成功。涂抹均匀后，将芥菜放进大池子里，层层压紧压实，不留缝隙。

每一种食物的制作，水都在扮演着重要角色，藤县咸酸菜的制作也不例外。取当地纯净井水，倒进池子内直至淹没芥菜，再用塑料薄膜盖着，压上巨石，使之与空气隔绝。

每一种美食的诞生，都需要时间的沉淀。那些有风味的美食，都是经过岁月的淘洗而成就的。藤县咸酸菜也需要时间的携手，经过漫长的发酵，方能成就芳香浓郁、风味独特的魅力。大约10天后，池子里的芥菜经过盐、水的交融，已初具酸菜的模样了。这时，就得把芥菜一棵棵翻出来，装进另一个干净的大池子，再次加盐和黄姜粉，注满当地井水，封好。经过时间酝酿，腌制10天后，用同样的方法把芥菜翻过第三个干净的大池，约一周后再翻过第四个大池进行腌制。值得注意的是，在整个制作过程中，绝不能沾上一点油腥，要不然整池的酸菜就会变成烂菜，所有努力都将付之东流。

要说时间是藤县咸酸菜的天然配方，那么，气温则是它的催化剂。藤县咸酸菜腌制时间也视气温而定，一般夏季20天即可出坛，在气温较低的冬天，则需一个月甚至两个月。

经过如此三番两次的折腾，时间晃晃悠悠来到了20多天

藤县咸酸菜制作工艺

咸酸菜加工车间一角 / 何锦奋　摄

后或一个多月后，这时的芥菜，清爽脆口、色泽嫩黄、酸味十足、咸淡适宜，美味的藤县咸酸菜就成了。

每一种美食的诞生，都是有根源的。藤县咸酸菜的制作历史可以追溯到清朝，发源地在藤县太平镇新雅村江口组。据说，家住在江口组的一位农户的祖先从广东潮州那里学到了腌咸菜的技术，于是引进潮州芥菜的种子，在村里种植，并在潮州咸菜的腌制基础上不断地摸索、改良腌制工艺，使之色泽黄亮、酸脆可口，于是就演变成了咸酸菜。后来发展到作坊和工场，批量生产咸酸菜，作为商品出卖和送礼佳品。现如今，藤县咸酸菜以太平镇、濛江镇的最为出名。

一酸解千忧，一菜融百味。咸酸菜炖排骨、咸酸菜蒸扣肉、咸酸菜水煮鱼、咸酸菜炒牛肉、咸酸菜炒猪大肠、咸酸菜炒猪肚等，每一道都是人们难以忘怀的人间美味。同时，咸酸菜含有大量的有机酸和乳酸菌，具有开胃健食、提神醒脑、去油腻助消化等功效。此外，每逢酒席，藤县人都喜欢上一道咸酸菜做成的菜肴，寓意着"好子好孙"。

2018年，藤县咸酸菜制作工艺列入第五批市级非物质文化遗产代表性项目名录。

藤县咸酸菜制作工艺传承谱系

代别	姓名	性别	民族	学历	学艺时间（年）	传承方式
第一代	陈嵩生	男	汉	不详	无从考究	家族传承
第二代	陈绪林	男	汉	不详	1920	家族传承
	陈祖财	男	汉	不详	无从考究	师徒传承
第三代	陈静基	男	汉	初中	1967	家族传承
	陈剑强	男	汉	高中	1988	家族传承
	许子新	男	汉	小学	1995	师徒传承
第四代	陈洪峰	男	汉	初中	1997	家族传承
	许景都	男	汉	初中	2000	师徒传承

The Technique of Making Pickled Mustard Greens in Tengxian County

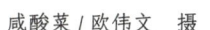

· Luo Jinxia ·

"Sour" is one of the oldest condiments in the history of human cuisine. According to *The Book of History*: "If you make a soup, you should season it with salt and sour plums, " where "plums" refers to sour plums, which are featured as a condiment in this text. The Chinese people have loved pickled foods since ancient times. Among the five basic flavors—sour, sweet, bitter, spicy, and salty—sour is often considered the most prominent. The pickled mustard greens of Tengxian County, with its yellow hue and bright color, offers a uniquely sour, crisp, and delicious flavor. It occupies a special place in the culinary spectrum and remains popular among the people.

Every region has its own distinctive culinary customs. Before the Qin Dynasty, Tengxian County belonged to the Baiyue region, a settlement of various ethnic tribes whose food culture reflected this diversity. Compared to the more economically and culturally advanced Central Plains, the local diet was relatively simple. When the Qin Dynasty unified China, Tengxian County fell under the jurisdiction of Nanhai County, which increased cultural and economic exchanges between the Central Plains and Lingnan. Influenced by the dietary culture of the Central Plains, Tengxian's cuisine gradually became more refined. Additionally, with the Xijiang and Beiliu Rivers running through Tengxian, the county served as a vital stop on the "Silk Road on the Water" in ancient times. As a result, the food cultures of the North and South merged in Tengxian, leading to the development of unique culinary traditions. One such tradition is the production of pickled mustard greens, which has become a hallmark of the local cuisine.

In China, the earliest recorded method for making pickled mustard greens dates to the Western Zhou Dynasty, thousands of years ago. *The Rites of Zhou* describes a dish made from pickled mustard greens, which was prepared for ancient banquets. According to Xu Shen's *Shuowen Jiezi* (an *Analytical Dictionary of Chinese Characters* from the Eastern Han Dynasty), pickled mustard greens refers to pickled vegetables. In *The Book of Songs*, there is a description: "There are residential houses in the middle of the field, and fruits and vegetables grow on the edge of the ridge. Peeled, cut into pieces, and pickled into pickled mustard greens to be dedicated to the great ancestors." Furthermore, in *Shiming* (a treatise written by Liu Xi during the Eastern Han Dynasty that traces the origins of various things), pickled mustard greens is described in more detail: "Pickled mustard greens should be preserved in a sealed manner. Fresh cabbage or mustard greens is directly pickled into pickled mustard greens. During pickling, it must not be placed in hot or cold areas to prevent spoilage." The people of Tengxian County have long had a tradition of making pickled mustard greens. The production in Tengxian County reflects an ancient method of food preservation. It not only extends the shelf life of the mustard greens but also enriches the region's culinary diversity. The process mirrors the method described in *Shiming*, where fresh cabbage or mustard greens is directly transformed into pickled mustard greens.

Tengxian County, located in the subtropical monsoon climate zone, is an agricultural county with a warm climate that is highly conducive to crop cultivation, particularly mustard greens. This has provided ample raw materials for producing mustard greens. Every autumn and winter, fresh Chaozhou mustard greens, ideally suited for pickling, becomes available. Farmers take the surplus mustard greens and pickle it for personal consumption or sale.

The production of pickled mustard greens in Tengxian County is highly meticulous. First, whole mustard greens are harvested, manually selected to remove yellow leaves, then cleaned and sun-dried until slightly wrinkled. Ensuring the leaves are completely dry is crucial, as any moisture would ruin the subsequent steps. Once the leaves are prepared, the pickling process begins. The mustard leaves are evenly coated with salt and turmeric powder. Salt is essential for flavor, while turmeric gives the mustard its bright yellow color. The proportions of salt and turmeric must be carefully balanced. Too much or too little of either will result in pickled mustard greens that is either too salty or too bland, with a dark, unappetizing appearance. After the mustard greens is thoroughly coated, it is packed tightly into large vats or pools, leaving no gaps between layers.

Water plays a vital role in food production, and the pickled mustard greens of Tengxian is no exception. Locals use pure well water to submerge the mustard greens before sealing the vat with plastic sheeting and weighing it down with stones to ensure the mustard greens is fully isolated from the air.

The creation of any food requires time, and pickled mustard greens is no exception. The mustard ferments for about ten days, during which time the salt and water work together to transform the leaves into pickled mustard greens. After this period, the mustard greens is transferred to a clean vat, re-seasoned with salt and turmeric, and submerged in fresh well water. This process is repeated over several weeks, with the mustard greens being moved from one vat to another three or four times. Each stage must be carried out with precision to avoid contamination. Even a small amount of oil can ruin an entire batch, turning the mustard greens into rotten vegetables and rendering the effort futile.

Time and temperature are also key factors in the production of pickled mustard greens. During the summer, the fermentation process takes around 20 days, while in winter, when the temperature is lower, it can take a month or even two.

After these painstaking steps, the pickled mustard greens becomes sour, crisp, and yellow, ready to serve.

The history of pickled mustard greens production in Tengxian County can be traced back to the Qing Dynasty, with its origins in Jiangkou Group, Xinya Village, Taiping Town. It is said that a local farmer's ancestor learned the pickling technique from Chaozhou, Guangdong Province, bringing Chaozhou mustard greens' seeds to the area. Through experimentation and refinement, he developed a method for producing pickled mustard greens that is distinct for its bright yellow color, crisp texture, and deliciously sour taste. Over time, this method expanded from small workshops to factory production, making pickled mustard greens a popular local product and gift. Today, the pickled mustard greens of Taiping and Mengjiang Towns are the most renowned in Tengxian County.

Pickled mustard greens plays a central role in the region's cuisine. It is a versatile ingredient that enhances countless dishes. Pickled mustard greens is also used in dishes like stewed ribs, braised pork, boiled fish, stir-fried beef and stir-fried pig intestines and fried pork stomach slice, all of which are local favorites. Additionally, pickled mustard greens contains organic acids and lactic acid bacteria, which aid digestion and stimulate the appetite. Culturally, it holds symbolic meaning at banquets, representing the hope for good sons and grandsons.

In 2018, the technique of making pickled mustard greens in Tengxian County was listed in the fifth batch of Wuzhou municipal intangible cultural heritage items.

The Inheritance Pedigree of Making Pickled Mustard Greens in Tengxian County

Generation	Name	Gender	Nationality	Education Background	Year of Craft Leanring	Means of Inheritance
First	Chen Songsheng	Male	Han	Unknown	Unknown	Family inheritance
Second	Chen Xulin	Male	Han	Unknown	1920	Family inheritance
Second	Chen Zucai	Male	Han	Unknown	Unknown	Apprenticeship
Third	Chen Jingji	Male	Han	Junior high school	1967	Family inheritance
Third	Chen Jianqiang	Male	Han	Senior high school	1988	Family inheritance
Third	Xu Zixin	Male	Han	Primary school	1995	Apprenticeship
Fourth	Chen Hongfeng	Male	Han	Junior high school	1997	Family inheritance
Fourth	Xu Jingdu	Male	Han	Junior high school	2000	Apprenticeship

藤县抢花炮

○ 黄静

藤县抢花炮起于何时、源于何方已经难以考究，村中老人说，自古有村就有庙，有庙才有抢花炮。根据象棋镇甘村大社庙的存在历史推算，抢花炮在藤县应该有八九百年的历史了。

一个小铁环，状如钥匙圈，裹上红绸带，绑个漂亮的蝴蝶结，看上去像一朵花，置于火药筒上面，名曰"花炮"。吉时到，组织者一声令下，点燃火药筒，"砰"的一声铁环被冲上半空，参与者朝着铁环跌落的方向一拥而上，争相抢夺，是为"抢花炮"。

藤县是古百越聚居之地，各个氏族有不同的宗教信仰。他们相信，经过社庙开光的花炮拥有神秘的力量，可以帮助他们得到好运、心想事成。所以他们以自己的心愿来命名花炮，比如"添丁炮""发财炮""婚姻炮"等。参与者可以视自身需要选择抢哪一个炮。社庙组织的抢花炮活动，成为每年一次的盛会，吸引周边的群众前来参加或者围观。

藤县抢花炮的分布区域曾经遍及全县乡村，但是随着社会的发展变化，很多地方已经不举办了，现在是以藤县象棋镇甘村和岭景镇篁村为代表。这两处的抢花炮活动数百年来长盛不衰，与当地的社庙香火鼎盛、声名远扬分不开。

抢花炮一般在收割后的稻田等开阔的地方进行。用红绳围定一个圈，抢花炮者在这个圈定的位置内抢夺，抢到者要跑出红绳圈定的范围才算胜出。抢夺过程是有规则的，比如不能故意用脚踢人，不能使用管制刀具等。违反规则的话就算跑出了圈定的范围也不算数。

花炮 / 何家海 摄

藤县抢花炮

抢花炮 / 欧伟文　摄

这一天一般还有舞龙舞狮助兴。获胜者举着花炮，被龙狮簇拥着，在欢乐的锣鼓声中去到花炮管理委员会（简称"炮委会"）登记处登记，然后买肉杀鸡，带上贡品到社庙拜谢神灵，把花炮请回家中好生供奉。以后每一年到了抢花炮那天都要抬着花炮的牌位，带上贡品，有的人家还请狮队助兴，敲锣打鼓来社庙拜祭，叫作汇炮，意思是社庙历年放出去的花炮都来集中一下。等到主家愿望达成，就要自觉地把花炮还给炮委会，由炮委会当年放出，给别的人家来抢。依此类推。

抢花炮由各村社庙的炮委会统一组织进行，每个村抢花炮的日期不同，象棋镇甘村是在农历正月十四举行，俗称"十四炮"，岭景镇篁村是在农历正月初四举行。

抢花炮既是一项民间体育活动，也是一项群众祈福活动。近年来，为了照顾那些实在非常需要，但又没有体力、没有能力抢花炮的家庭，象棋镇甘村的炮委会通过抽签的形式把花炮送给这些家庭供奉。另外，有些远道而来的客人，只要有诚心，也可以向炮委会申请抽签，通过抽签的形式得到花炮。这也使得这个小山村的花炮更加闻名，每年的抢花炮活动更加隆重、热闹。

2018年，藤县抢花炮列入第五批市级非物质文化遗产代表性项目名录。

祭供花炮／杨定登　摄

藤县抢花炮

藤县抢花炮传承谱系

代别	姓名	性别	民族	学历	学艺时间（年）	传承方式
第一代	陈进杰	男	汉	私塾	1961	师徒传承
第一代	黎棣年	男	汉	私塾	1961	师徒传承
第一代	黎棣枢	男	汉	私塾	1966	师徒传承
第二代	陈进文	男	汉	初中	1972	师徒传承
第二代	陈进科	男	汉	初中	1978	师徒传承
第二代	陈家永	男	汉	高中	1983	师徒传承
第二代	陈永华	男	汉	初中	1997	师徒传承
第三代	程志佳	男	汉	高中	2004	师徒传承
第三代	甘浩光	男	汉	高中	2003	师徒传承
第三代	蒙敏英	男	汉	高中	2009	师徒传承

祭供花炮 / 杨定登 摄

Hua Pao (Fire Cracker Ball) in Tengxian County

· Huang Jing ·

The precise origins of fire cracker ball in Tengxian County are difficult to ascertain. According to local elders, a temple has existed in the village since ancient times, and it is the sole provider of fire crackers. Historical records from the Grand Temple of Gan Village in Xiangqi Town suggest that the practice of fire cracker ball may date back 800 to 900 years in Tengxian County.

The fire cracker ball used in this tradition consist of a small iron ring, resembling a key ring, wrapped in a red ribbon and tied into a decorative bow that resembles a flower. This item, known as "Hua Pao" (a type of traditional Chinese fire cracker), is placed atop a powder cartridge. When the time is deemed auspicious, the organizer signals for the cartridge to be ignited. A loud "Bang!" occurs as the iron ring is launched into the air, prompting participants to rush toward its descent, competing to catch it while shouting in excitement. This activity is referred to as "fire cracker ball".

Tengxian County is home to the ancient Baiyue people, whose clans possess diverse religious beliefs. However, they share a common practice of expressing these beliefs through their local community temples. Many villages are rich in stories and legends about the establishment and continuity of their settlements, with villagers believing that the deities they honor in the temples, who once provided assistance and good fortune, possess mysterious supernatural powers. Consequently, the fire crackers associated with the temple are also thought to carry these mystical attributes,

藤县抢花炮

believed to help fulfill the villagers' wishes. As a result, fire crackers are named according to their intended purposes, such as "fire cracker ball of child" (symbolizing the birth of children), "fire cracker ball of wealth" (representing fortune), and "fire cracker ball of marriage". Participants select which fire cracker ball to pursue based on their individual needs. The annual fire cracker ball event organized by the community temple has evolved into a significant festival, drawing large crowds from neighboring areas.

Historically, fire cracker ball was practiced across numerous villages in the county. However, with societal changes, many such events have ceased. Currently, the tradition is primarily represented by Gan Village in Xiangqi Town and Huang Village in Lingjing Town. These two locations have maintained the practice for centuries, closely linked to the prosperity and reputation of their local community temples.

The event typically takes place in open areas, such as rice fields after harvest. A circle is delineated with a red rope, designating the area where participants compete to grab the fire cracker ball. To win, a participant must exit the confines of the rope circle. Specific rules govern the event, such as prohibitions against intentionally tripping competitors or using controlled knives. Violating these rules results in disqualification, even if the participant successfully escapes the designated area.

The festivities are often accompanied by loong and lion dances.

The winner, holding the fire cracker ball, is surrounded by dancers and proceeds to the registered office of the fire cracker ball committee, accompanied by the joyous sounds of gongs and drums. Upon returning home, the winner slaughters a chicken, purchases meat, and brings offerings to the community temple to pay homage to the deities. The fire cracker balls are then taken home for a ceremonial sacrifice. Subsequently, every year on the day of the event, families carry the memorial tablet of the fire cracker balls and present tributes. Some families even invite lion dancers to perform and play drums and gongs in celebration at the temple, a practice known as "Hui Pao", symbolizing the gathering of fire cracker balls over the years. When a family's wish is fulfilled, they are expected to return the fire cracker balls to the committee, which then releases them for others to compete for in subsequent events.

The game of fire cracker ball is organized by the administrative committee of the temple in each village. The dates of the event vary by village; for instance, Gan Village in Xiangqi Town holds its event on the 14th day of the first lunar month, commonly known as the "the 14th fire cracker ball", while Huang Village in Lingjing Town celebrates on the fourth day of the first lunar month.

Fire cracker ball serves not only as a folk sport but also as a communal blessing activity. In recent years, to assist families in need who may lack the physical ability to participate, the Gan Village Fire Cracker Ball Committee has introduced a lottery system to distribute fire cracker balls to these families. Additionally, sincere guests from afar can also apply for fire cracker balls through this lottery system, further enhancing the significance and recognition of the fire cracker ball in this small mountain village, making the annual event more solemn and lively.

In 2018, fire cracker ball in Tengxian County was included in the fifth batch of Wuzhou intangible cultural heritage representative items.

The Inheritance Pedigree of Fire Cracker Ball in Tengxian County

Generation	Name	Gender	Nationality	Education Background	Year of Craft Leanring	Means of Inheritance
First	Chen Jinjie	Male	Han	Old-style private school	1961	Apprenticeship
	Li Dinian	Male	Han	Old-style private school	1961	Apprenticeship
	Li Dishu	Male	Han	Old-style private school	1966	Apprenticeship
Second	Chen Jinwen	Male	Han	Junior high school	1972	Apprenticeship
	Chen Jinke	Male	Han	Junior high school	1978	Apprenticeship
	Chen Jiayong	Male	Han	Senior high school	1983	Apprenticeship
	Chen Yonghua	Male	Han	Junior high school	1997	Apprenticeship
Third	Cheng Zhijia	Male	Han	Senior high school	2004	Apprenticeship
	Gan Haoguang	Male	Han	Senior high school	2003	Apprenticeship
	Meng Minying	Male	Han	Senior high school	2009	Apprenticeship

藤县木偶制作技艺

○ 陈志锋

多姿多彩的木偶造型 / 梁斯瑜 摄

木偶在古代叫傀儡、魁儡子、窟儡子，指木刻偶像（用木头雕刻的人像或者形似其他生物的小东西）。木偶制作技艺和木偶戏在藤县具有悠久的历史。

藤县位于广西壮族自治区东部，东接龙圩、长洲，南连岑溪、容县，西邻平南，北靠蒙山、昭平。浔江自西向东流贯穿藤县中部，特殊的地理环境使得藤县水路畅通，码头货运便利，从唐朝至清朝末期这里便已成为全国商品的集散地。南北商贾云集，文武官员、骚人墨客汇聚，沟通了中原与南越的文化交流。木偶戏也随经贸往来，由水路登陆玉林，最后由陆路传到藤县。据老艺人世代相传，木偶戏是明末清初传入藤县的。木偶是木偶戏的道具，也是"演员"，因此木偶与木偶戏如影随形，相伴而生，而木偶制作技艺也因此产生。藤县木偶制作技艺也是从这时开始，后来经艺人在实践中不断完善、创新，形成今天的木偶。

木偶造型 / 何锦奋 摄

藤县木偶制作技艺

木偶制作技艺是一项集雕刻、涂色、配制头饰和服装于一体的复杂技艺。所需的材料主要有本地蓝木、柚子木、水彩涂料、青漆、布料、圆珠子、珠片、花、中国结、红绳、小棍子、铁丝，所需的工具主要有锯、刀、凿子、刨、砂纸等。木偶制作技艺主要是用木雕刻木偶模型和绘制脸谱，所以"刻"和"绘"是主要的制作技法。木偶脸谱上绘眼睛、眉毛、耳朵、嘴、鼻，有的木偶衣服上、头饰上有五颜六色的圆珠、珠片。

制作一个木偶首先要选用本地的蓝木、柚子木制成木偶模型。据木偶匠人说，蓝木木材是散孔材，纹理通直，结构细致，黄白色，纵切面色更淡，材质软而轻，极易加工，干燥后不变形、不开裂，材色雅致美观，纵切面有光泽，适于做轻巧上等家具和印章、雕刻版画，是做木偶的首选材质。制作时匠人会从深山老林选取上等的蓝木，趁木材生湿时加工成木偶的头部、躯干、手臂，等干燥后，用砂纸人工打磨，然后涂肉色，上脸颊胭脂，做出木偶的各个部件，再根据戏剧的不同角色画出五官，最后装上躯干、手臂，缝制衣服、装上头饰等。制作一个木偶一般耗时 10 天左右。木偶制作是一门高难度的、细致的纯手工技艺，这门技艺靠师傅言传身教来传承。学木偶制作这门技艺的学徒要有绘画基础，才容易学习和提高。木偶制作技艺与民间传统工艺美术紧密联系，通过木偶形象及道具来反映出角色的特征，对研究民间艺术发展史及藤县风情习俗具有重要价值。

木偶是演木偶戏的道具。受民俗审美风尚的影响，各地木偶造型呈现出不同的地域特征。藤县的木偶戏在藤县南部主要分布在同心镇、金鸡镇、新庆镇、天平镇，在藤县北部主要分布在濛江镇、和平镇、太平镇、东荣镇、大黎镇。与此相适应，这些地方都有木偶制作的作坊。木偶造型精巧，表演时，木偶的头部、手臂、肘、腕和腰等各部位都能灵活自如活动，极为

| 藤县非遗传录 |

老匠人与木偶 / 梁斯瑜　摄

木偶制作的部分工具 / 何柏　摄

生动形象。藤县木偶色彩丰富，根据人物在故事中的角色设定脸谱、头部饰物、服饰颜色。其色彩运用反映了不同历史年代藤县各乡的风土人情，具有浓郁的地方色彩。

　　藤县木偶制作技艺历史悠久。现在藤县比较出名的木偶作坊是藤县天平镇新大村的作坊，这个作坊一共有3个匠人。他们的木偶，制作技艺出类拔萃，具有地方特色。这个作坊的匠人，既能制作木偶，又能表演当地的木偶戏，自给自足。师傅林柱成说他从小对杖头木偶很感兴趣，有一定的美工基础，经过自学摸

藤县木偶制作技艺

木偶制作组图 / 何柏 摄

索制作木偶。他现在收有一个徒弟，言传身教传授木偶制作技艺，再由他传给下一代，使木偶制作技艺一代一代传承下去。

2022年，藤县木偶制作技艺列入第六批市级非物质文化遗产代表性项目名录。

藤县木偶制作技艺代表性传承人

级别	姓名	性别	出生时间（年）	认定时间（年）
市级	林柱成	男	1946	2023
县级	麦普壬	男	1956	2019
县级	黄桂荣	男	1961	2019

Puppet–Making Craft in Tengxian County

Chen Zhifeng ·

The craft of puppet-making, historically referred to as "*Kuilei*", "*Kuileizi*", or "*Kuleizi*", involves the creation of wooden idols and similar figures. This tradition has a long-standing history in Tengxian County.

Located in the southeast of the Guangxi, Tengxian County borders Cangwu to the east, Cenxi and Rong County to the south, Pingnan to the west, and Mengshan and Zhaoping to the north. The Xunjiang River, a major waterway in Guangxi, flows through the center of Tengxian County from west to east. The area's unique geographical features allow for unobstructed waterways, facilitating convenient freight transport. From the Tang Dynasty to the Qing Dynasty, Tengxian County became a hub for trade, attracting merchants from both northern and southern regions, as well as civil and military officials, poets, and writers. This vibrant exchange of goods and culture fostered significant cultural interactions between the Central Plains and South Vietnam. Puppetry, as a cultural form, spread alongside these economic exchanges, reaching Yulin by water and subsequently flowing north. According to local artists, puppetry was introduced to Tengxian County in the late Ming and early Qing dynasties. As the props of puppetry, puppets serve as the "actors" of this art form, resulting in the emergence of puppet-making techniques in the region. Over time, through continuous refinement and innovation by artisans, the contemporary practice of puppetry has evolved.

藤县木偶制作技艺

新制作的木偶 / 何锦奋 摄

Puppet-making encompasses a complex array of artistic skills, including carving, coloring, and the creation of headdresses and costumes. The primary materials used are local blue wood and pomelo wood, while the essential tools include saws, knives, chisels, planes, sandpaper, watercolor paints, cloth, beads, flowers, Chinese knots, red ropes, and more. Additional related products, such as small sticks and iron wire, are also utilized. The puppet-making craft primarily involves carving puppet models from wood and painting facial features, where "engraving" and "painting" are the main production techniques that define the craft. Artisans paint the eyes, eyebrows, ears, mouth, and nose on the puppet's face, and some puppets are adorned with colorful beads on their clothing and headdresses.

The puppet-making process begins with selecting local blue wood and pomelo wood to create the puppet model. According to artisans, blue wood is characterized by its loose texture, fine grain, and yellowish-white hue, with a lighter longitudinal section. This material is soft, lightweight, and easy to process, showing no deformation or cracking upon drying. Its elegant color and glossy longitudinal section make it ideal for crafting delicate and fine furniture, seals, prints, and engravings, rendering it the optimal

形态各异的木偶 / 欧伟文　摄

choice for puppet-making. When the wood is still moist, artisans shape the head, torso, and arms of the puppet. After the pieces have dried, they are polished manually with sandpaper. Next, flesh tones are applied, and the upper cheeks are painted with rouge to define the puppet's features. The five sensory organs are painted according to the character's role in the play, and finally, the body and arms are assembled, and the clothing and head ornaments are tailored. The entire process typically takes about ten days to complete. Puppet-making is a highly skilled and meticulous craft passed down through the teachings and practices of master artisans. Apprentices seeking to learn this art must possess a foundation in painting, facilitating their understanding, learning, and improvement. Puppet-making crafts are closely related to traditional folk arts, with puppet designs and props reflecting the characteristics of the characters, thereby holding significant value for the study of the development of folk art and the customs of Tengxian County.

　　Puppets serve as props in puppet shows, and regional folk aesthetics influence their shapes, resulting in distinct characteristics across different areas. In Tengxian County, puppetry is primarily concentrated in Tongxin Town, Jinji Town, Xinqing Town, and Taiping Town in the southern part, while the northern region includes Mengjiang Town, Heping Town, Dongrong Town, and Dali Town. Workshops dedicated to puppet-making exist in these towns. The puppets are often exquisitely crafted, allowing for flexibility and expressiveness in their movements during performances. Tengxian County's puppets are known for their vibrant colors. The colors of facial makeup, hair ornaments, and clothing are uniquely decorated according to each character's role in the story. The use of color reflects the historical context of Tengxian County, emphasizing local characteristics.

With a long history of puppet-making, Tengxian County is home to many skilled artisans. The most notable workshop is in Xinda Village, Tianping Town, which comprises three craftsmen. The puppets produced here exhibit maturity and distinctive local traits, and the craftsmanship is outstanding. The artisans not only create puppets but also perform puppet shows, aiming for self-sufficiency. One prominent master, Lin Zhucheng, who possesses a solid artistic foundation, has a keen interest in rod head puppetry since his childhood and has learned the craft through self-study. He currently has an apprentice, to whom he plans to impart the skills of puppet-making, ensuring the continuity of this art form for future generations.

In 2022, the puppet-making craft in Tengxian County was included in the sixth batch of Wuzhou intangible cultural heritage representative items.

The Representative Inheritors of the Puppet-making Craft in Tengxian County

Level	Name	Gender	Year of Birth	Time of Certification
Municipal	Lin Zhucheng	Male	1946	2023
County	Mai Puren	Male	1956	2019
County	Huang Guirong	Male	1961	2019

藤县赛龙舟习俗

○ 卢瑞昌

藤县赛龙舟习俗由来已久。浔江沿岸的藤城、濛江、南安、赤水、白马,蒙江沿岸的和平、太平,北流河沿岸的老鸦塘、金鸡、双竞等地,每年农历五月初五(端午节)都以自发组织赛龙舟的方式纪念屈原。新中国成立后,多由政府组织赛龙舟活动。

藤县赛龙舟习俗曾见于明朝翰林学士解缙《双竞驿》那首脍炙人口的诗篇"双竞驿前双小洲,年年于此竞龙舟。翻思夺锦青天上,河汉江声共北流"。诗中描述的就是双竞驿(今藤县象棋镇双竞村)旁的北流河上民间赛龙舟的画面。

旧时的龙舟与普通船只不同,长短大小不一,龙舟一般狭长细窄。藤县龙舟一般长约10米,中舱最宽处0.96米左右。桨叶长0.5米,宽0.16米,桨全长1.38米。船头装上一个木雕龙头,船尾装上一个龙尾,船身画上彩色,有金龙、黄龙、青龙、白龙、黑龙等,惟妙惟肖,栩栩如生,精气神十足,特别吸引人们的眼球。如今,赛龙舟已与国际接轨,有统一的舟、桨标准和竞赛规则。

藤县赛龙舟有一整套习俗。每年的农历二月初二龙抬头这一天,择吉时将去年赛事结束后埋在泥

藤县赛龙舟习俗

力争上游 / 霍雨锋 摄

新龙下水 / 霍雨锋　摄

水里的龙舟起出水面，谓升龙。升龙仪式一般由龙舟队牵头，会同各界热心人士参与。吉时到，龙舟队员焚香鸣炮，狮鼓助阵，祭拜河神龙母，祈福人民安居乐业，顺风顺水，水头十足（意为财源滚滚）。接着龙舟运动员进入江中把龙舟起出水面，清理冲洗干净后，便进入开龙仪式。开龙仪式是先把龙头龙尾安装在龙舟上，邀请德高望重者点睛（用朱砂圈涂龙头的眼珠）。点睛毕，由点睛者宣布"开龙"，龙舟上早已准备好的运动员齐声欢呼"开——龙——"。龙舟满桨奋飞，顺水顺时针转上一圈，寓意万事顺利！然后会进行一场友谊赛，升龙、开龙仪式结束，便进入为期3个多月的全面系统训练，迎接五月初五（端午节）的龙舟大赛。

　　藤县赛龙舟的赛场设在县城边的浔江上，起点为旧港务站旁边的游泳码头，终点在旧中胜火电厂泵站，保持传统的全程5000米的长距离竞赛。端午节的龙舟大赛现场，一河两岸、屋顶甚至树上，人头攒动，人声鼎沸。河中，随着裁判的发令枪"呼"的一声，敲锣打鼓，鞭炮齐鸣，龙舟如离弦之箭，运动员吆喝声声，你追我赶，赛道里桨人合一，水花翻飞，赛道外的裁判船、工作船、观摩船也在不断调整最佳角度、速度，犹如另一个竞赛场景，难怪解学士写出了"翻思夺锦青天上，河汉江声共北流"。龙舟比赛结束，胜者烧鞭炮庆贺，领奖品（烧猪等），抬回祠堂拜祭，然后团队聚餐，集体吃烧猪狂欢。之后，把龙舟重新埋进河边的泥水里。至此，整套仪式结束。

藤县大地山水相依，境内江河密布，水系发达，赛龙舟习俗代代相传。"海纳百川，力争上游"的理念深深地烙印在藤县人民的精神血脉里。藤县龙舟队在梧州市举办的历届龙舟赛中都有获奖。特别是在 2022 年 10 月 26 日至 27 日，在贵港市平南县江北公园边的浔江江面举办的广西壮族自治区第十五届运动会群众赛事活动"禾乐杯"龙舟比赛。本次比赛参赛队伍分别来自柳州市、梧州市、防城港市、贵港市、百色市和贺州市。由藤县人组成的梧州市代表队在男子 22 人 100 米、200 米、500 米直道赛，男子 12 人 100 米、200 米、500 米直道赛中囊括了所有男子项目的冠军。

"藤县年年竞龙舟，百舸争流竞上游。"这是藤县民间广为流传的俚语。赛龙舟作为藤县人民喜爱的一种传统体育活动，很好地保留了一套赛龙舟习俗。

2022 年，藤县赛龙舟习俗列入第六批市级非物质文化遗产代表性项目名录。

The Custom of Loong Boat Racing in Tengxian County

· Lu Ruichang ·

The custom of loong boat racing is an ancient traditional folk activity with a rich history in Tengxian County. Every year, on the fifth day of the fifth lunar month, spontaneous loong boat races are held along the Xunjiang River in Tengcheng, Mengjiang, Nanan, Chishui, and Baima, as well as along the Mengjiang River in Heping and Taiping, and along the Beiliu River in Laoyatang, Jinji, and Shuangjing. These races commemorate Qu Yuan. Since the founding of People's Republic of China, many of these races have been organized by the government as competitive events.

The history of loong boat racing in Tengxian County is documented in the well-known poem *Shuangjing Post*, written by the esteemed Ming Dynasty scholar Xie Jin. Xie Jin, who was demoted to Guangxi in February during the fifth year of the Yongle reign, composed the poem while residing in Tengcheng. His verses vividly capture the folk tradition of loong boat racing in Tengxian County: "Shuangjing Post, located in front of two small islands, is the site of annual loong boat races. One cannot help but envision victory under the vast blue sky, as the Milky Way seems to flow in harmony with the Beiliu River."

Distinct from ordinary vessels, loong boats in Tengxian County measure about 10 meters in length, with the widest part of the middle cabin approximately 0.96 meters. The blade measures 0.5 meters long and 0.16 meters wide, while the total length of the paddle is 1.38 meters. The bow is adorned with a loong head, and the

藤县赛龙舟习俗

奋勇争先 / 欧伟文　摄

stern features a wood-carved loong tail. The hulls are painted in vibrant colors, depicting golden, yellow, green, white, and black loongs, creating an eye-catching and dynamic appearance. Currently, these loong boats comply with international standards, featuring uniform specifications for both the boats and paddles, along with established competition rules.

　　Loong boat racing in Tengxian County is accompanied by a rich array of customs. On the second day of the second lunar month each year, the loong boat that was submerged after the previous year's race is ceremoniously retrieved at an auspicious time, a practice known as "loong-raising" (a local dialect term signifying the retrieval of the loong boat). This ceremony is typically led by the loong boat team and attended by enthusiastic community members. A large audience gathers to witness the event. When the auspicious moment arrives, participants burn incense and fire guns, using lion drums to honor the River God and Loong Mother, while praying for the well-being of the community and wishing for peace, contentment, and prosperity for all. Following this, the loong boat athletes enter the river to lift the boat out of the water. After cleaning and washing, they commence the Kailong ceremony (another local term referring to the traditional painting of the loong's eyes on the boat, symbolizing the eye-opening of the loong). Once the finishing touch is completed, the individual who performed the task announces "*kailong*", and all on board cheer in response. The loong boat then glides swiftly along the river, turning clockwise to signify good fortune. A friendly match may follow. After the "loong-raising" and Kailong ceremonies, the teams engage in comprehensive and systematic training for over three months in preparation for the loong boat races held during the Duanwu Festival on the fifth day of the fifth lunar month.

The loong boat races in Tengxian County take place on the Xunjiang River in the county town, starting opposite the swimming dock near the old port station and ending at the pumping station of the old Zhongsheng Thermal Power Plant, maintaining a traditional long-distance race of 5,000 meters. During the races, crowds gather along both banks of the river, with some spectators even climbing onto rooftops to view the event. The Kailong ceremony involves assembling the loong head and tail on the boat and inviting esteemed guests. With the sound of the referee's starting gun, gongs and drums echo, and firecrackers are set off. The loong boats surge forward like arrows, with athletes shouting and vying for position. The oarsmen coordinate their efforts, splashing water as they race. Meanwhile, the referee boat, work boat, and observation boat maneuver to capture the best angles and speeds, creating an exhilarating atmosphere. As Xie Jin wrote, "One cannot help but envision victory under the vast blue sky, as the Milky Way seems to flow in harmony with the Beiliu River." After the loong boat race, the winning team celebrates with firecrackers. Their prizes, including a roast pig, were carried to the ancestral hall for worship, followed by a communal meal. Afterward, the loong boat was ceremoniously buried in the mud by the river, marking the end of the ritual.

Tengxian County, a region of mountains and rivers, boasts a well-developed water system, making the loong boat race a beloved traditional sport. The spirit of the loong boat race—embodied in the saying "Absorb all rivers into the sea and strive for the upper reaches"—runs deep in the people of Tengxian. The Tengxian County loong boat team has consistently won prizes in previous races held in Wuzhou City. Notably, from October 26 to October 27, 2022, the team participated in the "Hele Cup" loong boat race, a major mass sporting event of the 15th Games of Guangxi. This competition, held on the Xunjiang River in Jiangbei Park, Pingnan County, Guigang City, featured teams from cities such as Liuzhou, Wuzhou, Fangchenggang, Guigang, Baise, and Hezhou. The Wuzhou team, composed of people from Tengxian County, has secured victories in all twenty-two men's races, including the 100-meter, 200-meter, and 500-meter straight races.

Every year, Tengxian County competes for loong boats, with hundreds of boats vying for the upper reaches. This traditional sport is deeply ingrained in the county's culture.

In 2022, the custom of loong boat racing was listed in the sixth batch of municipal intangible cultural heritage items in Wuzhou City.

藤县彩龙编织技艺

○ 孙燕凤

藤县民间流行舞龙活动，以此为节日营造欢乐祥和的氛围。藤县彩龙编织技艺随舞龙活动而生。

藤县彩龙编织技艺起源于何时没有文字记载，但民间不乏编织彩龙的高手，使这一纯手工活得以世代相传。

彩龙编织主要的工具和材料有竹篾、铁丝、白色纱纸、纱布、立德粉、油漆、龙头饰物（玻璃珠、照妖镜、吊球等）、龙被以及竹竿等。

竹篾是主要材料，一般选取较老的单竹。为了增加竹篾的柔软度、韧性和防虫，民间艺人有的烧开水将竹篾煮15分钟，有的也将竹篾放进水中浸泡2~3天，捞起晾干后便可以使用了。

彩龙的编织要经过砍竹、破篾、熏篾、织龙头、织龙尾、扎龙身、弯龙鳍、安龙珠、装龙头撑竹、平整龙头、龙头上色、上枣（装饰品）、缝制龙被、画龙鳞、装龙、开光16道工序，全靠手艺人手工制作，历时一个半月左右。彩龙编织是精细活，对技术的要求较高，每道工序都需要细磨慢做，才能编织出栩栩如生的彩龙。

彩龙由龙头、龙身、龙尾3部分构成，其中龙身有5节，因此彩龙又称为"七节龙"，每一节独立存在。龙身用3条绳子串起来，这3条绳子像人的筋骨一样贯穿全身，俗称"龙筋"。

首先从龙头开始，这是彩龙编织中难度最大、最复杂的。龙头长约1.3米，有龙角、龙眼、龙嘴等，像人的五官一样生动有趣。龙颈由7个圆箍组成，从后面往前数，在第5个圆箍前编织龙喉，最前面开龙口，有下巴和上、下腭。上腭还要编织出

藤县彩龙编织技艺

彩龙 / 何柏 摄

龙髻、龙鼻子、龙角、龙眼睛（装上灯泡），这样一个栩栩如生的龙头便编织好了。

其次是龙身。龙身编织相对简单些，由5节圆柱形圆筒组成，有点像农人织的箩筐，长度不一：第一节略长，第二、第三节同长，第四、第五节略短。这样织出来的彩龙结实匀称，舞动时灵活，游刃有余。

最后是龙尾。龙尾呈弯弯的圆锥形，长约2.1米，由13个圆箍组成，并用纱纸扎实，收尾时聪明的手艺人向外编织出一朵花的形状，昭示人们的生活如花般幸福美好。

新制作的龙被 / 何锦奋　摄

制作龙身 / 韦相　摄

彩龙编织好后，接着是上色和画龙鳞。上色即是在龙头、龙尾上绘画。在编织好的龙头、龙尾里外覆盖上一层纱纸，用糨糊粘稳，将各种涂料画上去：以黄色作为底色，再涂抹上红、蓝、绿等几种艳丽且有强烈视觉冲击力的色彩，特别是龙头，要用大红、大绿、亮黄等颜料，画出龙角、龙耳朵、龙牙齿等，还有各种装饰纹，色彩鲜艳，惟妙惟肖。尤其是张开的血盆大嘴，伸出一条长长的舌头，四周锋利的牙齿，形象逼真。涂抹了涂料的龙尾，红黄黑相间，活像一片片金光闪闪的鱼鳞，色彩斑斓，鲜艳夺目。龙鳞画在覆盖龙脊的龙被上。龙被中间选用黄色（也有用红色）布料，两边取红色（或其他颜色）布料，在中间画上惟妙惟肖的龙鳞，红色花边保留原来布料的花草蝴蝶等图案。舞龙时红色的花边恰似少女的裙裾散开，飘逸潇洒，红红火火。彩龙编织好并上色后，套上龙被并扎稳，再选吉日开光，一条活灵活现的彩龙便诞生了。

2022年，藤县彩龙编织技艺列入第六批市级非物质文化遗产代表性项目名录。

藤县彩龙编织技艺代表性传承人

级别	姓名	性别	出生时间（年）	认定时间（年）
县级	麦宏玉	男	1946	2019
县级	周家旺	男	1976	2019

The Weaving Technique of Colorful Loong in Tengxian County

· Sun Yanfeng ·

To enhance the festive, joyful, and peaceful atmosphere, folk loong dance activities are prevalent in Tengxian County, distinguished by their vibrant loong totems and rhythmic drumbeats. These celebrations, full of life and renewal, inspire excitement and joy among the people.

While there are no written records of when the colorful loong weaving technique originated, numerous folk artisans have preserved this tradition, passing down the techniques of this entirely handmade craft through generations.

The primary materials and tools for colorful loong weaving include bamboo strips, iron wire, white yarn paper, mosquito netting, instant glue, various paints, and loong head ornaments (glass beads, demonic mirrors, and drop balls), loong quilt and bamboo poles.

Bamboo strips are the essential material, with artisans typically selecting mature Dan bamboo for its flexibility, strength, and resistance to pests. Some artisans boil the bamboo strips for about 15 minutes and then soak them in water for two to three days before allowing them to dry.

The process of creating a colorful loong involves sixteen distinct steps, including cutting bamboo, preparing bamboo strips, smoking the strips, weaving the loong's tail, tying the loong's body, bending the loong's fins, installing bamboo supports, leveling the loong's tail, adding decorative elements, sewing the loong quilt, painting loong

藤县彩龙编织技艺

活灵活现的彩龙 / 韦相 摄

scales, and finally, "opening the light" — a ceremonial completion. This intricate process takes about one and a half months, during which meticulous attention to detail is required. Only through dedication to craftsmanship can an artisan produce a high-quality loong.

The colorful loong consists of three main parts: the head, body, and tail. The body is divided into five sections, giving the loong its common name, "the loong with seven sections." Each section is independent but connected by three ropes that run through the loong's entire body, functioning like its muscles and bones, colloquially referred to as "loong tendons".

The most challenging part of the process is weaving the loong head, which is approximately 1.3 meters long and features vivid loong horns, eyes, and a mouth, resembling lifelike human expressions. The loong's neck consists of seven round hoops, with the loong throat woven at the front of the fifth hoop. The front of the head is intricately designed with an upper and lower jaw, a loong bun on the palate, a nose, horns, and illuminated eyes (where light bulbs are installed). The result is a vivid and lifelike loong head.

The loong body, though simpler to create than the head, consists of five cylindrical sections resembling farmers' baskets. Each section varies slightly in length: the first section is the longest, the second and third are equal in length, and the fourth and fifth are shorter. This structure ensures the loong's strength, symmetry, and flexibility during performances.

The loong's tail, a curved cone approximately 2.1 meters long, consists of 13 round hoops. Once woven, it is consolidated with gauze paper. At the end of the tail, the artisan skillfully shapes it into a flower-like form, symbolizing happiness and prosperity.

After weaving, the loong is decorated through a process known as "coloring". The loong head and tail are first covered with yarn paper inside and out, glued to increase stability. A base coat of yellow paint is applied, followed by vibrant red, blue, green, and iron red hues. Special attention is given to the head, where red, green, and bright yellow are used to accentuate the loong's features, including its horns, ears, and teeth, as well as decorative patterns. The result is a ferocious yet vivid loong, with a long tongue and sharp teeth. The loong's tail is painted in red, yellow, and black, resembling glittering fish scales. The loong quilt, which covers the spine, is adorned with painted scales. Typically, the middle section of the quilt is made of yellow or red cloth, with other colored fabrics on either side. Decorative patterns, such as flowers and butterflies, are painted on the cloth, while red lace, reminiscent of a girl's skirt, adds to the loong's lively appearance during the dance, symbolizing prosperity and abundance. Once the weaving and coloring are complete, the colorful loong is set in place and fixed. A ceremonial event is held on an auspicious day to celebrate the loong's creation, marking the birth of a vibrant, lifelike loong.

In 2022, the weaving craft of colorful loong in Tengxian County was listed in the sixth batch of Wuzhou intangible cultural heritage representative items.

The Representative Inheritors of the Weaving Technique of Colorful Loong in Tengxian County

Level	Name	Gender	Year of Birth	Time of Certification
County	Mai Hongyu	Male	1946	2019
County	Zhou Jiawang	Male	1976	2019

木面筛

○ 黄锦飞

木面筛是古代聚居太平镇一带的先人流传下来的一种戏曲,类似傩戏,主要流行于太平镇狮山周边村庄。

表演木面筛时,表演者戴木制面具。面具用樟木雕刻而成,刻有人、神、鬼怪、野兽等脸谱,其中人的面具分男人、女人两种类型。表演者边跳边唱,唱腔固定,曲调较为简单。一般由两个表演者戴面具,身穿大红或大绿、大蓝袍服,以对话形式自唱、自白(唱词分上下句式,有韵律),或一问一答。表演者手持单打(小手鼓类乐器),边唱边打,配以表情、动作,滑稽搞笑。所唱内容丰富,有表演驱逐妖魔鬼怪和野兽的情景,也有劝人与人为善、积极向上、辛勤工作等。木面筛表演常见于庙会、社公安龙建醮等活动中,表演者多为道公,演唱时长视内容而定。

木面筛表演 / 周雄　摄

木面筛

木面筛面具 / 周雄 摄

　　木面筛表演不用搭戏台,在地面即可表演,所以又叫地戏。近代庙会说唱、民间丧葬也唱木面筛,庙会时所唱的内容多为祈福之类,而丧葬时唱的内容主要是逝者的事迹和美德,劝勉逝者的子孙后代传承其美德。

　　太平镇柴咀村都更一组的木面筛传承人覃庆荣家保存有较完整的木面筛面具。太平镇柴咀村的村民覃德权以及太平镇德胜街石子垌的吴宏海等都是演木面筛的好手。20世纪50年代后,木面筛鲜少出现。直至20世纪80年代后,农村庙会、社公安龙建醮等活动又兴起演木面筛助兴。

　　木面筛是一种传统色彩浓厚的艺术形式,对于了解藤县本土的生活风情和人文习俗很有帮助。

　　2008年,木面筛列入第一批县级非物质文化遗产代表性项目名录。

Mumian Shai: A Wooden Mask Performance

· *Huang Jinfei* ·

Mumian (wooden mask) Shai is a form of opera that has been passed down by the ancestors of the Taiping area in ancient times. (It bears similarities to Nuo opera, a folk genre that evolved from Nuo dance, which was traditionally performed to expel malevolent spirits.) Mumian Shai is primarily popular in the villages surrounding Lion Mountain in Taiping.

During a Mumian Shai performance, the actors don wooden masks, carved from camphor wood and adorned with facial makeup representing humans, deities, ghosts, and animals. The masks representing humans are classified into two categories: male and female. Performers engage in dance and song, utilizing a fixed and relatively simple melodic structure. Typically, two performers don props (wooden masks) and wear red, green, or blue robes while engaging in dialogue. Their exchanges are structured into upper and lower sentence patterns, often rhythmical, incorporating questions and answers. Accompanied by props such as tambourines, performers sing and play while expressing various facial expressions and movements, which tend to be humorous. The lyrical content often carries an instructive message, addressing themes such as driving away monsters and beasts or encouraging kindness, positivity, and hard work, such as constructing sacrificial altars for ceremonies. Most performers are Taoists, and the duration of the performance varies based on its content.

藤县的木面筛木制面具 / 何锦奋 摄

木面筛

Mumian Shai can be performed on the ground without a stage, which is why it is sometimes referred to as "ground opera". In modern times, it has also been featured in puppet shows, temple fairs, and folk funerals. The performances at temple fairs generally involve prayers for blessings, while those at funerals primarily recount the deeds and virtues of the deceased, encouraging future generations to honor and inherit their legacy.

Qin Qingrong, the inheritor of Mumian Shai in the Dugeng Group of Chaizui Village, Taiping Town, possesses a relatively complete set of Mumian Shai props. Villagers Qin Dequan from Chaizui Village and Wu Honghai from Shizidong, Desheng Street, Taiping, are also skilled practitioners of Mumian Shai. Following the 1950s, performances of Mumian Shai became scarce, but in the 1980s, the tradition was revived at rural temple fairs and Taoist sacrificial ceremonies as a form of entertainment.

Mumian Shai serves as a cultural activity rich in traditional significance, offering valuable insights into the local customs and cultural practices of Tengxian County.

In 2008, Mumian Shai was included in the first batch of county-level intangible cultural heritage representative items.

藤县黑米饭制作工艺

○ 苏海

"三月三"是壮族、黎族、畲族等多民族共同欢庆的重要节日。农历三月初三前后几天，男女老少都会聚集街头村尾、江边、山头欢歌饮宴，甚是隆重热闹。"三月三"在广西主要有以下习俗：制作五色糯米饭、抢花炮、抛绣球、打扁担、赶歌圩、打铜鼓等。

藤县的"三月三"具有浓厚的节日氛围。当地有制作五色糯米饭的习俗，其中以黑糯米饭最为常见。藤县本地还有在农历四月初八（又叫"寒食节"）这一天做黑糯米饭的习惯。黑糯米饭惯称黑米饭、乌黑饭、乌米饭。黑米饭历史由来已久，据说最早出现于唐代，本是道家的养生食物和佛家的斋食。嘉庆二十一年（1816年）版《藤县志》记载："三月三上巳亦作乌米饭相饷""四月八日为三宝佛诞士民用黄花渍米炊饭或乌米饭备香楮酒礼作佛诞会。"清朝亦有诗文记载：

黑米饭 / 霍雨锋 摄

制作黑米饭的鲜嫩枫叶 / 欧伟文 摄

藤县黑米饭制作工艺

黑米饭的历史记录 / 何锦奋　摄

藤江四时风景竹枝词之三

清 · 何耀庚

佳节刚逢三月三，木棉花放遍江潭。

枫叶汁炊乌米饭，沙糖伴食有余甘。

　　黑米饭一般用枫叶捣汁泡米蒸煮而成。吃黑米饭，是一种习俗，家乡的老人们都说，吃了黑米饭，男女老少身壮力健，家族人丁兴旺。"三月三"正是枫树新叶盛长之时，此时采摘枫叶制作黑米饭正合时宜。

　　制作枫叶黑米饭，村里的年长者都是好手。三月初一上午，太阳升起，晨雾散去，乡亲们到山里采摘枫叶。他们会挑选一枝一米左右的枝条折断，连枝带叶带回家中。待到家中，去枝摘叶，将枫叶清洗干净后，放在石器或者铁器里捣杵，直至枫叶被捣杵出汁液。

做黑米饭要用白糯米。一般是选取米粒细长，米身椭圆，色泽乳白或蜡白，不透明的糯米。这种糯米煮熟后，胶结成团，黏性大，不易散开，光亮透明。

把捣碎的枫叶装在大容器里，放上没过枫叶表面的清水，同时放进一两块铁器，如菜刀等一起浸泡，目的是让枫叶汁与铁元素加速反应，这样的枫叶水煮出的米饭会更黑。枫叶里面含有丰富的鞣酸，又叫单宁酸，和铁在常温下就能发生化学反应，使水变成更透亮的黑色。

装枫叶水的容器要放在阴凉通风处，加盖子防虫防鼠，确保干净卫生。

枫叶经过两天的浸泡，发生了一系列的化学反应。到了"三月三"那天，对枫叶水过滤，一般取 80～100 目的滤网进行过滤，去除碎叶。过滤后的枫叶水就可以用来浸泡糯米了。

如果时间允许，把糯米清洗一到两遍，用簸箕或带小孔的篮子沥干，再将沥干水分的糯米放进装枫叶水的容器里浸泡着色，水的高度以过米面一节手指为宜，浸泡时间约两小时后，加上三五滴植物油拌匀，便可煮饭。这个方法的米水比例相对容易控制，煮出的黑米饭软硬适中，清香四溢，晶莹剔透，油黑发亮。

有的人家是先把过滤好的枫叶水煮热，然后把洗好沥干水分的糯米投进去，浸泡至糯米变黑再直接煮成黑米饭。这种方法的用水量比前一种方法的用水量相比更难准确控制，水少了，会出现夹生饭，熟得不够透；水多了，会成烂饭，味寡淡，难以下咽。

还有一种方法是直接用过滤好的常温枫叶水煮饭，但效果相对较差，做出来的黑米饭没有那么清香、透亮发黑。

最基础的黑米饭就是这样煮出来的，俗称斋饭。

藤县黑米饭制作工艺

随着人们生活水平的提高,黑米饭有了升级版。一种是把一些食材诸如芋头粒、红薯粒、玉米、花生、板栗、肉丁、虾仁、瑶柱、腊味等,直接放到锅里同煮。另一种是待黑米饭煮到饭水初干,再把上述食材铺放饭面一起焖煮。

还有一种是炒黑米饭。用枫叶水煲出的饭,黑黝黝的,一粒一粒晶莹透亮,弥漫着枫叶的清香。这时不要急着吃,还要加配料炒香才是真正升级版的黑米饭呢。先把肉丁、香菇、腊肉、腊肠、玉米、花生、青豆、咸鱼、虾仁、瑶柱等自己喜欢的配料炒熟炒香,起锅待用。把黑米饭炒干至粒粒不黏连后,再加入先前准备好的配料炒至香气四溢,最后加入葱花或韭菜,翻炒均匀就可以起锅了。

吃饭之前要先行祭祖之礼,而后一家人围坐一起,吃着香喷喷的黑米饭,尽享天伦之乐。

一碗地道的黑米饭,是"广西好嘢"的产品品牌,也是传承藤县非遗的一道美食。

2013年,藤县黑米饭制作工艺列入第二批县级非物质文化遗产代表性项目名录。

Preparing Black Rice in Tengxian County

Su Hai ·

The day of "Sanyuesan" is an important festival jointly celebrated by many ethnic groups such as the Zhuang, Li, and She ethnic groups. During this time, men, women, and children gather in the streets, villages, by rivers, and on mountains to sing, feast, and celebrate in a lively and solemn atmosphere. In Guangxi, the customs associated with "Sanyuesan" include making five-colored glutinous rice, participating in fire cracker ball competitions, expressing love through hydrangea tossing, engaging in pole games, singing to find romantic partners, and playing bronze drums.

In Tengxian County, "Sanyuesan" also carries a strong festive spirit, with the tradition of making five-colored glutinous rice being particularly widespread. Among the various types, black glutinous rice is the most popular. This tradition also extends to the eighth day of the fourth lunar month (also known as the "Cold Food Festival"), when locals in Tengxian County prepare black glutinous rice. Historically, black glutinous rice was known as black rice, *wuhei* rice, or simply *wu* rice. Its history is rich, with roots tracing back to the Tang Dynasty, when it was considered a Taoist health food and a Buddhist vegetarian delicacy. The 1816-year-eidtion of *Tengxian County Chronicle* notes: "Black rice is also served as a delicacy on the third day of the third lunar month." The same text records that on the eighth day of the fourth lunar month, scholars would prepare incense, wine, and either yellow-flower-dyed rice or black rice as offerings to celebrate the Buddha's birthday. A poet named He

Yaogeng from the Qing Dynasty also captures the festival's spirit in his poem *Third Bamboo's Poem of Teng River's Seasonal Scenery*: "The festival of Sanyuesan has arrived, hibiscus flowers bloom along the riverbanks. Black rice, cooked with maple leaf juice, leaves a lingering sweetness when eaten with sugar."

Black rice is traditionally made by cooking glutinous rice soaked in maple leaf juice. According to traditional Chinese medicine, this type of glutinous rice is believed to have various health benefits, such as promoting digestion, strengthening the spleen and stomach, relieving pain, and supporting kidney function. It is believed that consuming black rice brings health and prosperity to the family. Thus, the production of black rice on Sanyuesan coincides with the budding of new maple leaves, forming a strong association with the festival. Year after year, this dish remains a favorite among locals.

The elders in Tengxian County are skilled in making black rice using maple leaf juice. On the first day of the third lunar month, villagers head to the mountains to collect fresh maple leaves. They break off branches no more than a meter long after the morning fog has lifted and the dew has dried. These branches are brought home, where the leaves are separated and cleaned of any debris. The fresh maple leaves are then pounded in a stone or iron mortar until the juice is extracted.

The main ingredient for cooked black rice is locally grown white glutinous rice. The selected grains are slender, elliptical, and milky white, offering a sticky texture that holds together well after cooking, producing a bright and translucent appearance.

Once the leaves are mashed, the maple leaf juice is placed in a large container and mixed with cold water. One or two iron objects, like a kitchen knife, are submerged in the liquid to trigger a chemical reaction with the maple leaf juice. This process helps enhance the black color of the rice. Maple leaves are rich in tannic acid, which reacts with iron to form ferrous tannate, the main component of iron gall ink. The iron promotes oxidation, making the juice turn a transparent black.

The container is then stored in a cool, ventilated area with a lid to protect the liquid from insects and rodents.

After two days of soaking, the maple leaf juice is filtered using an 80 to 100 mesh sieve to remove any small leaf particles, leaving the liquid ready to soak the glutinous rice.

The glutinous rice is typically rinsed once or twice and then drained. The rice is placed in a container filled with the maple leaf juice, with the liquid level just above the rice. The rice is soaked for about two hours, and a few drops of vegetable oil are added before cooking to enhance the rice's texture and flavor. The ratio of rice to water is easy to control, resulting in perfectly cooked rice that is moderately firm, fragrant, and deep black in color.

Some people prefer to boil the filtered maple leaf juice first, adding the washed and drained glutinous rice to the boiling liquid (commonly known as "shrimp eyes water"). However, this method makes it more difficult to control the water content accurately. Too little water results in undercooked rice, while too much water yields a mushy and flavorless dish.

In some variations, the rice is cooked directly in room-temperature maple leaf juice, although this method produces rice that is less fragrant and lacks the vivid black color.

Initially, black rice was prepared in its simplest form, known as "*zai fan* vegetarian meal", but as living standards have improved, the dish has evolved.

Today, black rice is often cooked with additional ingredients such as taro, sweet potatoes, corn, peanuts, chestnuts, diced meat, shrimp, scallops, and seafood. In one method, the black rice is cooked until the water has evaporated, then topped with the ingredients. Another approach involves stir-frying the rice with these ingredients after the rice is cooked, enhancing both flavor and texture.

When stir-frying black rice, ingredients such as diced meat, mushrooms, sausage, corn, peanuts, shrimp, and salted fish are first cooked until fragrant. The rice is then stir-fried separately until the grains are dry and separate from each other. The prepared ingredients are mixed with the rice until the aroma fills the air. Lard is often used for frying, adding richness to the dish. Finally, scallions or leeks may be added for extra flavor.

The authentic black rice made with maple leaf juice is a specialty of Guangxi cuisine and an essential part of the culinary heritage of Tengxian County. However, it is more than just a dish—it is deeply rooted in the tradition of ancestor worship, with families gathering to share a meal of black rice after honoring their forebears.

In 2013, the preparation of black rice in Tengxian County was listed in the second batch of the county's intangible cultural heritage items.

藤县龙母诞

○ 郑彬昌

龙母在西江流域被奉为河神，不少地方都建有龙母庙奉祀龙母，龙母文化沿着西江流域，一路流传到中国香港、澳门及东南亚等国家和地区。据考证，闽港澳及东南亚的妈祖文化，其实与龙母文化是一脉相承的。

龙母文化在藤县是最具影响力、最深入民心、受众最广泛、历史最久远的传统文化，已经融入了民众的血脉之中。在龙母文化中，龙母诞是重要的内容。

相传龙母生于楚怀王辛未年（前290年），卒于秦始皇三十六年（前211年），为古藤州一都水东街孝通坊（今藤州镇胜西村）人，距今有2300多年。龙母姓温，名媪，其父为藤州水东街孝通坊人，母亲是广东德庆县悦城人氏。民间传说龙母是古代的女英雄，她率领百越民众与自然灾害斗争，使黎民安居生息繁衍，她"利泽天下"的民本思想深得民众拥戴，被推为仓吾氏族领袖。传说她豢养五龙，相助造福黎民，被尊称为"龙母"。

龙母去世后，人们为了纪念这位有德于民、有功于国的女中英杰，便为她立庙，岁岁祭祀。

龙母诞的诞期有"生辰诞"和"升天得道诞"两个，都成了人们纪念龙母的隆重节日。

"生辰诞"是为了庆祝龙母降生，因而庆典活动隆重而热烈，活动从农历五月初一至初十共10天，以农历五月初八为正日；"升天得道诞"以农历八月十六日为正日，是为了纪念龙母"得道升天"。龙母"生辰诞"和"升天得道诞"是龙母文化中的重要内容，要举行隆重的庆祝和纪念活动。

藤县龙母诞

龙母像 / 胡永 摄

在每年农历五月初七晚上 12 点，由 4 位品行优良的妇女进入龙母庙龙母像的帷帐内，给龙母像沐浴更衣，换上新的龙袍。沐浴更衣时，有一群道公在外面喃经诵道。

沐浴更衣完毕，开始上头炷香，接下来就是所有香客排队上香拜祭了。除了拜祭龙母像，还有摸龙床、求子等祈福项目。随后还有引龙、放河灯等一系列活动，以示纪念。活动当天，万人空巷，盛况空前。

"生辰诞"从农历五月初一到初八活动期间，几队八音队轮流吹奏表演。

千百年前藤县民间形成的龙母诞，不但备受当地民众推崇，而且影响到西江流域、珠三角及港澳台地区，乃至东南亚等国家，很多人在当天到藤县龙母庙参加敬崇龙母活动。

广东省德庆县每年都要举办龙母诞庆祝活动，事前要派人到藤县龙母娘家，先到藤县龙母庙参拜龙母，随后为龙母更衣沐浴。从藤县出发前，他们要举行更衣沐浴的送行仪式，有颂道、龙母出巡、引龙、放河灯等一系列敬崇龙母活动，

龙母诞活动盛况 / 胡永 摄

预示平安吉祥、健康如意。

据统计，藤县境内西江及其支流流域至少有 10 座龙母庙，而其中影响力较大的有 3 座，位于胜西村的藤县龙母庙是其中之一。藤县龙母庙现存有龙母庙印章一枚、蛇身狮面神兽一尊、莲花柱墩两个，以及雕刻有"龙母娘娘"的香炉等，这些都是珍贵的文物。

由此可见，龙母文化之龙母诞活动，深入西江流域民众的血脉之中，寄托了当地民众对龙母大爱的崇敬和对美好生活的向往。

2013 年，藤县龙母诞列入第二批县级非物质文化遗产代表性项目名录。

Loong Mother's Birthday Celebration in Tengxian County

· Zheng Binchang ·

Loong Mother is revered as the river deity of the Xijiang River Basin, and her cultural legacy has spread throughout the region, extending to Hong Kong, Macao and Southeast Asian regions and countries. Numerous Loong Mother temples have been erected in these areas for worship. Research indicates that the Mazu culture, which venerates the ancient Chinese goddess of seafaring, prevalent in Fujian Province, Hong Kong, Macao, and Southeast Asia, is a derivative of Loong Mother culture.

The Loong Mother culture is particularly influential in Tengxian County, where it has deep roots among the local population. This culture has not only the widest following but also the longest history, becoming an integral part of the community's identity. Central to Loong Mother culture is the celebration of her birth.

According to legend, Loong Mother was born in 290 BC during the Xinwei year of King Huai of Chu, and she died in 211 BC during the 36th year of the First Emperor of Qin. She was born in Xiaotong Lane on Shuidong Street, Shengxi Village of Tengzhou, which boasts a history of more than 2,300 years. Her surname was Wen, and her given name was Ao. Her father hailed from Xiaotong Lane, while her mother came from Yuecheng in Deqing County, Guangdong Province. Folk legends depict Loong Mother as a heroine who led the Baiyue people in their fight against natural disasters and ensured the well-being of the local population. Her guiding principle, "benefit the world", endeared her to the people, who elevated her to the status of leader of the Cangwu Clan. She is said to have raised five loongs to assist and protect the people, thus earning the title "Loong Mother".

After her death, locals constructed temples in her honor and offered sacrifices year after year to commemorate this heroic figure who had made significant contributions to the welfare of both the people and the country.

The celebration of Loong Mother's life includes two key events: her birthday, referred to as "Loong Mother's Birthday", and her death, known as "Loong Mother Ascension Day". These are grand festivals that hold great significance in Loong Mother culture.

The birthday celebrates her birth, with festivities running from the first to the tenth day of the fifth lunar month, with the eighth day being the official observance. The Ascension Day, commemorated on the sixteenth day of the eighth lunar month, marks her passing. Both events are observed with elaborate ceremonies and commemorations.

One of the key rituals takes place at midnight on the seventh day of the fifth lunar month, when four gentlewomen ceremonially dress Loong Mother in a new loong robe after she has been bathed and her clothes changed. While these rites are being performed, a group of Taoist priests chant scriptures outside.

After the dressing, the first incense is lit, and pilgrims line up to offer their own. Additional rituals include touching the loong bed for blessings, praying for children, and other acts of veneration such as loong drawings and floating river lanterns. On these festive days, the streets are crowded, and the spectacle is truly grand.

The Loong Mother's Birthday celebration lasts from the first to the eighth day of the fifth lunar month, accompanied by performances of traditional folk arts, such as eight-tone ensembles, playing in rotation.

Formed thousands of years ago in Tengxian County, Loong

Mother's Birthday is not only highly regarded by the local community but also has far-reaching influence throughout the regions of Xijiang River Basin, the Pearl River Delta, Hong Kong, Macao, Taiwan, and even Southeast Asian countries. Many people travel to the Loong Mother Temple in Tengxian County to participate in the festivities.

In Deqing County, Guangdong Province, an annual celebration of Loong Mother's Birthday is held. Prior to the event, delegates are sent to Loong Mother's ancestral home in Tengxian County to pay homage at the Loong Mother Temple and then assist in the ceremonial bathing and dressing of Loong Mother's statue. Before departing from Tengxian, a farewell ceremony is conducted, featuring a series of traditional activities such as Taoist chanting, loong parades, and the floating of river lanterns, all symbolizing peace, prosperity, and good health.

There are at least ten Loong Mother temples within the Xijiang River Basin and its tributaries in Tengxian County, three of which are particularly prominent. Among them is the Loong Mother Temple in Shengxi Village, Tengxian County, which houses valuable cultural relics, including a seal from the temple, a statue of a serpent with a lion's face, two lotus pillars, and censers engraved with the inscription "*long mu niang niang* (Loong Mother) ".

The activities surrounding Loong Mother's Birthday are deeply embedded in the spiritual life of the people in the Xijiang River Basin, reflecting their reverence for Loong Mother's compassion and their aspiration for a better life.

In 2013, Loong Mother's Birthday celebration in Tengxian County was included in the second batch of county-level intangible cultural heritage listings.

斗鸡

○ 黄锦飞

斗鸡在藤县民间流传的历史比较悠久,但源于何时无法考证。据藤县藤州镇的居民讲述,以前北方商人来到南方做生意,带来了这一游戏项目,一般在节庆日举行。刚开始时,只是富家子弟参与,后来普通百姓也参加。所用斗鸡规定是本地鸡,鸡种由裁判员鉴定、确认。

斗鸡多从天性好斗的赤毛鸡驯养得来,以体形魁梧、体质健壮结实、结构匀称紧凑、形似鸵鸟、性格强悍、好斗善斗为基本特征。斗鸡一般头小,便于攻击;脚直而大,站立更稳;眼大而锐,便于防卫。斗鸡的头、颈高昂,颈、胸、胫几乎成一直线,冠红色,颈粗长灵活,胸部发达;喙如鹰嘴,粗短、坚硬呈楔形,尖端微弯而甚锐;腿强劲有力,

斗鸡 / 欧伟文 摄

爪粗大、坚硬锋利。斗鸡全身羽毛短而稀薄，鸡毛富有光泽，羽色多样，以黑色羽居多，翼羽拍打有力。

斗鸡比赛开始前，用竹栏围出一个占地约10平方米，高约1米的圈，把鸡圈在中间相斗。比赛规则以约定俗成为准，一般是淘汰赛，两鸡相斗，放弃打斗不再反击并逃跑的一方为输方，赢方的鸡主便得到赛前公布的奖品。

斗鸡开始时，斗鸡引颈收翅，屈足抬尾，争斗一触即发。只见两只斗鸡相互追逐，上下翻飞跳跃，相互啄咬，一啄到适宜的地方，就牢牢咬住不放，再用爪来协助，不叼得对手鸡血长流绝不罢休。争斗中的斗鸡头上的羽毛都蓬松竖起，煞是好看，也为其增添了气势。斗鸡在任何情况下都主动找对方进攻，尤其战斗的最后阶段，哪怕斗到精疲力尽也宁死不屈，只要还有一口气，就要战斗到底，进攻中毫无后退表现，进攻积极主动，往往两鸡争斗10分钟，还难分胜负。

斗鸡是民间特色传统民俗游戏、群众性娱乐项目，观赏性、趣味性较强，因此民众乐于参与。近年来，随着藤县人民的生活水平的提高和娱乐活动的多样化，斗鸡活动逐渐减少，但在各地乡镇仍时有举办。

2013年，斗鸡列入第二批县级非物质文化遗产代表性项目名录。

斗鸡代表性传承人

级别	姓名	性别	出生时间	认定时间（年）
县级	李小金	男	不详	2018
县级	程毅展	男	不详	2018
县级	程毅松	男	不详	2018

Cockfighting

· Huang Jinfei ·

Cockfighting has a long history of folk tradition in Tengxian County; however, its exact origins remain unverified. According to residents of Tengzhou Town in Tengxian County, merchants from the north introduced the game to the south, where it was typically held during festivals. Initially, participation was limited to the wealthy, but over time, others were also allowed to join. The fighting cocks used are local breeds, and their classification must be confirmed by referees.

The fighting cocks are primarily domesticated from red-feathered chickens, known for their aggressive nature. These birds exhibit several key characteristics: they are large in size, robust in constitution, compact in structure, and resemble ostriches in form. Fighting cocks generally have upright, small heads that facilitate attacks. They possess straight, large feet for stability, and their prominent, sharp eyes help them remain vigilant. Their heads and necks are elevated, and their necks, chests, and shins form nearly straight lines. The crowns are red, the necks are thick, long, and flexible, while the chests are muscular. The beaks, slightly curved at the tips, resemble those of eagles: short, hard, and wedge-shaped. Their feathers are short and thin. Additionally, their plumage is glossy, varied, and predominantly black, while their well-feathered wings allow for vigorous flapping.

Before the fight begins, a circular arena measuring approximately ten square meters in width and one meter in height is enclosed with bamboo fencing, placing the cocks in the center to engage in battle. The rules are based on convention, typically following a knockout format. In each match, two cocks fight until one retreats, at which point the owner of the winning cock receives a pre-announced prize.

As the fight commences, the cocks bend their necks and draw in their wings, preparing for the imminent clash. Spectators observe as the two birds chase each other, aiming for critical points. When successful, one cock will firmly grasp its opponent with its beak, and with the aid of its claws, it will continue until blood is drawn. The feathers on both sides of the cock's head become erect and fluffy, enhancing the fight's intensity. Throughout the encounter, both cocks actively seek to attack one another, especially in the final stages of the battle. They will fight to the death rather than yield, exhibiting no retreat in their aggression. Even after ten minutes of intense combat, the outcome often remains uncertain.

Cockfighting is a traditional game characterized by folk elements and serves as a popular form of mass entertainment. Its ornamental appeal and inherent excitement attract participants. However, in recent years, with improved living standards of people in Tengxian County and diversified recreational activities, it has become increasingly rare. Fortunately, it continues to be held in some towns and villages.

In 2013, cockfighting was included in the second batch of the county-level intangible cultural heritage list.

The Representative Inheritors of Cockfighting

Level	Name	Gender	Year of Birth	Time of Certification
County	Li Xiaojin	Male	Unknown	2018
County	Cheng Yizhan	Male	Unknown	2018
County	Cheng Yisong	Male	Unknown	2018

斗蟋蟀

○ 卢瑞昌

斗蟋蟀 / 何锦奋　摄

　　大千世界，无奇不有。在藤县象棋镇道家村，有一座蟋蟀的坟墓。墓很小，如钵盂。在蟋蟀墓的旁边，是蟋蟀主人杨树福的坟墓。这个传奇的故事发生在 20 世纪 40 年代，杨树福把训练有素的蟋蟀带到平南县大洲镇参加蟋蟀擂台赛。这只"蓝颈珠头，龙须虎牙，眼碌腩收，腿壮羽釉"的蟋蟀一上场，就震住了很多人，最终连续击败近百只蟋蟀，夺得冠军，主人获奖黄牛 1 头、挂钟 1 座、布 8 匹、银票 12 万元等战利品。随后，这只蟋蟀又在两广的斗蟋蟀擂台赛上连夺三届冠军，为杨树福夺得了价值不菲的奖品，也为当地村民赢得了荣光，声名大噪，并获"蟋王"美称。"蟋王"死后，杨树福用盘装载，埋葬在他发现"蟋王"的思罗河边，并叮嘱自己的子孙，自己死后，把自己埋葬在"蟋王"旁边。

　　这个故事，在藤县广为流传，是藤县斗蟋蟀活动流行的见证。

斗蟋蟀

斗蟋蟀这一民间活动，据传原是北方富家人的游戏，北方商人到南方做生意便将其引入，并在南方民间流行。藤县的斗蟋蟀起于何时没有文字记载，坊间传闻最初是在天平镇富双村兴起，逐渐在藤县各乡镇流行。

藤县民间斗蟋蟀，大都是由热心者及有一定威望的两三人牵头作为会主，自发组建蟋蟀协会，定期举办斗蟋蟀活动。斗蟋蟀地点多数选择在圩镇中交通便利的仓库、空置民房甚至大树下，时间多选在圩日人最多的时段。斗蟋蟀者仅选用雄性蟋蟀，头大、颈粗、腿壮、须直、色亮的为上品。这样的蟋蟀体形矫健，凶猛强悍，顽强好斗。斗蟋蟀有一套由蟋蟀协会制定的规则，愿者入局，进出自由。一般按20盘蟋蟀为一组先打，再由各组胜者参加决斗，最后积分最多的为当届"蟋王"，"蟋王"的主人得奖金。奖金的来源是入会者的会费，也有热心人士的赞助。

斗蟋蟀的规则如下：

入场共3人，一个裁判与双方蟋蟀的主人，行话就叫作"三草两别头"。

裁判让蟋蟀的主人用棚户提供的草撩拨，激起蟋蟀的打斗性，待两方的蟋蟀起叫后（以1分钟为限，如到时间蟋蟀不叫，也得开斗）起闸开斗。在打斗过程中，蟋蟀的主人不得用草。打斗中把两蟋蟀分开，双方开叫（相差不过3秒）则被视为平局，继续比赛；如一方开叫，该方赢半局。失局的一方的蟋蟀主人可用草撩拨蟋蟀以激发其斗性（15秒为限），如有斗性则继续，如无斗性，则输一局。蟋蟀主人再继续用草撩虫（1分钟为限），到时能斗，起闸继续，不再有斗性，则输全局。如蟋蟀在先失半局后反败为胜，夺回半局，其余如上所述。若先失一局后转胜，也如上。每一场斗蟋蟀下来，第一名叫"头笼"，第二名叫"二笼"，第三名叫"三笼"。

斗蟋蟀这一民间游戏，是一项古老的娱乐活动，在藤县的乡村流行了很长时间，但如今日渐式微。

2013年，斗蟋蟀列入第二批县级非物质文化遗产代表性项目名录。

Cricket Fighting

· Lu Ruichang ·

The world is full of surprises. In Daijia Village, Xiangqi Town, Tengxian County, there exists a unique cricket tomb. This small tomb resembles an alms bowl and is situated next to the grave of Yang Shufu, the cricket's owner. The legendary story dates back to 1940s, when Yang Shufu brought crickets, he had trained to Dazhou Town, Pingnan County, to participate in the Cricket Challenge Tournament. Upon its arrival, the cricket—characterized by its "blue neck, pearl head, loong-like whiskers, tiger-like teeth, rolling eyes, folded belly, strong legs, and feathers as smooth and thin as porcelain"—captivated many spectators. Ultimately, this remarkable cricket triumphed over hundreds of others to claim the championship. The owner of the winning cricket received various prizes, including a yellow ox, a wall clock, eight pieces of cloth, 120,000 yuan of banknote, and numerous other trophies. Subsequently, this cricket went on to win the championship three more times in the Cricket Challenge matches held in Guangdong and Guangxi, earning significant accolades for Yang Shufu and bringing honor to the villagers. Consequently, it was dubbed the "King of Cricket". Following the cricket's death, Yang Shufu buried it in a tray beside the Silo River, where he had discovered it, instructing his descendants to bury him next to the "King of Cricket" upon his demise.

This story is well-known throughout Tengxian County, serving as a testament to the cricket fighting activities in the region.

Cricket fighting, a folk activity, is believed to have originated as a gambling game for the wealthy in northern China. It was introduced by merchants who migrated south for trade and subsequently gained popularity among the general populace. Although no written records detail the inception of cricket fighting in Tengxian County, it is rumored to have begun in Fushuang Village of Tianping

Town and gradually spread to various towns in Tengxian County.

In Tengxian County, cricket fighting is organized spontaneously by individuals who have recently experienced success, along with respected community members, forming a cricket association that takes the lead in organizing events. Most cricket fighting venues are located in warehouses, empty houses, or even under trees in towns and cities with convenient transportation. Events are primarily scheduled during the "Xu Ri (fair days) ", when market activity is at its peak. The cricket association has established a set of rules based on common practices, and participation is open to anyone willing to join. Generally, 20 crickets compete in initial groups, with winners advancing to subsequent rounds. Ultimately, the cricket that scores the most victories is crowned the champion. The owner of the champion receives a prize. Prize money is sourced from membership fees collected from participants, as well as sponsorship from enthusiasts.

Rules of cricket fighting: the competition involves three participants: a referee and the owners of two crickets. This arrangement is colloquially referred to as "three weeds and two ends".

At the beginning, the referee instructs each circkets' owner tease their crickets with grass provided by the organizers. After one minute, if both crickets start chirping, the match begins; if not, the fight commences regardless of chirping. During the match, neither side is permitted to tease their crickets with grass. If the crickets separate during the fight, both owners must yell within three seconds to call a draw; otherwise, the match continues. If one owner yells, that side wins half the game. The losing side may then use grass to tease their cricket for 15 seconds. If the cricket still has energy, the fight resumes; if not, the match is lost. If a cricket loses the first half but wins the second, the rules above apply accordingly. After each match, the winners are designated as follows: the first place is called "*tou long*", the second place is "*er long*", and the third place is "*san long*".

Cricket fighting was once a popular folk activity and served as a form of entertainment in ancient times. Although cricket fighting continues in rural areas of Tengxian County, its prevalence has declined.

In 2013, cricket fighting was listed in the second batch of county-level intangible cultural heritage items in Tengxian County.

藤县古龙舞豹节

○ 周雄

据史料记载，清末民初，每年农历七月十六日在古龙大王庙（现古龙镇中心小学旁）举办随化里（今古龙镇）民间传统节日舞豹节。

古时的古龙人口稀少，四面高山，原始森林茂密，野生动植物丰富，时有豹子出没伤害人畜，使人苦不堪言。人们每天辛勤劳作结束回到家中，唯一防备的办法是早早关门闭户，不敢轻易外出走家串户。每当发生豹子伤害人畜的事件，受害的人家往往束手无策，只好自认倒霉，到社庙神坊烧香拜佛，祈求神灵保护。

那时人们对自然界的认识有限，因此对豹子出没伤害人畜事件，有许多稀奇古怪的说法。有的人说，豹子出没伤害人畜是"豹反"，因为有人没有诚心拜神礼佛。因为，豹子出来之前都会事先得到社公、神灵同意。一些忙于生产，疏忽拜社、祭神的人家必定会被豹子伤害。这实际上是触犯了神灵，而不是遇到了豹子。

为此，村丁地保和族老们想出了一个很巧妙的办法，制订了一年一度求神消灾的活动计划——"舞豹"，每年农历七月十六日举行秋祭神明活动，由神明来惩治伤人害畜的豹子。

每年农历七月十三日开始进入舞豹节活动的准备阶段。由村丁地保分头到各村，做好广泛的宣传筹备工作，并由大庙里的主持负责安排舞豹表演的人员和道具，同时准备好一头大黄牛作祭豹时用。

农历七月十六日这天上午10时左右，大庙里摆着黄牛头祭品，庙前广场汇集了来自附近的三村六寨及苍梧岭脚镇和昭平木格乡等邻乡远道而来参加舞豹节的村民。

庙内则是一片八音锣鼓吹打之声，香烟弥漫，火焰冲天。大约到11时，只见大庙门户洞开，一行身着袈裟道袍的道士从庙内鱼贯而出。一道士手牵着由人扮演披着假豹皮的"豹子"，头戴竹扎纸糊的豹子头，低头闭目漫步，跟随着队伍走到庙前广场中间的神台前。号炮三声后，道士们分各方位落签定符，然后由3个道士施展法术降服"豹子"。

此时的"豹子"温顺地俯首低头在广场中，任由道士们施"降龙伏虎术"。前头一道士手执桃木剑，自始至终用三个手指按住"豹子"头，在这个时间内，那"豹子"的头是绝对不能抬起的，据说在舞豹的时间里如果"豹子"不慎抬了起来，当年村寨里一定会遭到"豹反"，伤害人畜的。左右两边道士分随后面。一帮道士双手合掌，口里念着道语，绕于人群围成的场子中间慢步行走，其间，也有道士们打令牌或吹符水的花样动作出现。一番舞弄后，一道士骑上"豹子"背，令"豹子"绕着大王庙转上一圈，时不时把"豹子"鞭打三下，喃呒道语一番。鞭打的频率随着锣鼓八音不断加快的节奏而提升，人声、鼓声、豹吟声此起彼伏，桃木剑飞舞，黄符灰飞烟灭，把"豹子"逼迫到神台底下，表示伏治，"治豹"大功告成。现场民众欢呼雀跃，鞭炮齐鸣。庙前场地集市又马上开始演地戏、卖艺、杂耍、山货贸易，好不热闹。

舞豹结束，道士、保丁、族老们进入庙内用餐、分享祭品。那个扮"豹子"的人劳苦功高，能分到3公斤牛肉和5公斤大米。

时至今日，每年农历七月十六日的舞豹节系古龙镇大圩日的传统习俗。

2013年，藤县古龙舞豹节列入第二批县级非物质文化遗产代表性项目名录。

Gulong Town's Leopard Dance Festival in Tengxian County

· Zhou Xiong ·

Historical records indicate that since the late Qing Dynasty and the early Republic period, the "Leopard Dance Festival", a traditional folk celebration of Suihuali (now known as Gulong Town), has been held annually on the sixteenth day of the seventh lunar month at the Temple of King Gulong, located next to the Central Primary School in Gulong Town.

In ancient times, Gulong was sparsely populated and surrounded by mountains with dense primeval forests and abundant wild plants, creating a suitable habitat for leopards. These leopards posed a serious threat to both livestock and residents, causing ongoing distress for the local community. People, upon returning home after a hard day's work, could only secure their safety by closing their doors early. Children and the elderly were often confined to their mud huts from morning until night, frequently falling victim to leopard attacks. The unfortunate victims had little recourse to deal with these threats, and many resorted to burning incense and praying at the temple, seeking divine protection for their peace of mind.

At that time, people's understanding of the natural world was limited, leading to various superstitions regarding leopard attacks. Some believed that these incidents were the result of "leopard retribution", arguing that such occurrences stemmed from a lack of sincere worship of the deities, which allowed leopards to emerge from the forest, day or night, to inflict harm. According to local beliefs, a leopard's appearance required approval from the communal lord and the deity. Thus, those who neglected their worship were often considered susceptible to leopard attacks. This was perceived as an offense against the deity rather than merely a consequence of leopard behavior.

In response to these fears, the township soldiers and village elders devised a clever solution by developing an annual ritual known as the "Leopard Dance" to ward off calamities. Each autumn, they offered sacrifices to the deity on the sixteenth day of the seventh lunar month. hoping that it would deter the leopards that threatened human and animal lives.

Preparation for the Leopard Dance Festival begins on the thirteenth day of the seventh lunar month. Township soldiers visit each village to conduct extensive publicity and ensure that the temple's overseer arranges the performers and the necessary props for the leopard dance. Additionally, a large yellow cattle is prepared for sacrifice.

On the morning of the sixteenth day of the seventh lunar month, the temple fills with cattle head offerings, and villagers from nearby towns, including Cangwu, Daoshui, Lingjiao, Zhaoping, Muge, and others, gather to participate in the Leopard Dance Festival.

Inside the temple, the sounds of gongs and drums fill the air, accompanied by smoke and flames. Around eleven o'clock, the temple doors open, and a procession of monks dressed in Buddhist and Taoist robes enters. A Taoist priest dons a leopard skin, and the "leopard", clad in a costume made of bamboo paper, enters the temple square, bowing its head as it strolls. Following the three sounds of fire crackers, three Taoist priests draw lots and attach amulets, using their magic to govern the "leopard".

At this moment, the "leopard" humbly bows its head in the square, allowing the Taoist priests to perform their rituals. The leading Taoist priest holds a peachwood sword and maintains a firm grip on the leopard's head with three fingers, preventing it from lifting. It is believed that if the leopard's head rises during the dance, the village will suffer from "leopard retribution". The other two Taoist priests, walking slowly around the courtyard while chanting prayers and performing water tricks. After the dance, a Taoist priest mounts the back of the leopard and circles the altar, occasionally whipping the leopard three times and muttering incantations. The whipping frequency increases with the rhythm of the gongs and drums, intensifying the excitement. By dancing with swords, shouting, and lighting amulets, they compel the leopard to hide under the table, symbolizing their successful control over it. The crowd cheers, and firecrackers are set off, bringing the event to a climactic finish. Following the festivities, market activities commence, featuring busking, juggling, and trading, creating a lively atmosphere.

At the conclusion of the Leopard Dance, the Taoist priests,

township soldiers, and elders gather in the temple to partake in the offerings. The individual who portrayed the "leopard" receives three kilograms of beef and five kilograms of rice for their efforts.

Today, the annual Leopard Dance Festival on the sixteenth day of the seventh lunar month remains a cherished tradition of the grand fair day in Gulong Town.

In 2013, Gulong Town's Leopard Dance Festival was included in the second batch of county-level intangible cultural heritage list.

藤县太平二帝庙装色出游

○ 罗金霞

藤县太平二帝庙（又称文武二帝庙）建于清道光十九年（1839年）。二庙合邻而建，故名二帝庙。太平镇的人们把庙宇落成之日作为文武二帝的诞辰，每年的农历八月十六日二帝诞辰这天，人们都会举办一次巡游活动，称为装色出游。

中国人对自然万物有一种信仰，其中对星宿和历史人物的崇拜尤其明显。在中国人的心中，每个星宿都有自己的属性和代表物，文昌帝君是中国民间星辰信仰中的神。一般认为他是主管考试、命运及助佑读书撰文之神，是读书文人、求科名者所尊奉的神祇。以前皇帝把拜祭文昌帝君列为重要祭典之一，凡是读书人必须奉祀文昌帝君。

关圣帝受人们的尊崇。他本名关羽，字云长，是三国时的名将。他一生策马横刀，驰骋疆场，征战群雄，辅佐刘备完成三分天下的大业，谱写出一曲令人感慨万千的人生壮歌，被后人推举为"忠、信、义、勇"集于一身的代表性人物。

在我国古代，从文从武皆重要。人们一边追求文采斐然，一边又追求身强力壮、武艺超群，于是形成了崇文尚武的氛围。藤县太平镇对于文武双全的推崇，绝不会比任何一个地方逊色半分，所以藤县太平二帝庙供奉的自然也是文昌帝和关圣帝。

藤县太平二帝庙装色出游活动因庙而起，就是由人扮演成所信仰的神和历史上有影响力的各种人物的游街活动，类似于庙会活动。装色的"色"原意是饰，指精心巧妙的装扮，就是打扮、修饰、装点。《后汉书·梁鸿传》中写道："（孟光）及嫁，始以装饰入门。"意思是孟光出嫁时，修饰打扮了一番

藤县太平二帝庙装色出游

过门。参加巡游活动的人们也得盛装打扮一番,其隆重程度丝毫不逊于嫁女儿。

每年的农历八月十六日到来之前,藤县太平二帝庙的负责人就会在信士当中敲定演员名单,定好各人所扮演的角色。角色一般有文昌帝、关圣帝、文武二帝的太子、女娲、伏羲、观音、唐僧师徒、周仓等。一般挑选五官端正、身材高大或苗条之人来出演。

到了农历八月十六日这天,天才擦亮,信士就从周边的乡镇赶来,聚集在藤县太平二帝庙前,根据各人所扮演的角色描眉画眼,傅粉施朱,戴头饰,着华服,为装色出游活动作准备。

装色出游盛况 / 覃永森　摄

众人扮演的正待出游的各路神仙 / 欧伟文　摄

　　至早上 10 时，一切准备妥当，出游活动正式开始。拜过正殿里的文武二帝神像，人们列队从庙前广场走出。走在第一位的是持着书写着"文武二帝"大字庙旗的庙旗手，几名手提灯笼的童子紧随其后，舞狮、敲锣打鼓的一帮人也一并跟着。紧接着的是扮演文昌帝和关圣帝的演员并肩而行。扮演周仓的演员扛着大刀伴在关圣帝的身侧。由小孩子扮演的文帝太子、武帝太子则坐在轿子上，由大人们抬着，跟在文武二帝身后。再后面跟着的依次是云鬓峨峨、瑰姿艳逸的女娲，长头修目、龟齿龙唇的伏羲，手托净瓶、慈眉善目的观音，以及丰姿英伟、气宇轩昂的唐僧，古灵精怪的孙悟空，憨态可掬的猪八戒，红发蓬松的沙悟净等一众角色。更有舞龙队、扭秧歌队和手举着"五谷丰登""风调雨顺""百姓安康"等寓意美好的字牌的队伍的一路相随。百余人的游行队伍浩浩荡荡，从藤县文武二帝庙走到上元街，经石子街、上园岭，到康城居，过环城路、车站，走至西瓜市场，再绕回河塘市场，经河塘一路，到上元街，回藤县文武二帝庙，游行活动才算结束。游行期间，遇社拜社，敲锣打鼓，龙狮共舞，好不热闹。游行活动一般从上午 10 时持续到下午一二时，有时还会

藤县太平二帝庙装色出游

二帝庙出游中的部分角色 / 欧伟文 摄

持续到下午 5 时。当然,这还不是整个装色出游活动的结束,人们往往会在游行活动结束后,在庙前的空地上,搭起戏台子,美美地唱上一场牛歌戏,剧目多为《金玉满堂》《状元郎》等。至晚上 7 时,牛歌戏结束,整个装色出游活动才算落下帷幕。

藤县太平二帝庙装色出游来自民间,是一种比较独特的文化记忆,也是一种人们寻找心理慰藉的载体。它展现了中华优秀传统文化的魅力,具有重要的民俗学、人类学和社会学价值,对文艺样式的发展和民间传统习俗形成了一定的影响。

2013 年,藤县太平二帝庙装色出游列入第二批县级非物质文化遗产代表性项目名录。

Taiping Two Emperors' Temple Parade in Tengxian County

· Luo Jinxia ·

Taiping Two Emperors' Temple (also known as the Temple of Emperor Wen and the Temple of Emperor Wu) were built in 1839. These two temples, constructed side by side, are collectively referred to as the Two Emperors' Temple. The residents of Taiping Town regard the temple's completion date as the birth anniversary of the two emperors, and every year, on the sixteenth day of the eighth lunar month which is the birth day of the two emperors, a grand parade is held in their honor. This event is known as the "Zhuang Se Parade (Two Emperors' Temple Parade)".

Chinese culture is rich with reverence for natural elements, and this extends to the worship of stars and historical figures. In Chinese cosmology, each star embodies specific attributes, and Wenchang Dijun, is especially venerated as the god of academic success, fate, and intellectual pursuits. As the patron deity of scholars, Wenchang was historically honored in major imperial rituals, and scholars of all levels paid homage to him.

Similarly, Emperor Guan Sheng, a historical figure revered as a god, commands great respect. Known in life as Guan Yu, with the courtesy name Yun Chang, he was a celebrated general during the Three Kingdoms period. Renowned for his loyalty and martial prowess, Guan Yu played a pivotal role in assisting Liu Bei to establish one of the three major kingdoms of the era.

In ancient China, both literature and military prowess were esteemed, and people aspired to excel in both. This cultural ideal is

藤县太平二帝庙装色出游

农历八月十六日二帝庙装色出游的部分角色 / 欧伟文　摄

reflected in the town of Taiping, where the temples of Wenchang and Guan Sheng were erected to honor both the literary and martial traditions.

The Taiping Two Emperors' Temple Parade (Zhuang Se Parade) is a celebration that blends devotion to these deities with elements of a traditional street fair. The Chinese character "*se*" here refers to elaborate decorations and costumes. The tradition of dressing up for such events is recorded in ancient texts like the *Book of the Later Han Dynasty*, where it is noted that "Meng Guang adorned herself for marriage, " symbolizing the preparation and embellishment associated with important rituals. Similarly, participants in this parade don elaborate attire, lending the occasion an air of grandeur comparable to a wedding procession.

In the days leading up to the sixteenth day of the eighth lunar month, temple organizers select actors from among the faithful to portray key figures in the parade. Commonly represented characters include Wenchang Dijun, Guan Sheng, the Princes of Wen and Wu, Nuwa, Fuxi, Guanyin, Tang Monk and his disciples, Zhou Cang, and others. The chosen participants are typically those

二帝庙装色出游场景 / 吴瑞文　摄

with striking physical characteristics, such as strength or elegance, befitting the roles they will play.

At dawn on the sixteenth day of the eighth lunar month, believers from neighboring towns gather in front of the Two Emperors' Temple, where participants apply makeup, don headdresses, and dress in elaborate costumes, preparing for the grand procession.

By 10 a.m., the parade begins with a formal offering of incense before the statues of Wenchang Dijun and Guan Sheng. The procession is led by a flag bearer holding the temple banner inscribed with "*Wenwu Erdi*" followed by children carrying lanterns, lion dancers, and drummers. Next, Wenchang Dijun and Guan Sheng, both depicted with commanding presence, march side by side. Zhou Cang, tall, black-faced, and bearded, carries a large sword beside Guan Sheng. The Princes of Wen and Wu, portrayed by children, follow in sedan chairs carried by adults. The procession continues with Nuwa, magnificent and graceful; Fuxi, with long features, turtle teeth, and loong lips; Guanyin, serene with a vase in hand; and the Tang Monk, along with his clever disciple, the Monkey King, and the lovable Pigsy. The parade is completed by traditional loong and lion dance teams, as well as groups holding banners symbolizing agricultural prosperity, good weather, and general well-being. The parade route winds through the streets of Taiping, passing landmarks such as Shangyuan Street, Shizi Street, Shangyuan Ridge, Kang Cheng Ju, bus station and the watermelon market, before returning to the Two Emperors' Temple. Along the way, participants pause at various temples to offer worship, accompanied by lively performances of drumming, lion dancing, and loong dancing. The parade typically lasts from 10 a. m. until 1 or 2 p.m., and sometimes as late as 5 p.m. The celebration does not end with the parade. In the evening, an opera stage is set up in front of the temple, where traditional performances such as *Golden Jade Full Hall* and *Scholar* are staged. The event concludes around 7 p.m., marking the end of the day's festivities.

The Taiping Two Emperors' Temple Parade is a distinctive cultural tradition, offering a vital link to local folklore and serving as a source of psychological and communal solace. This event showcases a variety of traditional cultural elements, with significant folkloric, anthropological, and sociological value. It has influenced the development of local literary styles and folk customs.

In 2013, the Taiping Two Emperors' Temple Parade was listed in the second batch of county-level intangible cultural heritage items.

上灯

○ 卢颖莹

上灯 / 黄武朝 摄

在古代，人口数量是衡量一个国家实力是否强大的重要标准之一。"添丁"（添男丁，生儿子）是古代发展生产力的重要途径。

很早以前，藤县各地流行祝贺添丁的民俗节日——上灯。在当地方言中，"灯"是"丁"的谐音，也是希望、光明的象征，灯灯相继象征着种族繁衍的绵绵不绝。灯，是带有照明灯具的灯笼，上灯是把灯笼挂上去的一整套仪式。

在藤县濛江、象棋、新庆、金鸡等乡镇，上一年生育了男孩的家庭，在第二年春节正月十日凌晨0时，即为去年新生男儿挂上花灯，点亮直至正月十五日止，谓之上灯，以示祝贺新生男儿。藤县流行的上灯，有一套很讲究的程序，分为"上灯""暖灯""落灯"。

过去上灯用的花灯，多为手工竹篾纸糊，八角形，外吊纸花八串，灯托下部呈四方形，吊着的彩纸写有祝福的吉祥语，比如"少似芝兰时时欢，老如松柏天天翠，寿比南山日日新，福如东海年年

上灯

有""百家添子万家欢,子爱读书好做官,千般下品书中宝,孙孙子子着皇冠"等。从 20 世纪 90 年代开始,市场上出现的现代塑料镀金铜龙凤走马组装电灯动力花灯,因其具有美观、轻巧、精致和防火安全等优点,很快便取代了传统竹扎纸糊花灯。

"添丁"的人家,把花灯扎在现砍的新鲜竹子最上面的一段,该段竹子要保留竹叶,寓意开枝散叶,青云直上。需要注意的是,竹子不能取断头竹。到了正月十日0时,男孩父亲就要从自己的家门开始放鞭炮,一直放到本村的社或宗祠,挑着花灯,拿上祭品(水果、糖果、饼、熟鸡、熟猪肉等)去拜祭,拜完后,就把花灯挂在社旁的大树上或宗祠里。有些乡镇则是把花灯拿回家里再拜一次,拜完之后,就直接把灯挂在厅堂正中央。

也有人家在正月初九下半夜去祭拜社和宗祠的,说是为了"头炷香"。民间有说法是去得越快越好,越早越好,最好是第一个去祭拜。而负责写族谱的长辈见到花灯后,就会把花灯上男丁的名字写到族谱中。上灯这天,男孩父亲要先拜列祖列宗,接着拜长辈,长辈则给利市表示祝愿,拜完后便由男孩父亲

藤城花灯摊 / 胡永 摄

挂上的花灯 / 杨定登 摄

设宴招待亲朋好友，是谓"请灯酒"。饮灯酒的人数在从几桌到一百多桌不等，甚是热闹喜庆。

上了灯，接下来的几天就要"暖灯"了。从正月十一日到十五日，男孩父亲早晚都必须到社上香，给灯添油，一则保证花灯日夜不熄，二则以表添丁祝酒、香火不断之意。

最后是"摧灯棚"，又称"落灯"。到了正月十六日，男孩父亲杀鸡敬奉祖宗和社公之后把花灯取下，挂回本宗族的祠堂或自家厅堂里，寓意父母已将祈愿告知天神，希望天神保佑自己的小孩健康成长。

上灯起源于何时已经无从考证。《藤县志》（1984年版）有"每年正月初十，藤县南部乡镇流行上灯……"的记录。上灯作为一种传统民俗文化在藤县一直传承下来。

2016年，上灯列入第三批县级非物质文化遗产代表性项目名录。

Shang Deng: The Lantern Lighting Ceremony

· Lu Yingying ·

In ancient times, population was a crucial measure of a nation's strength. Due to physical limitations, women were generally unable to participate in daily agricultural labor or serve in the military. "*tian ding* (the birth of a son)" was highly valued in society.

An old festival, known as Shang Deng (lantern lighting), was celebrated throughout Tengxian County to mark the birth of a baby boy. The Chinese word for lantern, "*deng*", shares a homophone with "*ding*", which symbolizes hope, prosperity, and lineage. Lighting and hanging lanterns one after another during this ceremony represents the wish for an unbroken line of descendants. The term "Shang Deng" or "Lantern Lighting", refers to a set of ceremonial practices centered around the hanging of lanterns.

In the towns and villages of Mengjiang, Xiangqi, and Jinji in Tengxian County, families that welcomed a baby boy in the previous year would participate in the lantern lighting ceremony on the tenth day of the first lunar month, during the Spring Festival. The lanterns remain lit until the fifteenth day of the first lunar month. The Shang Deng festival is essentially a way of celebrating and congratulating the family for the birth of a son. The customs surrounding this event are characterized by three main stages: "lighting", "warming", and "lowering" the lanterns.

In the past, these lanterns were handcrafted from bamboo strips and paper, often octagonal in shape, with eight strings of paper flowers hanging from them. The lanterns were square at the bottom and adorned with auspicious inscriptions. Common blessings included phrases like: "May you thrive like irises and orchids in youth, and endure like pine and cypress in old age. May you live as long as the Southern Mountains and enjoy a new life every day, with blessings

上灯 / 欧伟文 摄

as vast as the East Sea." Another common inscription expressed the hope that the newborn would grow to become a scholar or official, with lines such as: "Wherever a son is born, joy follows. May the child have a love for learning and become an official, for in all trades, only scholarly achievements and government service are esteemed. May future generations rise to office and success." Since the 1990s, modern plastic lanterns, often gold-plated and featuring motifs of loongs and phoenixes, have become popular. These electric lanterns, being more beautiful, lightweight, and fire-safe, quickly replaced the traditional bamboo and paper varieties.

The family celebrating the birth of a son ties a lantern to the top section of freshly cut bamboo, ensuring that the bamboo leaves remain intact. This sharp and unbroken bamboo symbolizes the continuity of the family line and the success of future generations. Broken bamboo is never used. At midnight on the tenth day of the first lunar month, the father of the newborn boy sets off firecrackers from his home to the village ancestral hall. He carries the lantern, along with offerings such as fruit, candy, cakes, chicken, and pork, to pay respects to the family's ancestors. After the ancestral worship, the lanterns are hung on large trees or at the ancestral hall. In some villages, the lanterns are taken home for a second round of worship, after which they are hung in the center of the family's main hall.

Additionally, some families visit the ancestral hall late at night on the 9th day of the first lunar month to "light the first incense", believing that being the first to offer prayers will bring good fortune. There is a local saying: "The earlier, the better." Elders responsible for maintaining the family genealogy will inscribe the names of newborn boys onto the lanterns. On the day of Shang Deng, the father of the newborn first honors his ancestors, then visits his elders, who give him red packets as a gesture of blessing. Afterward, the father hosts a celebratory banquet, known as a "male feast", for friends and relatives. The scale of this banquet can range from a few tables to over a hundred, creating a lively and festive atmosphere.

Following the lantern lighting ceremony, the lanterns are "warmed" over the next few days. From the eleventh to the fifteenth day of the first lunar month, the father of the newborn must go to the temple each morning and evening to burn incense and add oil to the lanterns. This ensures that the lanterns remain lit day and night, symbolizing both the birth of the son and the continuation of the family line.

The final stage is known as "destroying the lantern shed" or "lowering the lanterns". On the sixteenth day of the first lunar month, the father removes the lanterns after performing rituals involving the sacrifice of a chicken and worship of the ancestors. The lanterns are then placed in the ancestral hall or family home, signifying that the prayers have been offered and the deities will now bless the child with health and prosperity.

The origins of the Shang Deng ceremony are unclear, but it has been passed down through generations in Tengxian County. According to the 1984 edition of the *Tengxian County Chronicles*, "On the tenth day of the first lunar month each year, it is customary to perform the Shang Deng ceremony in the villages and towns of southern Tengxian County".

In 2016, Shang Deng was officially included in the third batch of county-level intangible cultural heritage list.

藤县发糕制作技艺

○ 苏海

据说在清末民初年间，村中一位农家小媳妇在拌粉蒸糕时，不小心将搁在灶头上的一碗酒糟碰翻流进米粉中，小媳妇怕遭到公婆的责骂而不敢声张，只得把沾了酒糟的米粉拌匀后继续放在蒸笼里蒸。谁知由于酒糟的发酵作用，这一笼糕蒸得特别松软可口，还有一股淡淡的酒香，味道更特别了。拌酒糟蒸糕的法子从此流出。

据统计，中国糕点品种有3000多种，历史悠久，南北有异，而藤县本地最常见又最广泛用于喜事的要数发糕，寓意恭喜发财，步步高升。发糕发糕，越发越高。

藤县的糕点，以新庆发糕与太平米饼两大代表品牌雄踞南北，声名远播。

藤县发糕，一般分两种。一种是糕内气孔柱直如蜂窝状（也称莲藕孔），俗称实糕；另一种是糕内气孔如气泡状，俗称松糕。

各地做得最多的是松糕，其制作原料广泛，米粉、面粉、杂粮粉等都可以使用，工艺简单，如用干粉加酵母粉，按一定比例用水、糖调和均匀，隔水蒸熟即可。

实糕的做法是传统工艺，不太容易掌握，全凭制作人的经验。藤县有名的荣和发糕属实糕，自1993年开始，至今已有30多年的制作经验。荣和发糕的经营者坚持传统工艺，经过几十年的摸爬打滚，反复试验，不断探索，积累经验，终得其法，才把一整套技法稳定下来，保证了发糕出品的质量。

发糕的主要原料是大米，且必须是粘米，糯米不宜。这主要取自粘米的黏性，而不需要糯米的糯性。

藤县发糕制作技艺

藤县发糕 / 韦相 摄

选米。粘米的选取,以晚造米为宜,早造米稍有硬性,不够软熟。

洗米。选好粘米后要进行淘洗,淘洗一两次,以大水快淘为原则。利用缸桶淘洗,速度要快,水量宜多,也可以直接把粘米放到箩筐里,直接用清水冲洗。

泡米。粘米洗好后,把粘米放到容器里重新加水(最好是山泉水)浸泡,水位高出米面10厘米左右,浸泡时间1~3小时,以用拇指与食指压住米粒,轻轻揉捻,米粒自然塌落为度。

晾干。把已经泡好的粘米放在大簸箕上摊开,放置阴凉通风处自然晾干,多次翻动,直至米粒表面的水分干透。

磨米（又称磨浆）。将沥干水分的粘米放到石磨上磨浆，磨浆时要适当添加清水，投米量宜少不宜多，水、米的比例合适，磨出的米浆更幼滑。如有必要，可再过磨一次，以达到嫩滑细腻。

发酵。这是最为关键的一道工艺，发糕的好坏、口感、味道全在其中，决定其成败。发酵是把磨好的米浆放置桶缸之类的容器内，加入酒饼，再添加纯碱，充分搅拌调和均匀。酒饼、纯碱要求纯天然制作，酒饼的原料取自酒饼树（学名叶被木）、淡竹叶、辣蓼草等一些天然植物，作用是发酵。纯碱由花生苗秆、花生壳、稻草等一些天然植物晒干烧灰滤水所得，作用是中和酒饼发酵出来的酸味。酒饼、纯碱的用量最为关键，多一分则过，少一分不够。米浆经充分搅拌调和均匀后，再次加入清水，可适当多加，以不溢出为宜，用作阻隔空气、吸收废气，然后进入发酵。发酵的时间受温度、湿度、通风条件、季节变化等影响而时日不同。一缸缸的米浆水排兵布阵，贮立于阴凉通风之处，水面近乎平静，水底春潮涌动，酒饼中的酵母菌吸收米粉的营养成分迅速生长繁殖，将米粉中的葡萄糖转化为水和二氧化碳气体，这种气体又被粘米的黏性筋度所包裹，不能破水而出，开始形成孔洞，但气力有限，戛然而止。这时候要进入下一道工序——蒸糕，浴火重生。

蒸糕。米浆经过几天浸泡发酵，第一阶段使命完成。清除发酵缸中的上层废水，只保留米浆，加入黄糖（不用其他糖类、甜蜜素）。黄糖自带清香，颜色金黄。再次搅拌，装上托盘准备

晾晒浸泡过的粘米／韦相　摄

藤县发糕制作技艺

新出炉的发糕 / 何柏　摄

蒸糕，托盘内先涂抹清油，利于脱模。托盘习惯做成圆形，取团团圆圆、幸福圆满之意；托盘直径一般在30厘米左右。放米浆时不宜太满，比托盘高度低1厘米。蒸糕要隔水密闭进行，水沸始放入托盘，现在多用蒸柜，火力宜猛，充分激发二氧化碳的活力，一气冲天，成就柱状蜂窝、莲藕条孔，火力保持旺盛，蒸一个小时左右，开盖出糕。发糕的香味立刻扑面而来，清香满屋，清甜扑鼻，令人食欲顿来，吃上一口，糕质爽滑弹，唇齿留香。闭上眼睛，咀嚼回味，浮想联翩，意犹未尽。

2022年，藤县发糕制作技艺列入第五批县级非物质文化遗产代表性项目名录。

The Craft of Making Fagao in Tengxian County

· *Su Hai* ·

According to legend, during the late Qing and early Republic period, a farmer's daughter-in-law in a village accidentally spilled a bowl of vinasse (fermented rice wine residue) onto some rice flour. Afraid of being scolded by her in-laws, she kept quiet and proceeded to steam the mixture as usual. However, due to the fermentation effect of the vinasse, the fagao (steamed sponge cake) turned out to be exceptionally soft and delicious, with a slight aroma of Chinese baijiu, giving it a unique flavor. This incident is said to mark the origin of the traditional method for making fagao.

Historically, there are over 3,000 varieties of pastries in China, with notable regional differences between the north and south. In Tengxian County, one of the most popular and widely used pastries for celebratory events is steamed sponge cake. The cake carries symbolic meanings such as "Congratulations on your prosperity!" and "Step by step to greater heights!" The Cantonese pronunciation of "*fa gao*" (meaning "fortune" and "high") reflects the cake's association with wealth and success.

Tengxian County is renowned for its pastries, particularly the Xinqing fagao and Taiping rice cake, both of which enjoy wide recognition and prestige throughout the region.

There are two main types of fagao in Tengxian County. One variety has pores that resemble a honeycomb (also known as "lotus root holes"), commonly referred to as "*shi gao* (solid cake)". The other type has larger, bubble-like pores and is known as "*song gao* (loose

藤县发糕制作技艺 341

cake)".

  Songgao is widely made, using a variety of ingredients including rice flour, wheat flour, and other grain powders. Its preparation is relatively simple: dry flour and yeast powder are mixed with water and sugar in specific proportions before being steamed.

  The craft of making shigao, however, is a traditional technique that is more difficult to master. It requires extensive practice and experience. The famous "Ronghe" brand from Teng County has been producing shigao since 1993, accumulating nearly three decades of expertise. Adhering to traditional methods, this brand has perfected its technique over time, ensuring the consistent quality of its steamed sponge cakes.

  The key ingredient in fagao is sticky rice, not glutinous rice, which provides the necessary viscosity. Only late-harvest brown rice is suitable, as early-harvest brown rice tends to be too hard and lacks the softness needed for this craft.

  Rice Selection: The appropriate rice for fagao is late-season glutinous rice. Early-season varieties tend to be harder and less

石磨磨浆 / 何锦奋　摄

mature.

Rice Washing: Once the sticky rice is selected, it must be washed quickly one or two times. The process requires swift washing with plenty of water. Washing can be done by placing the rice in barrels, where it is rinsed thoroughly, or directly in baskets where water is poured over it.

Soaking the Rice: After washing, the rice is soaked in water, preferably mountain spring water. The water level should remain approximately 10 cm above the rice, and the soaking time ranges from one to three hours. When the rice can be gently rolled and pressed between the thumb and index finger, it is ready for the next step.

Drying: The soaked rice is spread out on a large dustpan to dry naturally in a cool, ventilated area. It should be turned multiple times to ensure all surface moisture evaporates.

Grinding: The rice is then ground using a stone mill. Water is added gradually during the grinding process, with careful attention to maintaining the correct ratio of water to rice, ensuring a smooth, even rice paste. If necessary, the rice paste can be ground a second time to improve texture.

Fermentation: This is the most critical step, as the quality of fermentation determines the success of making fagao. The rice paste is placed in a container, such as a barrel, and mixed with a natural leavening agent (wine yeast) and soda powder. Both the wine yeast and soda are traditionally made from natural ingredients, including Phyllostachys, bamboo leaves, and Polygonum spicatum. The soda powder is derived from burning peanut shells, straw, or other plant materials, and its purpose is to neutralize the sourness produced by the fermentation process. Precise measurements of the yeast and soda are essential. Once the rice paste is mixed and homogenized, additional water is added to create a barrier between the paste and the air, aiding in fermentation. The mixture is left to ferment in a cool, well-ventilated area for several days, during which yeast ferments the glucose in the rice, producing carbon dioxide that forms holes in the cake structure.

Steaming the Cake: After fermentation, the surface water is removed, and the rice paste is mixed with golden sugar, which adds a natural fragrance and color. The paste is poured into oiled circular trays, symbolic of unity and happiness, and prepared for steaming. The trays are typically 30 cm in diameter and filled to about 1 cm below the rim. Once the water in the steamer is boiling, the trays are placed inside, and the cakes are steamed at high heat to activate the carbon dioxide, creating honeycomb-like holes. After approximately one hour, the cakes are ready, filling the air with a sweet, appetizing fragrance. The result is a cake that is soft, elastic, and fragrant, leaving a pleasant aftertaste.

In 2022, the craft of making fagao in Tengxian County was listed as a representative item in the fifth batch of the county's intangible cultural heritage.

藤县山歌

○ 周羽兵

处在丘陵地带为主的藤县，一条蜿蜒的浔江穿越其中，人们以农耕为主，主要从事水稻种植、林牧业、竹排河运等生产活动，生活单调乏味。为消除疲劳、宣泄情绪、表达意愿，又或是为驱赶野兽、迎击强盗、抗击灾害等，藤县人用本地方言高声歌唱。就这样，在长期的生产劳动过程中产生了藤县山歌。藤县人民有唱山歌的习俗，从3岁的小孩到八九十岁的老人都会唱。藤县山歌已经大众化，山乡处处传唱不绝。

藤县山歌大都源于生活而高于生活，在历经数百年的精雕细琢之后，形成自己的特色，成为民间文化百花园中鲜艳亮丽的奇葩。

藤县山歌体裁种类多样，有赋体山歌、比喻山歌、起兴山歌、谐趣山歌等。赋体山歌直接叙述，表现人事，生动形象。例如：

> 送妹送到家婆屋，
> 好多家产妹有福。
> 我劝阿妹要珍惜，
> 冇要争跤偷偷哭。

> 远远睇到靓妹来，
> 五官端正好身材。
> 唔肥唔瘦侬中意，
> 年尾有钱娶转来。

比喻山歌通过明喻、暗喻、借喻、隐喻、讽喻、反喻等形式生动、贴切地借喻言情，非常具有艺术魅力。例如：

藤县山歌

　　大姐不如二姐娇，
　　三寸金莲四寸腰。
　　抹点香香靓又靓，
　　如意郎君任你招。

起兴山歌借景借物起兴，抒情写意。例如：
　　五只手儿捏田螺，
　　你拾我拣边个（哪个）多。
　　斧头劈入烂牛屎，
　　边知（哪知）失意一箩箩。
　　勤俭持家一朵花，
　　娶得妹转会当家。
　　一年镰转两造谷，
　　隔壁邻舍赞不差。

谐趣山歌的歌词诙谐有趣。例如：
　　阿妹好比枝上鸟，
　　飞上飞落任哥撩。
　　两腮冇够四两肉，
　　诱倒阿哥把脸丢。

　　阿军面上一窝窝，
　　冇知边度（哪里）鹊儿窝。
　　对面山上挖个坑，
　　比比边个装水多。

　　歌词每一句可能用"豆""嘟"等本地土话、俚语作助词调节。一些俚语是方言中的象声、状物的联绵词，多是后世方言内部产生，没有古今字词传承，只有用与方言相同或相近的字词代替。

面对异常恶劣的生存环境，面对凶禽猛兽的侵害，藤县人民生活艰辛，在痛苦之余也想寻找一种生活情趣以抵御危难与痛苦，他们顺口吟几句顺口溜，以缓解苦涩悲哀的情感。

淘金佬儿挣钱难

淘金公啊淘金公，十日淘金九日空。
腊月赤脚水里浸，难得两文度寒冬。

老了难

老了难，
老了唱歌嘟口腾弹。
冇并阿年都十七八，
唱歌应过九重山。
老个好，
八角还是老个香。
老个识情都识义，
吾中嫩个有金镶？

渴望美好生活是人类生存、延续和发展的永恒主题，藤县人民用对山歌表达喜怒哀乐的情感。

对歌

问：睇牛佬儿我豆问你，
　　一条牛尾豆几多毛。
　　一只筛箕豆几多眼，
　　一埕烧酒豆几多煲？
答：讲你听，

藤县山歌

牛尾论条冇论毛。
筛箕论只冇论眼，
烧酒论埕冇论煲。

执稔歌

石表山顶豆尖又尖，
十八姑娘豆去执稔。
你冇熟执稔豆兄教你啊，
黄蜂注过龈牙甜。

对歌相睇

男问：小姐你生得白漂漂，
　　　好似石灰豆初出窑。
　　　若是阿妹你嫁俾我啊，
　　　冇使你担水劈柴烧。
女答：我冇信啊，
　　　冇信阿哥你敢冇行。
　　　若是真正有敢好啊，
　　　我愿嫁俾你作妻房。

注：相睇就是相亲，古时候适龄未婚男女通过对歌相互了解对方性格、智慧、胆识、人品、家庭条件等。如果唱得情投意合，相互喜欢，男方就会选择吉日提上礼品去提亲。

情深深

阿哥谋生去远方，阿妹思哥守空房。
薄被难过落霜夜，鸳鸯分飞心惊慌。
一年到头冇信转，阿妹心中乱忙忙。

现今突然回了乡，阿妹开心喜若狂。

从此共侍父母亲，不分不离偎身旁。

牛郎织女睇夜景，双双对对喜洋洋。

男耕女织俩恩爱，勤俭持家好时光。

藤县山歌简易通俗、押韵隽永、寓意深刻、教益无限、广为传唱，历经数百年历史积淀，成为深厚的乡土传统文化。

2022年，藤县山歌列入第五批县级非物质文化遗产代表性项目名录。

Folk Songs of Tengxian County

· *Zhou Yubing* ·

Tengxian County, situated in a mountainous and hilly region, is traversed by the meandering Xunjiang River. The people of this county primarily engage in rice farming, forestry, animal husbandry, bamboo rafting, and various other labor-intensive activities. Life in this area is generally monotonous. To relieve fatigue, express emotions, ward off wild animals, or face threats like bandits and natural disasters, the people of Tengxian County sing loudly in their local dialect. Through these activities, the rich tradition of Tengxian County's folk songs has evolved over time. Folk songs are deeply ingrained in the lives of the people of Tengxian County, and from the youngest children to elders in their 80s or 90s, everyone can sing. These songs resonate throughout the mountains and villages, becoming a pervasive part of everyday life.

Folk songs in Tengxian County originate from life but beyond it, and after hundreds of years of refinement, they have formed their own characteristics and become the bright and colourful flowers in the garden of folk culture.

Folk songs in Tengxian County encompass various genres, including fu-style folk songs, figurative folk songs, Qixing (inspired) folk songs, and humorous folk songs. Fu-style folk songs are akin to prose poetry—where Ci Fu occupies a form between poetry and prose. As Ci Fu transitions from the middle to the end of a line, it takes the form of "fu-style poetry", whereas it appears as "fu-style prose" when closer to prose. Fu-style folk songs narrate straightforward stories about people and events, creating vivid imagery that allows listeners to feel as though they are part of the scene. For example:

"Sending my sister to her in-law's house,

With so many family possessions, she's truly blessed.

I advised my sister to cherish what she has,

Avoid disputes and tears."

"Seeing a beautiful girl approach from afar,

With perfect appearance and graceful figure,

She embodies the ideal—neither too fat nor too thin.

When you've prospered at the end of the year, you can marry her."

Figurative folk songs vividly express emotions using similes, metaphors, allegories, and even reverse metaphors, endowing them with artistic charm. For example:

"Little sister is prettier than big sister—

Three-inch golden lotus feet and a four-inch waist.

With her sweet fragrance, she's even more enchanting,

And ready to marry the perfect husband."

Qixing folk songs use scenery and objects to evoke emotions. For example:

"Picking a field snail with five fingers,

You selected the best one for me.

Striking an axe into rotten ox dung,

Who could've known it would uncover a basket of sorrow?

A hard-working, thrifty woman,

Whoever marries her is truly fortunate.

Her family will reap rich rewards,

And the entire village praises her."

The lyrics of humorous folk songs are witty and playful. For example:

"A Mei is like a bird on a branch,

Flitting up and down beside my brother.

Her face is so thin, weighing less than four *liang*.

In the end, she lured the shy young man."

"A'jun's face is full of wrinkles.

Nobody knows where the magpie's nest is.

He digs holes on the opposite hill,

And compares which one holds more water."

Many folk songs incorporate local dialects and slang, such as the words "*dou*" or "*du*". These dialectal expressions often feature words that imitate sounds or describe objects and are passed down through the generations, though they lack direct connection to ancient and modern words, relying instead on similar dialect terms as replacements.

In the past, life in Tengxian County was harsh, marked by a challenging environment and threats from predatory animals. In such difficult times, people sang these folk songs, even doggerels, to alleviate their feelings of bitterness and sorrow.

The Gold Digger

"Gold diggers find it hard to earn a living,
Digging for ten days, only to come up empty for nine.
Barefoot in the water in December,
Earning barely enough to survive the winter."

The Hardships of Aging

"Growing old is tough, and even singing becomes difficult.
But without illness, everyone feels like they're seventeen or eighteen again,
Singing so loudly that their voices carry across nine mountains.
Yet, aging has its virtues—old anise grows more fragrant.
The elderly understand true friendship,
While the young flaunt their youth, oblivious to life's deeper values."

Despite their hardships, the people of Tengxian County expressed their emotions, including their hopes for a better life, through folk songs that conveyed their happiness, sorrow, and dreams for a brighter future.

Duet

Question: "I ask the ox farmer—how many hairs are on an ox's tail?

How many holes are in a sieve?

How many pots in a bottle of liquor?"

Answer: "Listen closely—an ox's tail is counted by its strands, not hairs;

A sieve is measured as a whole, not by its holes;

And liquor is counted by bottles, not by pots."

The Song of Holding Myrtle

"Peak beans grow pointed on Shibiao Mountain,

And an eighteen-year-old girl goes to gather myrtle.

If you don't know how to gather myrtle,

Your brothers will teach you—its sweet sap touched by bees."

The Song of Xiangdi

Male: "Miss, your skin is white as freshly fired lime.

If you marry me, you'll never need to fetch water or chop firewood."

Female: "I don't trust you—how can I believe you're so capable?

But if you truly are, I would consider marrying you."

(Xiangdi refers to the tradition of dating through songs, where unmarried men and women of marriageable age would sing to one another, assessing each other's character, wisdom, courage, and family background. If they felt a connection, the man would later propose with gifts on an auspicious day.)

Deep Love

"A Ge left to earn a living far away,

While A Mei remained home, missing her husband.

The cold nights were unbearable with only a thin quilt,

And the loving couple was stricken by separation anxiety.

No letters arrived for a year,

Leaving A Mei nervous.

Then, suddenly, A Ge returned to the village,

And A Mei was overwhelmed with joy.

From that moment on, they served their parents together,

Vowing never to be separated again.

Tender couples, like the cowherd and the weaver girl,

Enjoy the fragrance of a beautiful night.

Together, they work diligently—the man plows, the woman weaves—

Building a future through hard work and frugality."

Folk songs in Tengxian County are simple, yet rich in meaning, with rhythmic patterns, profound themes, and boundless inspiration. They have been passed down through generations, embodying the deep local culture accumulated over centuries.

In 2022, Tengxian County's folk songs were included in the fifth batch of representative county-level intangible cultural heritage list.

唱山歌 / 周雄　摄

藤县上灯歌

○ 曾春凤

我国民歌历史悠久，源远流长。在原始社会，我们的祖先在狩猎、祭祀、节日或生产劳动中开始用歌声表达情感。《诗经》中的《国风》，是我国最早的民歌选集。藤县上灯歌不知起源于何时，据新庆镇建新村朝岭的老人介绍，清咸丰年间（1851—1861）已有流传。

每年正月十日，藤县大多数乡村都有上灯的习俗。20 世纪 80 年代，象棋镇、新庆镇的民间上灯户均有举行对唱花灯歌活动，惯称上灯歌。每年村里少则也有几户添丁上灯的人家，而上灯歌歌队有两三队，歌手没有化妆，没有戏服，更没有乐器伴奏，只是辅以简单的手势进行清唱，歌声纯净如天籁之音。一队一队轮流唱，先在村边或东家屋对面较远处唱，唱词大多是对小孩的褒奖和祝福。唱道：

> 贺喜贺新正，
> 今晚星光月又明。
> 今晚星光月又好，
> 大家喜庆过新正。

这是歌手（即贺客）的开场白，新正即新年正月。若东家没有回应，过一会贺客又唱：

> 贺喜贺新正，
> 祝贺东家添贵仔，
> 今年出有状元兄。
> 我队一班参高兴，
> 齐齐喜庆过新正。

藤县上灯歌

如果东家还是没有动静，贺客就有点催促的意味了：

> 贺喜贺新正，
> 敬请东家出贵声。
> 请我东家开金口，
> 大家喜庆得倾倾。

人逢喜事精神爽是事实，人逢喜事忙得脚不沾地也是常情，所以东家久不回应，有时确是忙，但有时是考考歌手的水平和歌喉。因为在物资匮乏的年代，普通人家大都缺衣少食，遇上上灯节日，歌手都想得到东家的邀请，进屋吃一顿丰盛的晚饭。断断续续唱了两三个小时，看看火候差不多了，东家开始应和：

> 贺喜贺新正，
> 今晚星光月又明。
> 今晚正是年宵节，
> 大家谈讲得心开。
> 听闻对面贵客到，
> 冇知边个贵客来。

然后，歌声回应，报上姓名，东家相邀进屋，好茶好酒招待。

传统花灯以竹篾、彩纸和细线为材料，由民间手工艺人制作而成，色彩斑斓，流光溢彩，既有薪火相传的寓意，又有生生不息的希冀。花灯挂在中厅的横梁下，饭后主人和宾客、歌手欢聚一堂，围着花灯用问答对唱式进行。上灯歌内容丰富，涵盖了对美好生活的歌颂，对村庄环境的赞美；对亲友的感恩，对东家上灯的小孩的祝福和期望等。贺客云：

> 朝岭人民风水好，
> 发财同时又添丁。
> 添丁就添白花仔，
> 北京大学有你名。
> 望你连生多贵子，
> 花根端正叶长青。
> 祝你成人快长大，
> 读书伶俐又聪明。

东家云：

> 不觉夜深已三更，
> 冇有灯火送君行。
> 过往我村要入屋，
> 冇茶饮水亦欢迎。

歌词通俗易懂，富含人情礼仪，弥漫着烟火气息。歌词皆朗朗上口，其结构以七言四句式为主，亦有三句式的，每句押韵。唱时添加助词"啊""啰"等，拉长语气，便于抒情。句与句之间衔接藕断丝连，又独具韵味。上灯歌声调平稳、舒缓，有种"日照芝麻口就开"的天然乡土味。

"添丁发财""丁财两旺"，添男丁是农村一大喜事，因此上灯歌是正月的重头戏。东家、亲友和歌手从正月十日开始唱，直到正月十五日（即元宵节）晚结束，正月十六日杀鸡宰鸭大吃一顿才散席。

现在，新庆镇建新村朝岭还保留唱上灯歌的习俗。

2022年，藤县上灯歌列入第五批县级非物质文化遗产代表性项目名录。

The Songs of Lighting Up in Tengxian County

· Zeng Chunfeng ·

The history of Chinese folk songs is both long and profound. In primitive society, Chinese ancestors began expressing their emotions through songs during hunting, rituals, festivals, and labor. *The Book of Songs* (*Shijing*) in the Zhou Dynasty is the earliest anthology of Chinese folk songs. The exact origins of the "Song of Lighting Up" in Tengxian County remain unknown, but according to elderly residents from Chaoling Ridge of Jianxin Village, Xinqing Town, these songs have been passed down since the Xianfeng period of the Qing Dynasty (1851 – 1861 AD).

Every year on the tenth day of the first lunar month, many villages in Tengxian County observe the custom of lighting up lanterns. By the 1980s, in Xinqing and Xiangqi Towns, families would host singing duets of lantern songs—commonly referred to as "lighting up songs". At least a few families in each village would have babies for whom lanterns were lit, and this often resulted in two or three singing groups forming. The singers had no makeup, costumes, or musical instruments. Accompanied only by simple hand gestures, their pure, natural voices created a serene atmosphere. They sang in turns, typically at some distance from the village or the host's home, with the lyrics focusing primarily on praising and blessing children.

The opening lines of the songs were usually: "Congratulations for the Xinzheng. The stars and the moon shine tonight, and we rejoice for Xinzheng." "Xinzheng" refers to the first month of the lunar new year. If the host did not respond, the singers would repeat:

"Congratulations for lively Xinzheng. We wish you a lucky child this year—perhaps a future Number One Scholar. Our group is happy to participate in this celebration and enjoy the Xinzheng festival together." If the host still did not respond, the singers would persist: "Congratulations for Xinzheng. We ask the host to honor us with his voice. Please, open your golden mouth so we may share this joyous moment."

As the saying goes, "happy events lift the spirits." Sometimes, a delayed response was simply due to the host's busyness, but at times, it was a playful test of the singers' skill. In times of material scarcity, families often lacked sufficient food and clothing, making singing on the day of lighting up an opportunity for singers to be invited to a lavish meal. After a few hours of singing, the festivities would reach their peak, the host began to respond: "The moon and stars shine brightly tonight—it is Lunar New Year's Eve, and we are enjoying lively conversation. I've heard that a distinguished guest has arrived on the other side, though I do not know who he is." With the singers finally introducing themselves to the host, who would then invite them inside, offering tea and Chinese baijiu.

Traditional lanterns, made from bamboo strips, colored paper, and thread, are crafted by local artisans. These colorful and bright lanterns symbolize continuity, happiness, and prosperity. Hung from the ceiling in the central hall, they serve as a focal point for post-dinner gatherings, where hosts, guests, and singers chant around the lanterns. The songs of lighting up are rich in content, covering topics like praising a better life, blessing the village, expressing gratitude to relatives and friends, and bestowing good wishes for the children's future. For example, the visitor sings: "The people of Chaoling Village enjoy favorable Fengshui. We wish you prosperity and success. May your children be white, tender, clever, and one day admitted to Peking University. May you have many noble children, may the roots and leaves of your family flourish, and may your offspring grow up to excel in their studies." And the host responds: "Without realizing it, it is already one o'clock in the morning, and a light is burning to bid you farewell. If you pass through my village and wish to visit my home, you are most welcome, though I have no tea to offer—we will simply drink water."

The lyrics are simple and comprehensible, yet they carry deep social meaning, rich in local flavor. The songs are often composed spontaneously or arranged in a catchy and rhythmic manner. Structurally, they are typically seven-character quatrains, although some use three-line stanzas, with each line rhyming. Singers frequently add auxiliary sounds like "*ah*" or "*lo*" to extend their tones and express emotion. The transition between sentences adds to the songs' unique charm, and the smooth, soothing melody reflects the rustic, unhurried pace of life.

In rural life, it was often said: "The more children, the more wealth" and "Prosperity comes with children and wealth." The birth of a male child was especially celebrated (the birth of a female child was referred to as "*Jiakou*", meaning the addition of a family member), and thus, the songs of lighting up were the highlight of the first lunar month. The celebration typically lasted from the 10th day until the Lantern Festival on the fifteenth day. And on the sixteenth day, the host would kill chickens and ducks to prepare a grand feast.

Today, the custom of singing the lighting up songs is still preserved in Chaoling Ridge of Jianxin Village, Xinqing Town.

In 2022, the "Song of Lighting Up" from Tengxian County was officially listed in the fifth batch of county-level intangible cultural heritage items.

藤县做社习俗

○ 甘丽云

做社的祭品 / 何锦奋 摄

社日，是一个古老而隆重的中国传统文化节日。在社日里举办各种纪念活动祭拜社神，藤县本地称为做社。做，白话，操办之意。

古人认为土生万物，对土地有着极其深厚的感情，所以土地神是广为敬奉的神灵之一，该神管理着五谷的生长和地方的平安。社字从示从土，"土"是土地，"示"表示祭祀，社就是祭土地神。早先的土地神只是神灵，后来逐渐被叫作"社"，俗称土地爷。藤县做社习俗起源于何时已经无法追寻，但其作为一种习俗流传至今，而且与历代群众的信仰和生活息息相关，有很高的历史研究价值。

藤县，古称藤州，历史悠久，源远流长，距今约一万年前已有人类活动。嘉庆二十一年（1816年）版《藤县志》记载："二月初二日乡民祭社祈穀群饮为欢。"又1996年版《藤县志》对社日记载："社日，农历二月二日为春社，八月初二为秋社，备酒肉、香烛等祭社神。"

藤县做社习俗

做社 / 黄明钊 摄

分社肉 / 黄位湘　摄

  每年春秋两季做社，祭祀、祈祷，是藤县民间的一种习俗。社的实物形态，最早是树木，后来改为石头、木牌和土堆。皇帝立的社叫"王社"，建筑高大恢宏。平民百姓立的社，一般称土地庙。城镇的社都由居民捐钱建造庙宇，建筑因地而异，一般不会太大，单层的三五开间，有别"王社"；乡间村头的社大多会选择在一棵或多棵大树下，砌个一两平方米的小庙，或干脆用四块石片，三块作墙，一块盖顶，盖上一块红布，捡块破缸片作盖顶的露天社坛。农家在厅堂正墙供奉了"天地君亲师神位"的墙根下，贴一张写有土地神位的红纸，摆个香炉，便算是请来了护家的土地神。社多由所在村的村民进行命名，比如大田社、石流社、镇安社等。

  藤县民间祭祀景象，是对神灵的敬畏，是对土地的感恩，是对丰收的希望，是对生活的憧憬。

  社的建立不是固定不变，有的是一个自然村就有一个，有

藤县做社习俗

的是几个自然村共有一个。社的辐射人群更是多种多样，一个村子不是固定祭拜自己村所属的社，还会祭拜周边的社。如果传说哪个社神灵验，会吸引周边甚至更远的村民，不论在社日还是其他日子都会前去祭拜。

藤县的做社，最隆重的是春社和秋社。各户户主进行抽签，确定今年春社、秋社的"社头"，或是由七八个不等的小组，每年每组出一家轮着当"社头"。"社头"顾名思义就是做社的头领。"社头"一般为几个人组成，主持做社的所有工作，在该次做社过程中又进行抽签来确定下一次做社的"社头"。

做社将至，"社头"聚集议事，确定这次社票的价格，收取每户的份子钱。社票，是每户作为参加社日活动领取社肉、社粥等的凭据。一般一户一份，也可以一户多份，份数以购买社票的多少为准，凭社票领取。社票的价格（也叫人丁钱）一般以这次计划购买的大猪、鸡、鱼、香火、鞭炮之类祭品进行估价，定出价格后，由各"社头"在村中上门到各家各户收钱出票。

做社 / 杨定登　摄

"社头"们提前采购做社所需的猪、鸡、鱼、香、蜡烛、衣纸等祭品。准备齐全后，各户代表如约而至，在社坛地坪升火开锅，劏猪杀鸡，分工合作，有条不紊。一边鸣锣开鼓，舞狮助兴，好不热闹；另一边支起一口大锅熬煮社粥（做社一般不煮饭）。一干人马，紧张忙碌：负责祭品的焖煎炒焗，刷洗锅碗瓢盆，将菜肴上桌摆台；负责劏猪的按社票分好份子社肉；负责熬煮社粥的，待粥滚米开，加入肉丁、姜、葱、豉油。一锅社粥香气弥漫，只待开锅分粥。负责祭拜仪式的，排布彩旗，摆好祭品，点香燃烛，由"社头"代表先行焚香祭拜，然后各家各户依次举香朝拜，祈求五谷丰登、人丁兴旺、身壮力健、村寨安宁。拜祭之后，双手取杯，滴茶洒洒，茶酒分三次平行倒在地上。然后烧元宝、衣纸等，鸣炮响鼓，舞动醒狮，好不喜庆。

拜祭完毕就是领社了，大家把社粥、社肉带回家中与家人分享，共祈安好，共享幸福。

2022年，藤县做社习俗被列入第五批县级非物质文化遗产代表性项目名录。

The Custom of Sacrificing to the God of Land in Tengxian County

· Gan Liyun ·

She Ri (an ancient festival for worshipping the God of Land, typically observed on the fifth day after the start of spring and autumn according to the lunar calendar) is a significant traditional cultural festival in China. On She Ri, people engage in various activities to honor the God of Land, a practice commonly referred to as "Zuoshe" (which means organizing the sacrificial ceremony) in Tengxian County.

In ancient times, people believed the land gave birth to all living things, and the God of Land was therefore widely revered. This deity was thought to oversee the growth of crops and maintain local peace, and as a result, people held deep reverence for the land. The Chinese character "*tu*" means land, while "*shi*" means sacrifice, and "*she*" refers to the act of sacrificing to the land. Initially, the God of Land was a singular deity, but over time, the term "*she*" came to represent the God of Land more broadly.

While the exact origins of the Tengxian County custom of sacrificing to the God of Land are unclear, it has been passed down through generations, maintaining a close connection to local beliefs and daily life, which lends it considerable historical value.

Tengxian County, once known as Tengzhou, has a long history, with human activity dating back over 10,000 years. According to *the Annals of Tengxian County* in the twenty-first year of Jiaqing period in the Qing Dynasty, "Villagers offer sacrifices to the God of Land with trees and communal drinking on the second day of the second lunar month." The 1996 edition of the *Tengxian County Annals* similarly records that on She Ri, sacrifices occur on the second day of the second lunar month (Spring She) and the second day of the eighth lunar month (Autumn She). On these days, offerings such as Chinese baijiu, meat, and incense are prepared for the God of

Land.

The practice of offering sacrifices in both spring and autumn remains a well-established folk custom in Tengxian County. Initially, sacrificial symbols (*She*) were represented by trees, but over time, these evolved into stones, wooden tablets, and earthen mounds. While emperors established grand sacrificial structures known as "She of Emperors", the common people typically built smaller shrines or temples. In towns, residents would pool resources to construct temples of varying sizes, depending on local conditions. In rural areas, people often built simple, small temples—sometimes no more than one or two square meters—beneath large trees, or constructed open-air altars with basic materials like stones, red cloth, and broken pottery. These altars, often named after their location (e.g., *Datian She*, *Shiliu She*, or *Zhen'an She*), served as communal spaces for worship.

The sacrificial rites in Tengxian County reflect both reverence for the gods and gratitude toward the land, along with hopes for bountiful harvests and a prosperous future.

The size and placement of She temples are flexible, with some villages having their own temple and others sharing one among several neighboring communities. If a particular She temple is believed to have miraculous powers, it may attract worshippers from far beyond the local area, regardless of She Ri.

The most elaborate She activities occur during Spring She and Autumn She. The head of each household draws lots to determine the "Head of She" for that year's ceremonies. The Head of She, a role often shared by several individuals, is responsible for overseeing all aspects of the sacrificial rites. After the ceremony, new lots are drawn to determine the next year's Head of She. In some cases, there are multiple groups, each taking turns to lead the ceremony annually.

As She Ri approaches, the Heads of She meet to set the price of She tickets, which are sold to households to cover the costs of the ceremony. A She ticket serves as proof of participation and entitles the holder to a share of the communal offerings, such as She meat and She porridge. Each household typically purchases one ticket, though larger families may buy more, depending on the number of social obligations they have. The ticket price is based on the cost of the offerings, which include pigs, chickens, fish, incense, and firecrackers. Once the price is set, the Heads of She will collect the money for tickets door to door.

In preparation for the event, the Heads of She procure pigs, chickens, fish, incense candles, paper clothing, ghost money, and other necessary offerings in advance. Once preparations are complete, representatives from each family gather as planned, lighting fires and opening the sacrificial pot in the She site. Pigs and chickens are slaughtered, and the offerings are prepared in an orderly fashion. On one side, gongs and drums are played, and lion dances are performed, creating a lively atmosphere. Meanwhile, a large pot is used to cook She porridge, as rice is typically not used to make offerings to the God of Land. A group of people busily attend to various tasks. Some are responsible for cooking and arranging pots and dishes on the table, while others handle the pigs, distributing She meat according to She tickets. Another group oversees the preparation of the porridge. Once the porridge is cooked, diced meat, ginger, and onions are added, along with soy sauce. The aroma of the porridge fills the air, enticing everyone to partake in it. Others are tasked with overseeing the worship ceremony, setting up offerings, arranging colored flags, and lighting incense candles. The Heads of She representative leads the ritual by burning incense to honor the god, followed by each family, who takes turns offering incense and praying for a bountiful harvest, population growth, strength, and peace in the village. After the prayers, participants hold a cup with both hands and sprinkle tea and wine drops on the ground. This is done in parallel three times. Paper ingots are then burned, and the sound of drums and lion dancing is accompanied by fire crackers, creating a festive and lively scene.

After the worship is completed, the community shares the She porridge and She meat among families. This tradition is known as "Everyone has a chance to enjoy the pork dispensed by the God of Land", symbolizing the collective prayers for peace and the sharing of joy.

In 2022, the custom of sacrificing to the God of Land in Tengxian County was listed in the fifth batch of representative items of county-level intangible cultural heritage.

藤县疳积散制药技艺

○ 李秋芳

古籍《慈幼新书·疳积》记载："小儿乳食不调，肥甘无节，积郁既久，则热生焉。热蒸既久，则虫生焉。有热有虫，而疳成矣。"疳者，甘也。小儿由于喂养不当或多种疾病影响，导致脾胃受损，饮食积滞，如不及时诊治，很容易成为慢性疾病，即患上疳症。患疳症的孩子通常神情呆滞，面黄肌瘦，毛发焦黄，没有健康孩子的活泼灵动。这时旁人便会提醒道："孩子生疳了，去找疳积散吧！"

疳积散（俗称甘积散），专门治疗小儿疳积之病，所以又称小儿疳积散。疳积散在藤县的起源，已不可究。20世纪，在藤南藤北的街上，经常听到这样的吆喝："小儿疳积散，有疳去疳，有积去积，无疳无积，开胃消食。"

藤县疳积散采用纯中药制剂，是藤县民间的制药技艺。一般用使君子、鸡内金、苦楝皮、小茴香、石燕、莲子、肇实、山药、茯苓等中草药研制而成。个别医家会根据自己所在地方的特点，特别加减几味中草药，研制成为独家家传秘方。

藤县积散所用的均是产自本地的中草药。如使君子（本地称病柑子）为君药，故取名疳积散，取当年9～10月成熟的果仁，待果皮变紫黑色时采摘，微火烘干去壳待用；鸡内金（本地称鸡肾皮），是家鸡胃内的砂囊内壁，至瓦片炒干待用；苦楝皮（本地俗称苦森木皮），取10年以上苦楝树老树皮晒干待用；小茴香（本地俗称松梢菜米），取成熟的果实，晒干待用；石燕，火煅醋淬7次待用；莲子，取干果去心待用；肇实（肇庆产的芡实，本地称鸡头米），去皮干果待用；山药，去皮切片晒干待用；

疳积散／何锦奋　摄

茯苓，去皮切片晒干待用。上述诸药按比例（配方保密）用碓舂或用中药的大盅锤碎碾碎，成为粉末，和匀，用细如针眼（约百目）的筛子过筛，留下细腻均匀的药粉，分成两钱（10克）一份，用纸包成一小袋（现在都用透明小袋子），放进盒子里密封，置室内阴凉干燥处，勿使受潮。

藤县疳积散是灰黄色粉末，嗅之微香，味微涩。通常医嘱加瘦肉隔水炖汤服用，或用热米汤加少量糖调服。服用时间一两天、三至七天不等，视疳症的轻重程度以及孩子个人的情况而定。

物华天宝，一方水土一方人。藤县疳积散制药技艺在藤县北部以濛江的吴氏比较有名，藤县南部则各有各的配方，且多是验方，历经数十年验证，君臣配伍得当，祖辈相传。

2022年，藤县疳积散制药技艺列入第五批县级非物质文化遗产代表性项目名录。

Pharmaceutical Technique of Making Ganji San in Tengxian County

· Li Qiufang ·

A child-caring medical book in the Ming Dynasty states: "If a child overeats, especially fatty foods, he/she may fall ill. Over time, roundworms can form in the stomach, leading to a condition known as gan." Today, this condition is known as infantile malnutrition, a chronic disease caused by improper feeding or other health issues. It impairs the spleen and stomach, depleting vital energy and fluids. A primary symptom is emaciation. Without proper diagnosis and timely treatment, infantile gan can develop into chronic wasting disease. Children with this condition often have a withered appearance, are skinny, dull, and have brownish hair. At this point, people would often say, "This child has gan; you need to find Ganji San!"

Ganji San is a specialized medicine for treating infantile gan. Its origins in Tengxian County are lost to history. However, in the last century, it was common to hear vendors on the streets of Tengxian County calling out, "Ganji San for infantile gan! It cures the disease, and if not, it will improve your child's appetite."

The production of Ganji San in Tengxian County follows traditional Chinese medicine practices and represents a valuable folk pharmaceutical craft. Generally, the medicine is made from a blend of herbs such as quisqualis indica, chicken gizzard lining, chinaberry bark, fennel, fossilia spiriferis, lotus seeds, gorgon fruit, yam, and poria. Some physicians modify the formula slightly, adding or removing herbs based on local customs, thus developing unique ancestral recipes.

All the ingredients used in Tengxian County's Ganji San are derived from locally sourced herbs. For example, quisqualis indica (locally called *bingganzi*) is a primary ingredient. The medicine is named after this herb, which is harvested between September and October when the kernels are ripe and the skins turn purplish-black. The seeds are lightly dried and hulled for use. Chicken gizzard lining (*jishenpi*) is made by frying the inner lining of a locally raised chicken's stomach on a clay tile. Chinaberry bark (*kusenmupi*) is harvested from trees at least 10 years old and dried for use. Fennel (*songshaocaimi*) is obtained from mature rapeseeds and dried. Fossilia spiriferis (*shiyan*) is roasted and calcined with vinegar seven times before use. Lotus seeds are dried, with the cores removed, while gorgon fruit (*jitoumi*), often sourced from Zhaoqing, is peeled and dried. Yam is peeled, sliced, and dried, as is poria. Once prepared, these ingredients are ground into powder according to a precise formula (kept secret). The powder is sifted through a fine sieve (approximately 0.150 mm) and collected. It is then measured into two *qian* (a traditional Chinese unit of weight, equivalent to ten grams) and packaged in small paper bags, though transparent plastic bags are more common today.

Ganji San is a grayish-yellow powder with a slightly sweet smell and a somewhat astringent taste. To make it more palatable, doctors often recommend mixing it with lean meat and stewing it, or dissolving it in hot rice soup with a small amount of sugar. The medicine is typically administered for one or two days, or in more severe cases, for three to five days, depending on the child's condition.

Ganji San is a treasured remedy, with each area of Tengxian County having its own unique variations. In the northern part of the county, the Wu family of Mengjiang is particularly renowned for their formulation. In the south, various families have developed proven recipes, passed down through generations. Over decades, these formulas have been refined to achieve an optimal balance of primary and secondary ingredients.

The pharmaceutical technique of making Ganji San in Tengxian County was included in the fifth batch of county-level intangible cultural heritage list in 2022.

藤县青砖烧制技艺

○ 苏海

砖瓦对建筑的保护作用和艺术效果是人类从原始进入文明的又一标志。在蓝田仰韶文化出土的5个残砖块，被确认为是至今发现的中国最早的砖，距今已有约5000年。可见，砖的历史深远，底蕴深厚。

藤县的青砖烧制始于何时，不得而知，但盛于20世纪70年代。这一时期，藤县乡镇的每个生产队都有砖窑。烧制青砖，以县城、镇区近郊交通方便之地居多。那时，生产队的劳动力，除了参加农活，其余时间都以打砖烧窑为主。

烧砖的传统技法，先是打造砖窑。砖窑的规格没有统一的标准，一般会按照当地的实际情况去决定，如黏土的储量、柴火的运输供给、砖坯的周期产量、天气因素等。砖窑越大装的砖就越多，烧制的时间相对较长，需用的柴火更多，需要的人手也更多。过去的砖窑容量从装十几筒（筒，是计量单位，每筒200块砖）到100多筒。现代的青砖烧制是改良创新过的龙窑、城窑，容量更大，不是传统的技艺功法，不在此论。

建造砖窑的选址，大多在较缓坡的山边或田头。传统的砖窑叫"望天窑"，一般是选择合适高度的土坡地，由地面向下挖一个既定尺寸的圆柱体，把圆柱体里面的土全部挖走后，称窑堂。窑堂四周用青砖砌24墙加固，达到设计高度后，再用大头砖（按设计窑顶的弧度计算出尺寸，事先烧制好的梯形方砖）拱成弧形窑顶。窑顶正中开圆形烟囱，在窑的后半圆边线三等分点再开3个方形烟囱，3个方形烟囱面积的和与中间圆形烟囱的面积相等。3个方形烟囱在窑堂砌砖时做成烟道，一气呵成，直通窑顶。而中间圆形烟囱只是一个圆形开孔，自成一体。人站在窑堂里，抬头见天，故称"望天窑"。

窑门开在圆柱体底部靠底坡的正前方，距窑堂边线约1米，高约2米、宽1米的圆拱形门洞，用青砖砌筑。窑门与窑堂有炉桥相连，炉桥底部比窑堂底部低40～50厘米。这是窑的基本构造。

砖坯的做法。砖坯的常规规格是24厘米×12厘米×6厘米的六面体方形结构，各地做法会略有加减。做砖坯的工具叫砖枷，是用较坚硬的木头做成井字形结构，中间开孔就是砖坯的尺寸。

和泥，俗称荡泥、熟泥。选好黏土堆成40～50厘米的高度，喷水湿润，慢慢让泥土吸饱水分，喷水速度不能太快，水分也不能太多，这一步骤叫润泥，是荡泥的基础工作，待泥土吸饱水分后，由人牵着牛进行反复踩踏，这就是荡泥。荡泥过程耗时耗力，5～7天时间，日出而作，日落而息，人牛轮流上阵，循环作战，每天荡泥时要安排人手把边沿的泥巴用一个叫刮弓的工具压割成块，再往中间垒叠，保持一定的高度，也是让泥土熟度更加均匀。泥荡得越熟做出的砖坯质量就会越好。

泥荡熟后，再次用刮弓把边沿或较高的泥巴压割成块，由人用双手捧起，举过头顶，用力往有牛脚印的地方摔填，直至泥巴之间再无孔洞，荡泥工序宣告完成。

接下来的工序是打砖，也叫出砖。打砖的工作台就地而建，大多是挖一个地坑，坑口地面嵌入与地面齐平的一块长约200厘米、宽约40厘米，厚

制作青砖的砖枷 / 何锦奋　摄

度 5 厘米以上的木板，木板与坑洞成 90 度，木板的左右两边挖有装上细沙的小坑，细沙的作用是涂抹砖枷四周，让砖坯容易脱模。打砖师傅有专人提供泥块。打砖讲究快、准、狠。打砖师傅双手高举泥块，快速、准确地往砖枷狠狠打摔，到边到角，满枷溢泥，整个动作行云流水，一气呵成，用小刮弓把多余的泥巴刮去，再把一块如砖枷尺寸的小薄板放进砖枷底部，顺势轻轻一敲砖枷的两个对角，砖坯脱落，有版有形的砖坯就可以搬去摆砖墙晾晒了。砖坯的晾晒，通常的做法是摆成一行一行的砖墙，便于通风晾晒，容易风干。风干好的砖坯就可以装窑了。

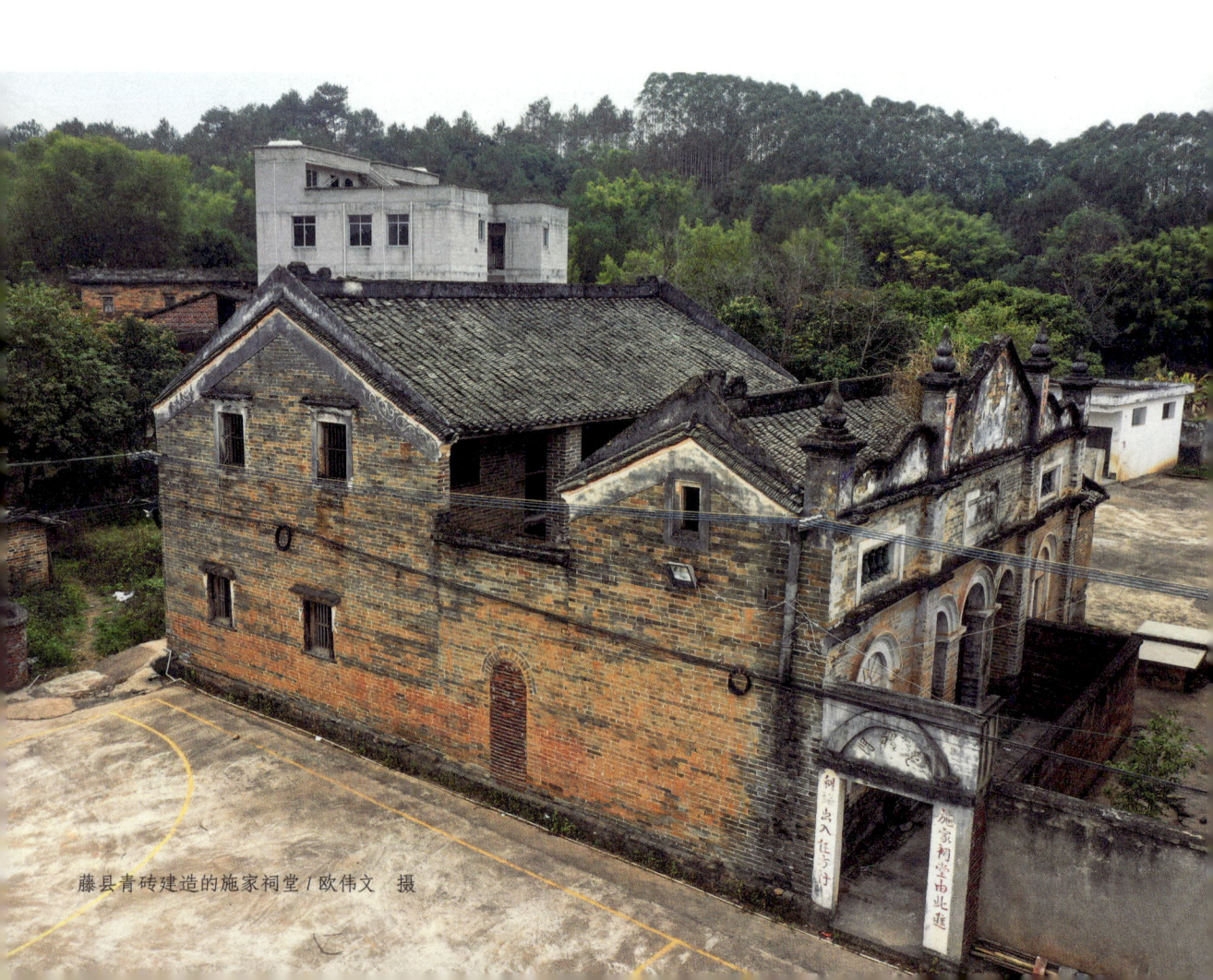

藤县青砖建造的施家祠堂 / 欧伟文　摄

藤县青砖烧制技艺

藤县青砖建造的房屋 / 霍雨锋 摄

装窑之前首先要在窑堂里烧上些许柴火，用于蒸去窑内水汽，俗称打冷火、暖窑。打冷火是小火慢蒸，需要一两天时间。

打冷火后开始装窑。装窑是个技术活，一般由几个有经验的人负责，其他人员只要把砖坯运送给他们即可。装窑时，砖坯的堆叠有讲究，要求达到通风透火，使不同位置的砖坯尽量受热均匀。既要留好火道，又要码堆稳当，如果码堆不好，在燃烧过程中由于砖坯受热收缩变化会容易引起坍塌，影响质量，甚至引发安全事故。因此，青砖烧制，装窑是关键。

装窑结束，封好窑门，只留一个边长20～30厘米的方形投柴口，接着进入烧窑环节。烧窑的时长视砖窑大小而定，一般在7～30天不等。

烧窑开始，又一次打冷火，这一次打冷火与上一次稍有不同。中小火慢烧，赶出砖坯内的水汽。烧窑师傅从观察烟囱的烟气量和颜色增减柴草，控制火力大小。

打冷火的时间根据烟气的颜色，烧个三五天，其时烟白，出来的是水汽。待烟色变黑，夹带着泥腥味，这时候说明砖坯的水分基本消散，便可柴薪交织。熊熊烈火，不舍昼夜，黑烟渐渐少去，青烟缕缕相继出，层层叠叠冲云天。再烧些时日，青烟袅袅已无色，红红火舌吐出来，这时火力最猛的时候到来了。在火龙喷薄而出、遥天响应的时候要先封上中间的烟囱，让火力遍布整个窑堂，窑内温度约1000摄氏度。此时要保持定力，再接再厉。数日后，火舌红到发紫，蓝白色的火焰，猎猎生威，呼呼作响，封窑的时刻就到来了。

封窑也讲究先后次序，先封中间的圆形烟囱，再到后面的三个方形烟囱。方形烟囱先封左右两个，再封中间的。用事先准备好的砖块、泥浆封堵，再盖上一层泥土密封。要时序分明，方能恰到好处。

窑顶封毕，再封窑门，和泥塞砖，封窑事结。

最为关键的一步到来了——灌水。

封窑一天后，灌水冷却。窑顶和窑门的灶膛同时进行，疾徐有致。窑顶的水位不越过烟囱顶部，窑门灶膛的水位控制在窑堂地面之下，这样还要连续7天保持水位不变。

这样富含铁元素的砖坯经过完全烘烧后，铁的化合物氧化为红色的高价三氧化二铁，而制得红色的砖。加水冷却，水蒸发成水蒸气，水蒸气和窑内高温的炭发生化学反应，密闭的煅烧窑内会产生大量的还原气体——氢气和一氧化碳，它们把红色高价三氧化二铁又逐渐还原成为青灰色的低价氧化亚铁而制得青砖。

窑温降至合适，便可开窑出砖，大功告成。

红衣褪去，只此青绿。

2022年，藤县青砖烧制技艺列入第五批县级非物质文化遗产代表性项目名录。

Firing Technique of Greenish-black Brick in Tengxian County

· Su Hai ·

Chinese architecture has long relied on Qin bricks and Han tiles, which played a crucial role in the evolution of buildings from primitive structures to the more advanced, aesthetically refined creations of later civilizations. The protective and artistic functions of these materials marked a significant transition in human history. Archaeological evidence, such as the five residual bricks unearthed from the Yangshao Culture site in Lantian, confirms that brick-making in China dates back 5,000 years.

The exact origins of greenish-black brick firing in Tengxian County remain unclear, but the craft became prevalent during the 1970s when every local production team had its own brick kiln. Brick production flourished in this period, especially in areas where transportation was convenient, such as towns and county centers. Production teams, in addition to their agricultural duties, managed brick kilns and handled the entire process of brick calcination.

The traditional process of brick firing begins with the construction of a brick kiln. Kiln specifications vary depending on local factors such as the availability of clay, the supply of firewood, brick output per cycle, and weather conditions. Larger kilns require more resources, both in terms of materials and labor. Kiln capacities in the past ranged from a dozen *tong* (approximately 200 bricks per *tong*) to over a hundred. In modern times, loong kilns and city kilns have larger capacities, but these innovations fall outside the scope of traditional craftsmanship.

The construction of traditional brick kilns typically takes place on hillsides or gently sloping fields. These kilns, known as "Wangtian Kilns", are cylindrical structures excavated into the earth on a suitable slope. Once the soil is fully removed from the cylindrical area, this space is referred to as the kiln chamber.

The kiln's roof is then constructed by arching large trapezoidal bricks, designed to match the curvature of the roof. At the center of the kiln roof, a circular chimney is built, while three square chimneys are placed equidistantly along the back semicircle of the kiln. The combined area of these three square chimneys is equivalent to the area of the central round chimney. During the construction of the kiln chamber, three square chimneys are built into flues that extend vertically to the roof, while the central round chimney remains a separate, self-contained opening. When standing inside the kiln chamber and looking upwards, one can see the sky through the circular chimney, which gives the "Wangtian Kiln" its name, meaning "sky-gazing kiln".

A black-brick arch forms the kiln door, which is located near the base of the kiln's front slope, approximately one meter from the side of the kiln chamber. The door itself is about two meters high and one meter wide, with a rounded arch shape. The kiln door is connected to the furnace bridge, the bottom of which is 40 to 50 cm lower than the floor of the kiln chamber. This design constitutes the basic structure of the "Wangtian Kiln".

The standard specification for bricks is a hexahedral structure measuring 240 × 120 × 60 mm, although slight variations exist depending on location. This specification has been consistently followed over time. The brick-making mold, known as the pillory, is made of hard wood and features a zigzag design with a central hole that matches the size of the brick.

The process of preparing the mud, referred to as swinging or cooking the mud, begins by selecting a suitable clay pile, which is built to a height of 40 to 50 cm. The pile is moistened by gradually spraying water to allow slow absorption. The water must be applied at a controlled pace to prevent oversaturation. This step, known as moistening, is the foundation of mud preparation. Once the soil is fully moistened, cattle are led to trample it repeatedly in a process called mud swinging. This labor-intensive procedure lasts five to seven days, from sunrise to sunset, with people and cattle alternating shifts. Throughout, workers use a scraping tool, known as a scraping bow, to press the edges into blocks, stacking them in the center to ensure uniform consistency. The quality of the mud is directly linked to the quality of the bricks.

Once the mud is fully prepared, the scraping bow is used again to cut and press the mud into blocks, which are carried by hand to fill any depressions left by the cattle's footprints. When the mud is evenly distributed and free of gaps, the mud-swinging process is complete.

The next step is brick formation, colloquially referred to as bringing bricks out of the kiln. A brick-making station is set up by digging a pit. A wooden board, 2 meters long and 40 cm wide, is embedded at the pit's opening, parallel to the ground. This board, set at a 90-degree angle to the hole, has small holes on either side filled with fine sand. The sand helps release the bricks from the mold more easily. Mud blocks are provided by designated workers. The brick-making process requires speed, precision, and force. The brickmaker molds the mud by hand, ensuring the brick form is filled to the corners, and scrapes off any excess with the scraping bow. Once molded, the brick is gently knocked free and transferred to a drying area.

Bricks are dried by stacking them into walls, and once air-dried, they are ready for the kiln.

Before loading the bricks into the kiln, firewood is burned inside to steam out the moisture, a process known as cold fire or warming the kiln. This takes one or two days with a slow-burning fire.

After the kiln is prepped, bricks are carefully loaded. The stacking process, managed by experienced workers, requires meticulous attention to ensure proper ventilation and even heat distribution during firing. Poor stacking can result in collapse due to shrinkage during combustion, which affects the quality of the bricks and poses safety risks. Proper kiln loading is key to successful greenish-black brick production.

After loading, the kiln door is sealed, leaving only a 20-30 cm square opening for airflow. The next stage is calcination.

Calcination begins with another round of cold fire, where a moderate, slow burn drives out any remaining moisture. Kiln masters monitor the color and volume of the chimney smoke, adjusting the fire accordingly.

The cold fire continues for three to five days until white smoke appears, indicating that the water has fully evaporated. As the smoke turns black, this signals the beginning of the main firing process, where strong, continuous flames burn day and night. After several days and nights, the black smoke diminishes, and clear smoke rises steadily. When colorless smoke and bright flames are visible, the kiln temperature reaches approximately 1000° C, marking the peak of the firing process. At this point, the

民间老宅的青砖灰雕 / 许旭芒 摄

chimneys are sealed to distribute the heat evenly throughout the kiln. Over the following days, the flames turn from red to purple, and eventually to blue and white, signaling the final stages of firing. At this moment, the kiln is about to be sealed.

The sealing process involves closing the chimneys in a specific order: the circular chimney is sealed first, followed by the square ones (side ones first and followed by the central one). Prepared bricks and mud are used to cover the chimneys, with a layer of soil added for insulation.

After sealing the kiln top and door, the most critical step, water quenching, begins.

A day after sealing, water is poured onto the kiln to cool it. This is done simultaneously on the roof and around the kiln door. The water level on the roof is kept below the chimney, and the level at the kiln door remains under the floor. This cooling process continues for seven days.

The water quenching facilitates a chemical reaction between the water vapor and the carbon in the high-temperature kiln. The process reduces the iron oxides in the bricks, transforming the originally red bricks into greenish-black ones.

Once the kiln cools to the appropriate temperature, the bricks are removed, completing the firing process.

The black bricks, now devoid of their red surface, emerge with a distinct green hue.

In 2022, the firing technique of greenish-black brick was officially listed in the fifth batch of Tengxian County's intangible cultural heritage list.

后记

中国有着悠久的文化传承，非物质文化遗产则是这一文化传承中不可或缺的一部分。它们是我们祖先留下的宝贵财富，蕴含着我们祖先千百年的智慧，承载着中国的历史与文化，寄托着人们的情感和记忆，是中华优秀传统文化的重要组成部分。

藤县是"海上丝绸之路"的一个重要交通节点，优越的地理环境和丰富的自然资源，孕育了这里的山水文明和多彩民俗。这本书就是从地域文化的视角，以图文并茂的形式，在时光里默默拾起那些代代相承的印迹，记录那些在岁月打磨中留下的璀璨的非物质文化遗产。

民族的就是世界的。为了做好非物质文化遗产保护传承工作，用有效的载体讲好藤县故事、梧州故事、广西故事，更好地传递中国声音，我们用一年多的时间收集、整理、书写、编辑了这本书。图书以文学的笔触，用中英文对照的方式，融文学性、史料性、工具性、欣赏性于一体，兼具可读性与生动性，让更多的人乐于徜徉其中，在缓缓叙述的文字和色彩鲜明的图片里，走进历史，触摸藤县深厚的文化脉搏和深藏的情感记忆，从而更好地传承与发扬我们独一无二的文化。我们试图用自己的热爱与坚守发出一些光亮，让藤县故事走向国际，为世界各地的人们提供一个了解广西、了解中华优秀传统文化的窗口。

这本书从收集、整理到拍摄、写作至成书，倾注了很多人的心血，也得到了很多人的关心与支持。藤县文化广电体育和旅游局及下属的藤县文化馆工作人员穿行在各乡镇默默收集、整理素材，藤县一批文化坚守者和文学爱好者倾情书写，摄影师们一次次奔赴各种非物质文化遗产活动的现场拍照。北京大学王娟教授欣然为此书写序。南京传媒学院的多位梧州籍学生担任了此书翻译，其导师对他们的翻译工作进行了精心指导。广西人民出版社在出版上给予我们大力帮助，他们对藤县文化的重视、热爱与支持让我们深为感动。在此，谨对给予帮助和支持的领导、专家、学者和其他朋友们表示衷心的感谢！

中华文明源远流长，地域文化多姿多彩。藤县的非物质文化遗产还有很多，在此我们只是做了阶段性的总结和展现。因我们学识、水平有限，在收集、整理和写作的过程中，还有很多不尽如人意之处，恳请大家批评指正。

编者

2024 年 8 月 8 日

后记

Afterword

China has a rich cultural heritage that stretches back through the ages, with intangible cultural heritage being an essential part of this legacy. These cultural treasures, passed down through generations, represent centuries of wisdom and embody the history and traditions of China. They encapsulate the emotions and memories of its people and are a vital component of China's exceptional traditional culture.

Tengxian County, a significant transportation hub on the southern "Maritime Silk Road," benefits from its strategic geographical location and abundant natural resources. These factors have nurtured a rich mountain and water culture, as well as vibrant folk customs. This book captures and presents these cultural legacies through the lens of regional culture, blending text and images to record the radiant intangible cultural heritage that has endured over time.

What is ethnic is also universal. To effectively preserve and promote intangible cultural heritage, and to share the stories of Tengxian County, Wuzhou, and Guangxi through modern media, we have spent over a year gathering, organizing, writing, and editing this book. Through a combination of literary expression, historical material, practical insights, and artistic appreciation, this bilingual book (in both Chinese and English) offers both readability and vividness. It invites readers to immerse themselves in the text and vibrant images, allowing them to explore the deep cultural currents and emotional memories embedded in Tengxian County. Our goal is to shine a light on these stories with our passion and dedication, bringing Tengxian's heritage to international audience and offering a glimpse of Guangxi and Chinese culture to people around the world.

This book reflects the collective effort and dedication of many individuals from the gathering and organizing of materials to the photography, writing, and eventual publication. Staffs of Tengxian County's Culture, Media, Tourism and Sports Bureau and its cultural center, worked diligently to collect and arrange materials from various towns and villages. A group of cultural enthusiasts and literary writers in Tengxian County poured their passion into the creation of this book, while photographers repeatedly attended intangible cultural heritage events to capture them on film. Professor Wang Juan from Peking University kindly provided the preface, and several students from Wuzhou, studying at the Communication University of China, Nanjing, served as translators under the careful guidance of their mentors. The Guangxi People's Publishing House offered substantial support for the publication of this work. Their dedication, care, and enthusiasm for Tengxian County's culture have touched us deeply. We extend our heartfelt gratitude to the leaders, experts, scholars, and friends who have supported and contributed.

Chinese civilization is ancient and profound, and its regional cultures are diverse and vibrant. Tengxian County is home to a rich tapestry of intangible cultural heritage, and this book serves as an initial summary and presentation of that richness. However, due to our limited experience and knowledge, there may be areas where the collection, organization, and writing could be improved. We welcome any criticism or suggestions.

Editor
August 8, 2024